Post-Soul
Nation

Post-Soul Nation

The Explosive, Contradictory, Triumphant,
and Tragic 1980s as Experienced by
African Americans (Previously Known as
Blacks and Before That Negroes)

Nelson George

VIKING

VIKING
Published by the Penguin Group
Penguin Group (USA) Inc., 375 Hudson Street,
New York, New York 10014, U.S.A.
Penguin Books Ltd, 80 Strand,
London WC?R ORL, England
Penguin Books Australia Ltd, 250 Camberwell Road, Camberwell,
Victoria 3124, Australia
Penguin Books Canada Ltd, 10 Alcorn Avenue,
Toronto, Ontario, Canada M4V 3B2
Penguin Books India (P) Ltd, 11 Community Centre, Panchsheel Park,
New Delhi — 110 017, India
Penguin Books (N.Z.) Ltd, Cnr Rosedale and Airborne Roads, Albany,
Auckland, New Zealand
Penguin Books (South Africa) (Pty) Ltd, 24 Sturdee Avenue,
Rosebank, Johannesburg 2196, South Africa

Penguin Books Ltd, Registered Offices:
80 Strand, London WC2R ORL, England

First published in 2004 by Viking Penguin,
a member of Penguin Group (USA) Inc.

10   9   8   7   6   5   4   3   2   1

Photograph credits
p. 1: Reprinted with the permission of *The Village Voice;*
p. 11: © Lynn Goldsmith/Corbis; p. 29: © 2003 *The Atlanta Journal-Constitution.*
Reprinted with permission from *The Atlanta Journal-Constitution;*
p. 45: © Owen Franklin/Corbis; pp. 63, 77, 143: © Bettmann/Corbis;
p. 107: © Jacques M. Chenet/Corbis; p. 123: Time Life Pictures/Getty Images;
p. 173: © S.I.N./Corbis; p. 197: Photo by Anthony Barboza

LIBRARY OF CONGRESS CATALOGING-IN-PUBLICATION DATA
George, Nelson.
Post-soul nation : the explosive, contradictory, triumphant, and tragic 1980s as
experienced by African Americans (previously known as Blacks and before that
Negroes) / Nelson George.
p.   cm.
Includes index.
ISBN 0-670-03275-1 (alk. paper)
1. African Americans—History—1964-   2. African Americans—Social conditions
1975-   3. African Americans—Intellectual life—20th century.   4. African Americans
in popular culture.   5. Popular culture—United States—History—20th century.
6. United States—Intellectual life—20th century.   7. United States—Social
conditions—1980-   8. United States—Race relations.   I. Title.

E185.615.G465   2004

973'.049607309'046—dc22
2003061606

This book is printed on acid-free paper.

Printed in the United States of America
Set in New York
Designed by Erin Benach

For Jade,
who will read this book one day
and wonder what the fuss was all about

Introduction: Affirmative Actions

For centuries the word "soul" was (pardon the pun) solely employed by religious leaders and philosophers to describe man's
spiritual core. The soul could be cursed to eternal damnation. The
soul could rise up to heavenly salvation. God and the Devil have
sparred over the soul of man since before the very devout Bible was
written. The soul has always been that region of consciousness that
truly defined us, not the temple of flesh we walk around in. To this
day the soul is, in popular consciousness, associated with one's
spiritual dimensions, as the ubiquitous best-selling *Chicken Soup
for the Soul* books testified to at the turn of the century.

It was no coincidence then that those black singers of the '60s
began describing the popular music as "soul music," since its musical base (rhythm, melody, vocal arrangement) all harked back to
the sounds heard in the Christian churches that nurtured them.
Though the subject matter of soul music was secular—usually love,
lust, and loss—soul was descended from gospel, and when performed by a queen like Aretha Franklin, the music possessed the
devotional intensity of a Sunday sermon.

From this simple linguistic transfer came a wider use of the
word. As the sixties progressed, soul signaled not simply a style of
pop music but the entire heritage and culture of blacks (or Negroes
or colored or Afro-Americans, depending on the year and context). We became "soul sistas" and "soul brothers" who dined on
"soul food," exchanged "soul shakes," celebrated with "soul claps"
as "soul children" marching for "soul power" while listening to

"soul brother number one," James Brown. This social use of soul quickly became commodified, resulting in soul magazines, soul barbershops, soul hair-care products, and an enduring TV show called *Soul Train.* Motown records founder Berry Gordy, never a man to miss a trick, even copyrighted the word and released records on the Soul label.

References to the '60s soul still pop up in music videos, commercials, and movies with great regularity. But they usually just skim the commercial surface of an era that for the black community had depth, substance, and edge. The sixties weren't about fried chicken—those ten years were the apex of the struggle of blacks for full citizenship—a battle that began the day President Lincoln signed the Emancipation Proclamation, but that took on a new urgency after World War II. That's when Americans of many hues (and too many foreign observers for the government's comfort) began pointing out the hypocrisy of a nation that battled Nazi hate but practiced institutionalized racism.

With a biblical ferver born of a desire to bring this country's everyday reality in line with our Constitution's soaring rhetoric, the civil rights movement remade America. Through legislation and marching, moral suasion and bloodshed, from 1946 into the 1970s, official barriers were smashed with the legislative and moral apex of the sixties.

I was a child during the '60s and I remember that "We Shall Overcome" energy with great affection. For me this historic period was absolutely about soul in its deepest spiritual meaning. It was about faith in the human capacity for change and a palpable optimism about the future. It's not necessary to recite the huge list of accomplishments of that epoch to say that period was witness to dramatic concrete action and a sense of commitment that defined the life of Martin Luther King Jr., Fannie Lou Hamer, Malcolm X, and thousands of others. And that hard, visionary work was all about soul.

The term "post-soul" defines the twisting, troubling, turmoil-filled, and often terrific years since the mid-seventies when black America moved into a new phase of its history. Post-soul is my shorthand to describe a time when America attempted to absorb the victories, failures, and ambiguities that resulted from the soul years. The post-soul years have witnessed an unprecedented acceptance of black people in the public life of America. As political figures, advertising images, pop stars, coworkers, and classmates, the descendants of African slaves have made their presence felt and, to a remarkable degree considering this country's brutal history, been accepted as citizens, if not always as equals.

Unfortunately, all that progress has not been as beneficial to the black masses as was anticipated in the '60s. The achievements of role models have not necessarily had a tangible impact on the realities of persistent poverty, poor education, and lingering, deep-seated social discrimination. A determined conservative backlash against the government's role in altering social conditions, heretofore repressed class tensions within the black community, widespread drug use, and a debilitating cynicism that runs counter to the spirit of the soul years are just some of the elements that make the post-soul years often seem a muddle.

Documenting the post-soul era is not about chronicling the straight line of a social movement, but collecting disparate fragments that form not a linear story, but a collage. Several trends—some direct reactions to the soul years, others revolutions that could not have been anticipated—drive this tangled narrative. An unprecedented number of black officials were elected in this period, men and women who were then challenged both to improve the race's well-being and to serve the needs of their other (presumably white) constituents. The post-soul period witnessed the ascendance, via high-visibility government appointments and jobs in media, of black conservatives who challenged the traditional views of black politics and values. The era fostered the creativity, desperation, and rage of the poor, communicated to the larger world through inspired artistry and destructive behavior, both on a scale never seen before; revealed the potency of black female writers and public intellectuals in the discourse of race and sex, and the often bitter backlash against these women from black men of many classes; and revived older notions of black nationalism and street protest as well as a critique of integration that encourages interest in African culture and non-Christian religions.

By decade's end "black" itself, as the verbal identification of race, would be, if not replaced, at least challenged or reinterpreted by the introduction of a new phrase. In fact the definition of blackness would be in play in the '80s, with terms like "buppie," "b-boy," "BAP," "underclass," "womanist," and "Afrocentricity" entering the lexicon. Some of these terms were sepia-tinted versions of white reality; others slang terms and academic inventions that captured new identities.

One of the safe assumptions of *Post-Soul Nation* is that the inventions, phenomena, and fads evolving out of the black community eventually shape the lives of nonblack Americans. That was true to a great degree during the civil rights movement in politics, law, and music. But in the more fully desegregated '80s, American society accepted this interplay without the same overt resistance, and, not surprisingly, the impact of black culture was magnified.

That said, *Post-Soul Nation* is not a simple slice of racially blind '80s nostalgia. There will be some '80s themes and events missing for those addicted to *Behind the Music* or the History Channel. There'll be no Rubik's Cube, no Members Only jackets, and as little of Mr. T as I can manage. Sorry. It is a very select vision of ten years (give or take twelve months) that emphasizes the achievement and dysfunction of people who suddenly decided it would be cool to be called African Americans.

Post-Soul Nation flows directly out of my life. The eighties were the first decade of my adulthood, and I lived through it with that mix of self-discovery and enthusiasm characteristic of one's twenties. Coming of age in the '80s made my peers and me extraordinarily lucky. The doors to opportunity in the United States opened wider than they ever had for black people. We accepted jobs our parents wouldn't have been offered. We probably made more money in that decade than entire black generations did in their lifetime. But were we '80s black folk better people? Were we stronger, braver, more courageous? I don't believe so. I believe we were often well trained and absolutely quite fortunate.

We were also greedy, self-dramatizing, and still stifled by racism's weapons: overcrowded, shabby schools and indifferent teachers; policing that could be either brutal or nonexistent, and was too often both; wretched, red-lined housing and putrid public services. Profoundly, despite our access and success, despite the possibilities integration offered, a cynical, isolationist attitude emerged in the populace, as if we were simultaneously under- and overwhelmed by this new America, a duality that would define us.

And then there was movie cowboy Ronald Reagan and the horse he rode in on—neoconservatism—that defined the national mood. His assumption of the presidency in 1980 was partially due to a backlash against black advancement that had been stirring throughout Jimmy Carter's troubled four-year term. Reading articles from the late '70s one finds there was a sense among many black leaders that President Reagan would be no worse for blacks than the Democratic incumbent President Jimmy Carter. A few prominent black leaders even endorsed the neo-con icon. To say these men were shortsighted is like arriving at the revelation that rapping involves rhymes.

Though told in a third-person narrative voice, *Post-Soul Nation* is in many ways autobiographical because the book's broad themes are the broad themes of my life. In January 1980, I was an unemployed freelance writer living with my mother and pregnant sister in a two-story row house in one of Brooklyn's most tattered neighborhoods. At the end of 1989, I was a newspaper columnist, noted music critic, and author living in a spacious brownstone in an arty Brooklyn area. My new bathroom was bigger than my old bedroom. The engine for improving my life in the '80s was the accelerated growth of black pop culture. The first actual disposable income I ever had derived from the royalties generated by a quickie Michael Jackson biography written breathlessly in the summer of 1983. I invested part of the proceeds from that endeavor in Spike Lee's film, *She's Gotta Have It,* my first involvement with the entrepreneurial side of culture. Between my writings and minor business ventures during the years 1980 to 1989, I benefited greatly from the access the post-soul era afforded.

But the trends that defined my life weren't only from the plus side of life. My family was scarred by the crack addiction of an immediate family member, which led to petty crime, awful lies, and a legacy of distrust and suspicion that my family still wrestles with. Hand in hand with drug addiction came an HIV infection to that same family member, visiting another '80s plague on our house. My family has survived all of that and, in many ways, is stronger than it has been in years. But the pain was real and will always linger with us.

To me, Charles Dickens's enduring phrase—it was the best of times and it was the worst of times—fits the '80s to a tee. All who lived through that decade were shaped by its lived joy and pain like a Frankie Beverly song. You don't know who Frankie Beverly is? It's an '80s thing.

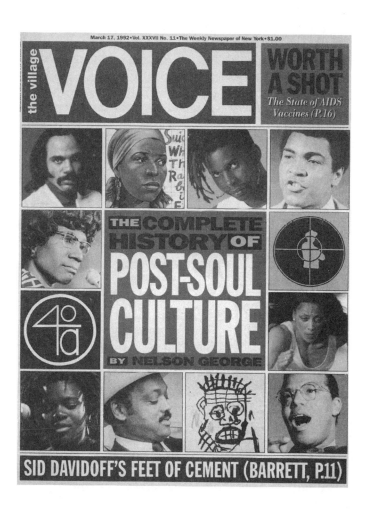

The *Village Voice* cover story that introduced the post-soul concept.

1979

1979

The year 1979 is the prologue, where we witness a few choice events whose impact spills over into the upcoming decade. A presidential election gets under way beneath the cloud of crisis—fifty-nine Americans being held hostage in Tehran after the fall of Iran's pro-American shah. An Islamic revolution has overthrown the old oligarchy and the Iranian people rightfully accuse America of supporting a corrupt, oil-rich tyrant. What no one in America realizes, except a few scholars, observant reporters, and close-mouthed government operatives, is that the bitterness that spews forth from enraged Iranians is the second big sign (the first being the 1973–74 oil embargo) that the political cold war is giving way to a hot religious one and that God-fearing America is to a lot of non-Westerners the great Satan.

In the American streets, where people wonder how a small Middle Eastern country can successfully disrespect us, there is a new drug epidemic. Phencyclidine (PCP, a.k.a. angel dust) is a test-tube drug that becomes popular as a kind of ghetto LSD, sending its users into a disorienting hallucinogenic state. The gray flaky substance is sprinkled either on regular cigarettes or marijuana cigarettes and then smoked. In addition to seeing weird, dreamy visions, dust smokers sometimes gain enough strength and aggression that it takes four or five policemen to subdue them. The hospital wards of big cities are dotted with "dusty" crazed, wild-eyed men and women who have to be restrained and injected with Thorazine, a cure that both calms victims down and often fries their brains. What's scary is that by the mid-'80s, angel dust will be to crack what herpes is to AIDS.

At our starting point, black culture is in the mainstream—to a degree. There are blacks in sitcoms and on local news. Several major cities have black mayors and desegregation is public policy in all fifty states. We are coming into a new era; Afros and dashikis can still be seen, but fades and baggy pants are on the rise.

JANUARY 25 American Mavericks, a festival of independent feature-length films, begins at an East Village theater in Manhattan. Among the young auteurs in the festival is Martin Brest with *Hot Tomorrows,* a film he writes and directs about the afterlife—very different from the movie that will make his reputation a few years later, *Beverly Hills Cop.*

The one black film in the festival is an hour-long documentary called *Streetcorner Stories,* made by Yale graduate Warrington Hudlin, which focuses on a group of men who congregate on a New Haven, Connecticut, street corner mornings before work. Using the popular cinema verité style with no narrator, *Streetcorner Stories* captures the rhythms and rituals of black working-class life by the careful accumulation of detail. Hudlin opens with a quote from Ralph Ellison about the "tragic comic" quality of the blues, which Hudlin, a product of the tough Midwestern working class of East St. Louis, uses as a template for this gritty film.

Hudlin, who lives in Harlem, is part of a community of black independent filmmakers on both coasts who've been toiling throughout the '70s, mostly ignored by Hollywood and mainstream (white and black) media. Melvin Van Peebles's *Sweet Sweetback's BaadAsssss Song* in 1971 was the last independent black film to get a significant commercial release and a large audience. Independent black filmmakers like Hudlin fund their films via grants from art organizations or family, or they make them at film schools they attend or teach at. Seen mostly at festivals or museums, the modest films rarely have stars, usually have very strong political or social themes, and never have an advertising budget, which is why popular black newspapers and magazines like *Ebony* give them token coverage. One of the recurring topics in the panel discussions of the Mavericks festival is how non-Hollywood black cinema can gain more exposure.

APRIL Jamaa Fanaka's movie *Penitentiary* is a whacked-out jailhouse version of *Rocky,* and sex symbol Leon Issac Kennedy is quite engaging as Too Sweet, the reluctant hero. Fanaka is a product of the serious Los Angeles school of black indie filmmaking but has his own warped world view. As a student at UCLA he became notorious for a short about a brother whose penis was so long it could be used to strangle his enemies. *Penitentiary* is a product of the same surreal mind-set and becomes a B-movie hit that spawns two sequels. Though unheralded by critics, Fanaka and Kennedy create the first black movie franchise of the decade.

MAY The Black Scholar, an important journal of black intellectual thought, dedicates the May/June issue to "The Black Sexism Debate." The issue is inspired by an angry review in the March/April issue by Robert Staples of Michelle Wallace's book *Black Macho and the Myth of the Superwoman.* Staples's essay was called "The Myth of Black Macho: A Response to Angry Black Feminists."

Wallace's book, published early in 1979, had been hailed by white feminists as a landmark look at male chauvinism in the black nationalist movement, placing black women under a double burden of white racism and black machismo. *Ms. Magazine* had featured the young author on its cover. Black men, still smarting from their damning portrayal in Ntozake Shange's Broadway hit, *For Colored Girls Who Have Considered Suicide When the Rainbow Is Enuf,* a few years before, viciously attacked Wallace. *The Village Voice*'s Stanley Crouch was typical, writing that whites in the media were "promoting a gaggle of black female writers who pay lip service to the woman's movement while supplying us with new stereotypes of black men and women." This issue of *The Black Scholar* boasts an impressive list of contributors: Ron Karenga, Askia Touré, Harry Edwards, Audre Lorde, June Jordan, Robert Staples, Ntozake Shange, Alvin Poussaint, Kalamu ya Salaam, Julianne Malveaux, and others.

Reflecting on this debate five years later in *The Sexual Mountain and Black Women Writers: Adventures in Sex, Literature, and Real Life,* Calvin Hernton observed, "it was clear that the men were the ones who were angry. . . . The men claimed that the women had fallen prey to white feminist propaganda. They said that black women, like white women, had been duped into turning against their men. The most truculent assertion was that the writings of black women were 'divisive' to the cohesion of the black community."

JULY The cries of "Disco sucks!" ring out across the land. Just a year after the massive pop cultural impact of the movie and soundtrack to *Saturday Night Fever,* a severe backlash against this musical-cultural movement is under way. Rock fans have always hated disco's self-conscious attempt at sophistication and faddish touch dancing. Others find its blending of the black, Latino, and gay club world frightening, upsetting, even dangerous.

At the dawn of the new decade, "disco" is still muttered by many as if a curse word, but the dance music scene it catalyzes will thrive and splinter into several dance genres driven by the DJs who would, as tastemakers and music makers, turn using turntables into a creative act.

New Jersey independent label Sugarhill Records releases *Rapper's Delight* by the Sugar Hill Gang, the first commercially successful expression of the rapping style that's been popular in New

York area parks and clubs for several years. Though it will evolve and, eventually, revolutionize world music, *Rapper's Delight* is at this point essentially just another approach to dance music. The groove the three performers talk over in rhyme—a.k.a. rap—is culled from one of the last great disco anthems, Chic's "Good Times."

Closer to the disco tradition is the scene at the West Village's Paradise Garage. Led by the visionary black gay DJ Larry Levan, the Garage becomes the most devout temple in a city that is the dance music mecca. Voted the best club with the best sound system in '79 and '80 at the *Billboard* Disco Convention, the Garage attracts a rabid, multisexual, multiracial throng every weekend. Because of its prominence in dance culture and the varied taste of Levan, the Paradise Garage is the spawning ground for a wide variety of dance music styles.

Halfway across the country, Frankie Knuckles, a black gay DJ from New York and intimate of Levan, spins at a club called the Warehouse in Chicago, where a huge crowd gathers on the weekends at a three-story factory on the city's west side. At the Warehouse dancing is known as "jacking" and the music, because of the club's name, is dubbed "house." Initially, the music played at the Warehouse is not very different from what dancers at New York's Paradise Garage might hear—Philly International dance hits, Euro-disco, and funk. But as the Chicago scene expands, drawing in more straights and musicians, "house" takes on a distinctive identity.

AUGUST　Michael Jackson's *Off the Wall,* produced by the former jazz and movie arranger Quincy Jones, sells several million copies, becoming the biggest-selling album by a male vocalist ever, establishing the former child star as an adult artist. Jackson, at the time of this album's release, is still remembered by most of America as the cute lead singer of Motown's bubblegum group, the Jackson 5. Michael and his four older brothers enjoyed a string of number-one hits at the beginning of the '70s ("ABC," "The Love You Save," "I Want You Back," "I'll Be There"), the last gasp of the production line that made Motown "the sound of young America."

Despite having enjoyed some solo hits, Michael struggled through adolescence as he searched for a grown-up identity (both on vinyl and off). The trick that underlies *Off the Wall* is how deftly veteran producer Quincy Jones matures the singer without losing his youthful quality. The dance jams are brilliant disco ("Don't Stop 'Til You Get Enough," "Working Day and Night"); the mid-tempo tracks sexy ("Rock with You"); and the ballads ("She's Out of My Life," "I Can't Help It") heartfelt. Vocally, *Off the Wall* is a tour de force that brings Jackson back to fans who'd grown up with the Jackson 5 and wins him the allegiance of a new generation.

Jackson appears in promotional videos for two songs, "Don't Stop" and "Rock with You," that are typical of the time—Michael singing and dancing alone before a cheesy blue-screened backdrop. The videos play on a few variety shows and fringe-time music programs, but basically they have no impact on record sales in the United States. They receive most of their play in the United Kingdom, where "promos," a.k.a. videos, had been commonplace since the '60s. As Michael goes back to work with his brothers on a Jackson 5 album, many wonder if *Off the Wall* will prove the peak of his solo career. After all, Jackson seems too old to play Peter Pan much longer.

SEPTEMBER The Feminist Press publishes *I Love Myself When I Am Laughing . . . and Then Again When I Am Looking Mean and Impressive,* edited by novelist Alice Walker, which brings obscure author-folklorist Zora Neale Hurston to national attention. Walker situates Hurston in the cosmology of black letters as *the* black female writer, the touchstone and artistic role model for all to follow. Hurston was a contemporary of and collaborator with Langston Hughes. Her work was regarded with disdain by the first black literary superstar, Richard Wright, and many of her books had been out of print for years. The attention given by Walker and other female writers to Hurston heralds a new prominence for black women writers and inspires many to use Hurston's work as an artistic template. Her novel, *Their Eyes Were Watching God,* would soon be reissued and enter the canon of great black (and feminist) (and American) novels.

SEPTEMBER Two of the most popular sitcoms of the '80s debut—*Benson,* starring Robert Guillaume on ABC, and *Different Strokes,* with Gary Coleman and Todd Bridges on NBC.

Benson, which debuts on the thirteenth, is a semi-dignified throwback to the age of movies and early sitcoms that featured the wise black servant. This show claims to subvert that tired concept by making the servant a male butler who works for (and usually outwits) a sitting governor. Guillaume is a solid comic actor who does his best to bring some class to what, in lesser hands, would be an all-out coon show. As it is, *Benson* runs for nearly seven seasons. By the last season Benson has risen from butler to lieutenant governor, the result a symbolic olive branch held out by its producers to its many black critics that should have been snapped in two. To its apologists *Benson* is a positive look at black servitude, the same people who think Margaret Mitchell's *Gone with the Wind* presents a positive view of black women.

Lacking the grace that Guillaume brought to *Benson* is the sad *Different Strokes,* the tale of a rich white widower and his two adopted black sons, which is first broadcast on September third. Todd Bridges plays a normal teenager, but the focus of the show is Gary Coleman, who many suspect is a midget but who is actually just a very irritating little boy. Coleman, with his toothy grin and "Lucy"-like antics, becomes a huge star during the show's eight-year run. He is the latest in a long line of caricatured black males who find success in American entertainment (Jimmie Walker's "J.J." on *Good Times* is his immediate predecessor).

The longevity of both *Benson* and *Different Strokes* (and the addition of *Webster* in 1983, another show about a black child being raised by white parents) speaks to Hollywood's comfort with stereotypes. Half the decade will be over before the black sitcom formulas that spawn these series are overhauled by a Philadelphia-born comedian who opens the '80s doing Jell-O commercials.

OCTOBER 5 Dudley Moore stars in the midlife crisis comedy *10* that introduces the white world to cornrows. Bo Derek, a twenty-two-year-old blonde with a frankly bodacious body, runs in slow motion on a beach, undresses, and beds the nerdy protagonist. Posters of Derek in a swimsuit adorn barbershops and car repair shops worldwide.

For black people, the sight of this Caucasian in long cornrows with decorative shells at their tips is a shock. The cornrow, an American adaptation of an African style, was a hairstyle intended to flaunt black pride. White women everywhere (albeit briefly) go to hair salons to get that "Bo Derek look."

A black cultural phenomenon is adopted by a white sponsor and spreads across the country—an old story in America. But in the '80s it all goes faster; there are more black faces in the mass media, and whites are freer to admit they like to borrow.

NOVEMBER Marion Barry takes office as mayor of Washington, D.C. The fiery leader had been a civil rights organizer in the South during the '60s and then evolved into a radical, dashiki-wearing nationalist in the '70s. During both incarnations Barry showed a charismatic flair for speaking forcefully for blacks. This is a man who would not be grateful for federal government handouts or accommodating to white liberals (at least in public). Because D.C. is the nation's capital, much goes on in the District that the mayor has no control over. But in his campaign, Barry makes it clear that what he can control, he'll control with gusto.

Yvonne Scruggs, executive director of the Black Leadership Forum, would later tell Barry biographer Jonetta Rose Barras that views of the mayor and his team on power were very different from those of the first generation of black politicians elected in the '60s: "Nobody gave them [Barry and his people] anything. They started out clawing and scratching. The style they developed was more confrontational, less ameliorative, more driven by quid pro quo than compromise. People like Marion Barry understood that the only way they got power was being in your face and making it clear there would be consequences if you didn't help them."

Unlike the previous wave of black mayors, such as Cleveland's Carl Stokes or Newark's Ken Gibson, who sought to accommodate the city's eroding but moneyed base of white voters, Barry's assertive national rhetoric has more in common with another relatively new chocolate city mayor, the curmudgeonly Coleman Young of Detroit.

Tom Wolfe had popularized the phrase "Mau-Mauing the Flak Catchers" to describe how black militants used threats of boycotts and rioting to appropriate power from white gatekeepers during the big-city turmoil of the late '60s. Barry had been the kind of loud, trash-talking advocate for the black agenda the journalist was referring to. Now, as mayor of D.C., Barry is the gatekeeper.

Eddie Murphy as Velvet Jones on *Saturday Night Live*.

1980

1980

Throughout this year there are many signs that the federal government has abandoned the struggle for equality for blacks. Discrimination continues in the workplace and a profound loss of hope develops among the nation's poorest (and darkest) citizens. President Jimmy Carter's election-year budget, which cuts spending for domestic programs while boosting the defense budget, is labeled a "disaster" by the Congressional Black Caucus. So is Carter's opposition to federal aid to poor people seeking abortions. Under his administration the unemployment rate among young blacks hovers somewhere between 20 and 30 percent. And when he does make proposals to aid the poor, as in a modest $288 million increase in a program that screens and treats children's health problems, Carter allows the Senate Budget Committee to knock off $88 million without either moral censure or political pressure.

Add to this the growing levels of violence in black neighborhoods. According to the Bureau of Justice Statistics annual report, 49.7 of every thousand black people are likely to be a victim of a violent crime, compared to 33.4 whites. Black males aged twenty-five to thirty-four are the most likely victims of homicide in the black community, at a rate of 145 deaths out of every hundred thousand people.

In the wonderful world of free enterprise, Amoco Oil is fined in a civil suit for discriminating against minorities in approving credit cards. But the tiny fine of $200,000 will scarcely intimidate the oil giant. The black poor's growing sense of isolation is evident in frequent clashes with police over their policing tactics. In the most serious race riot since the '60s, eighteen people are killed (eight white, ten black) and over two hundred are injured in Miami's Liberty City district after four cops are acquitted in the beating death of a black insurance executive.

Some good news is provided by the Supreme Court as it rules that Congress can impose racial quotas to counteract discrimination against blacks in federal job programs. This decision is part of a trend in federal and state government laws and court rulings that support affirmative action as a way to counteract years of racial discrimination. But the future holds little joy for proponents of affirmative action. As the power of the neoconservative movement grows, the momentum for affirmative action slows to a crawl. Moreover, the makeup of the Supreme Court, already tilting toward the right with appointees of Richard Nixon, is profoundly altered in the '80s.

Black progress in some visible areas, public battles over the fruits of the civil rights movement, conservative calls for a return to "traditional values" (a phrase sure to worry any black person with a memory of America's racist traditions): these are the seeds planted in the soul of the year.

The post-soul era begins to reveal its true nature in the fall of 1980 with two very different historic events: Ronald Reagan is elected president, and Eddie Murphy debuts on *Saturday Night Live,* elevating two men who truly encompass the schizophrenic nature of the American experience in the '80s.

For a nation of dysfunctional families (a new phrase in the '80s), broken homes, and insecure institutions, Reagan's grandfatherly demeanor promises security, certainty, and simplicity. He would make it "morning in America" again, which unfortunately for many means a return to states' rights and government indifference to poverty. In Reagan's world, the "great society" of the '60s is a moribund concept to be taken apart and then discarded like an old pair of pants. The old-style civil rights movement is viewed as largely irrelevant by Reagan, whose idea of spirituality in the public sphere isn't defined by Martin Luther King but by Jerry Falwell's Christian right. When Reagan turns down an invitation to address the National Association for the Advancement of Colored People during the campaign, he sends a clear message to friend and foe about his priorities.

For poor people of color this election will mean an accelerated erosion of government protections and a growing civic insensitivity to poverty; the enforcement of rigid rules governing programs and government spending would replace treatment of social ills, enterprise zones would be offered in lieu of job training, and the chasm between the middle and working classes would grow. These effects, and many others, would be Reagan's and the GOP's legacy to its darker citizens. Sadly, during the presidential campaign, two heroes of the civil rights struggle, Reverends Ralph Abernathy and Hosea Williams, who both toiled with Dr. King through years of marches and protest, endorse Reagan over their fellow-Georgian Jimmy Carter, stung by the Democrat's weakness on social issues. Thankfully, few blacks take their misguided advice; blacks vote overwhelmingly against the GOP in the November elections.

Reagan receives 51.6 percent of the popular vote to Carter's 41.7 percent, and the remaining 6.7 percent goes to third-party candidate John Anderson. Only 54 percent of all the eligible voters pull the lever. As a result, Reagan would get to implement a philosophy that would weaken the social fabric that connects Americans, based on the support of only 27 percent of eligible voters.

During the same November that brings the Californian to Washington, Eddie Murphy strengthens the threads that knit blacks and whites together on Saturday nights. Unlike Richard Pryor and Bill Cosby, the men he would succeed as the nation's most celebrated funny man, Murphy is a product of the post-soul world—television, movies, and a relatively color-blind world define his life experience. Like his white *Saturday Night Live* peers, Murphy's point of reference is pop culture, not a Midwestern brothel or an inner-city 'hood. Murphy grew up on the same cartoons and sitcoms as every other suburban kid. Blessed with an innate talent for mimicry, good looks, and personal charisma, Murphy doesn't so much create a formula for "crossing over" (a phrase we'll come back to repeatedly in this narrative) as just live out his influences in his art, influences he has in common with his vast suburban audience.

JANUARY 8 Black Entertainment Television debuts, the first cable network devoted to programming oriented toward black viewers. It is founded by D.C.-based black businessman Robert L. Johnson. Most of the programming at this early juncture is old movies with black cast members, '70s sitcoms, and lots of examples of the relatively new phenomenon of infomercials. BET's biggest struggle from its inception through the late '80s is simply being seen, since few cable systems carry it. Though Johnson founds a truly contemporary enterprise, his business practices and vision are very old-fashioned. With his monopoly position in black media, Johnson decides to focus on expanding his access to cable systems and not on potentially costly programs. Using the free programming that record companies begin to provide in the form of music videos, BET develops very few original shows in the '80s that do not revolve around music videos. Through this conservative strategy BET prospers while offering little new to a community starved for images of itself.

MARCH Random House publishes *The Salt Eaters* by Toni Cade Bambara. The novel is set in Claybourne, Georgia, and takes place in the span of a two-hour conversation between two women, ex-activist and recent attempted suicide (Velma Henry) and local spiritual leader (Minnie Ransom). In Bambara's impressionistic, nonlinear narrative we travel back and forth in time and into the minds of Velma and her friends and family. The goal of this journey is to "re-center" Velma, who, through the tumult of the civil rights struggle, has lost touch with herself.

Bambara, forty-one, taps into the collective exhaustion of the generation that fought furiously for black advancement but now finds itself confronting an unfinished agenda and middle age. Bambara, who'd previously published two short-story collections (*Gorilla, My Love* in '72 and *The Sea Birds Are Still Alive* in '77), does a superb job of capturing the psychic fallout from militancy and the yearning for spiritual connection so many ex-activists feel in the '80s. The themes and style of *The Salt Eaters* will influence not just other writers but filmmakers as well (for example, Julie Dash's 1991 film *Daughters of the Dust* is also set in Georgia and employs a visual strategy that echoes Bambara's prose).

MARCH The Jacksons release *Triumph,* their third post-Motown album, which is highlighted by the intense dance jam "Shake Your Body" and the anthemic "Can You Feel It," both of which feature Michael on lead vocals. Ultimately the most interesting song on *Triumph* is Michael's only solo composition, "Heartbreak Hotel," which echoes the cinematic production of his solo album and has as its subject a tortured, clandestine love affair. The *Triumph* tour that supports the album balances Michael's solo material with that performed by him with his brothers, and there's a palpable tension on stage between the two sets of songs. Many of the staging techniques (explosions, lighting cues, Michael's moves) recur in the singer's live shows to this day.

MARCH 2 A four-day conference of black political leaders ends after spotlighting several significant trends: a presidential forum is cancelled when all the invited candidates (Democrats Jerry Brown and Edward Kennedy, Independent John Anderson) decline, a slap in the face that infuriates the Reverend Jesse Jackson and illustrates the need for someone to articulate the black agenda on national issues; and the collected pols predict that the trend of federal budget cutbacks that started under Carter and would obviously continue under a Republican administration will endanger the social and economic progress of their constituents. At the convention, Detroit's feisty mayor Coleman Young gets booed for endorsing President Carter and argues that for the black community not to rally around the Democratic president is a profound mistake. The conference attendees aren't swayed by the stubborn Coleman's arguments, but do agree that pressing for economic and political sanctions against South Africa's apartheid government is a top priority for the black political class in this country.

MAY 16   In the NBA title-clinching game six against the Philadelphia 76ers, Earvin "Magic" Johnson starts at center for an injured Kareem Abdul-Jabbar. During the course of the 123–107 victory, Magic plays center, forward, and guard, scores forty-two points, grabs fifteen rebounds, and passes for seven assists. This game caps an amazing rookie season for the smiling six-foot nine-inch point guard who is revolutionizing the game by bringing a forward's body to a position traditionally played by men four inches shorter. His size causes teams to rethink how big a point guard should be. His no-look passes and deft ball handling encourage a generation of big men to develop a complete game, as dependent on skill as on size. Just ten years earlier, men of Magic's height, like Celtics great Bill Russell, played center and did little ball handling. No more.

But there is more to Earvin Johnson. With his bright smile and easy laugh, Magic charms fans all across the country and brings a fast-paced style dubbed "Showtime!" to the Los Angeles Forum. Endorsement deals pile up (Sprite, Converse) and movie stars become staples at Laker games. After winning the NCAA title at Michigan State, Magic comes into the pros with an aura of success that continues when he sparks the Lakers (who, despite the presence of Kareem Abdul-Jabbar, were late '70s also-rans) to the title. Under Johnson's leadership the Lakers will become the dominant professional basketball team of the '80s, driven by a flamboyant, exciting brand of basketball with an appeal across racial lines that is as broad as Magic's smile.

MAY 30 TransAfrica, a black lobby for Africa and the Caribbean, holds a very successful fund-raiser in the nation's capital. The organization, led by executive director and founder Randall Robinson (brother of ABC anchor Max), is relatively young (this is only its third dinner) but is already energizing the infant American antiapartheid movement. In his keynote address Robinson speaks of Nelson Mandela "languishing in a South African dungeon" and of the three hundred American corporations that have invested nearly $2 billion in South Africa. Liberian ambassador H. R. W. Brewer tells *The Washington Post,* "It's about time that Afro-Americans got involved. We know what Jewish people have done for Israel. It's a shame that in a country with 30 million blacks, there's no strong Africa policy." TransAfrica will help change that.

JUNE 1 Swashbuckling Atlanta-based millionaire Ted Turner introduces a twenty-four-hour-a-day cable news network known universally as CNN. Bernard Shaw, a sober black man with a James Earl Jones–like baritone, is a news anchor and a signature member of this ambitious enterprise that eventually affects how news is consumed, as well as how it is covered, all over the world.

JUNE 2 Richard Pryor and Gene Wilder star in *Stir Crazy,* directed by Sidney Poitier, which earns over $100 million at the box office, the first time a black-helmed feature has crossed the century mark. The film, about two New Yorkers who end up in a

Southwestern prison, reunites the two funny men whose collaboration in *Silver Streak* (1976) made that film a surprise hit. As with his direction of earlier comedies (*Uptown Saturday Night, Let's Do It Again*), Poitier's work is capable but hardly inspired. Still, *Stir Crazy* becomes another landmark in Poitier's historic career, and it also confirms Pryor as a bankable Hollywood star.

JUNE 9   Richard Pryor is severely burned while cooking cocaine in his home. The great stand-up (and longtime drug addict) was about to get high in his Columby Hills, California, residence by inhaling the fumes from heated cocaine. This technique, known as freebasing, is all the rage among "hip" users on both coasts. It is the next step up from snorting cocaine, since cooking coke intensifies the high. It is called freebasing because the process "frees" base cocaine from the cocaine hydrochloride powder. Making freebase is a cumbersome process that requires a butane or acetylene torch, but produces an intense, incredibly addictive high. Freebasing apparently was first done in South America and appeared in California around 1974.

Pryor, whose genius in comedy had led him to a lucrative but unimpressive film career, becomes the first high-profile American to publicly fall victim to freebase. The irony is that Pryor's near-death experience acts not as a cautionary tale, but as an advertisement. In the tragically colorful tale of America's love affair with narcotics, Pryor plays a starring role, because his life-threatening accident announces that we are leaving the era in which heroin and angel dust are the dominant drugs. Those interested in finding an easier-to-market version of the freebase high begin seeking an alternative.

Around the time of Pryor's accident, drug users on the small Caribbean island of Netherlands Antilles and in the Bahamas begin experimenting with a cocaine derivative created by mixing powdered cocaine with baking soda and heated water. The water is poured off and from the pasty residue chips or rocks are broken off and smoked. These drug pioneers have many names for their nefarious discovery—"roxanne," "base rock," and "baking soda base" were all used. Then someone comes up with "rock," and for a while, it is known primarily as rock cocaine. The high is brief, unlike the high from freebase, lasting only ten seconds or so. But rock is simple to make and easy to sell—addicts take one hit and are hooked. It will be a couple of years before this substance, which makes a crackling sound when smoked, reaches the mainland.

JULY 25 In New York City the Black Filmmaker Foundation begins screening a series of black independent fictional films and documentaries; their venues include a church, a hospital, and a discotheque. BFF codirector and filmmaker Warrington Hudlin tells *The New York Times* (which gives the event some minor coverage), "We want the filmmakers to understand the concerns of the audience and the audience to have a better understanding of the process—to understand that filmmaking is not just magic from Hollywood."

AUGUST To celebrate its tenth anniversary, *Black Enterprise*'s publisher Earl G. Graves has his staff ask readers to answer questions about their views on a wide range of issues. The replies from nearly 5,000 respondents paint a broad picture of the black middle class in America.

Seventy percent say black Americans "need a leader in the image of Martin Luther King Jr.," but 73 percent think the race doesn't have effective leadership at the moment. When asked, "Who speaks for the aspirations of black Americans today?" readers mention Reverend Jesse Jackson (30.3 percent) and former UN ambassador Andrew Young (20.9 percent). Both men, significantly, are lieutenants of the slain King. The only other person to reach double figures is National Urban League head Vernon Jordan.

The traditional civil rights organizations fare poorly (NAACP 1.8 percent, Southern Christian Leadership Conference 1.1 percent, the Urban League 0.8 percent). Getting the same number as the National Urban League is Minister Louis Farrakhan of the Nation of Islam, who receives no mainstream media coverage and precious little in the black press. Farrakhan's chief means of reaching his constituents is via a weekly radio broadcast and appearances at mosques around the country. To the *Black Enterprise* reader, Farrakhan was nearly invisible.

Yet the magazine points out that "there is a pivotal subclass within the black community which is sick of the political status quo and is beginning to reject the 'lesser of two evils' syndrome. They want new faces, new approaches, and new attitudes." In those words is an opportunity for someone.

The magazine's readers are very aware of their post–civil rights era economic gains: 52.3 percent believe employment opportunities have increased for blacks and 50.9 percent think their present jobs would not have been available to them ten years before. Which is why 93.6 percent think affirmative action "would be necessary one year from now." The readers of *Black Enterprise,* college educated, many with master's degrees, are precisely the group that has benefited most directly from affirmative action and whose children figure to as well.

There is no question among readers that black Americans feel they should participate more in the South African struggle for liberation. Almost 85 percent say so, though only 76.8 percent think American firms should divest their interests there, which the magazine interprets as "uncertainty about the impact of U.S. corporations on the struggle in southern African and their role in maintaining apartheid."

What is surprising is a deep ambivalence about school busing. While a solid 72.9 percent favor it as a tactic to ensure a quality education for black children, 57.3 percent do not support it if the sole goal is to achieve racial integration. Racial equality in school, and in all walks of life, had been the driving philosophical force of the civil rights movement. But just a scant fifteen years since the movement's peak, the majority of the college-educated *Black Enterprise* audience do not feel it is enough to support busing black kids to white schools. This is one reason that old-line civil rights organizations, for whom integration is the institutional goal, have fallen so far out of favor. The crucial issue for the respondents isn't busing—it is quality education for their children.

The relative vacuum in leadership, the sense of progress, worries about white retrenchment, and ambiguity about educational issues all speak to a collective black consciousness that is uncertain, hardly optimistic, and somewhat at war with itself. Only on support for South Africans and the continuing need for affirmative action is there anything approaching unison in thinking.

Black Enterprise reporter Isaiah J. Poole sums the survey up by saying, "Like the rest of the country, the black community is divided into several sectors, each grouping in a different direction to find its own elusive American dream . . . The only common binding element is a nagging—and potentially volatile—unhappiness with the way things are."

AUGUST Two icons of funk, George Clinton and Sly Stone, are arrested on a Los Angeles freeway for freebasing cocaine in a moving vehicle. Charges are later dropped when it is determined the amount of white powder recovered is too small to test. Sly then makes a guest appearance on Funkadelic's next album, *The Electric Spanking of War Babies*. Throughout the early '80s there are many fleeting glimpses of Sly doing unfinished concerts, making lackluster albums, and experiencing a steady stream of drug arrests. The sad irony is that while Sly flounders, so many acts obviously influenced by his Family Stone (Prince, Rick James, Parliament) prosper.

SEPTEMBER Eddie Murphy debuts on NBC's *Saturday Night Live*. After most of the members of the original breakthrough cast moved on to feature films, the sketch comedy show had lost its cachet. Creator and executive producer Lorne Michaels had moved on and was replaced by a young producer named Jean Doumanian. Many observers think the broadcast is on its way to oblivion.

The casting of twenty-year-old Murphy revitalizes the show and establishes it firmly as an ongoing comedy franchise. Murphy, a product of the black middle-class suburb of Roosevelt, Long Island, cut his teeth in white comedy clubs on the Island and in Manhattan. Because of his youth, his background, and the fact that he has only a passing connection to the old-school black comedy circuit, Murphy's views of what is funny and how to articulate that sense of humor differ from those of black comedy stars of the '70s. He isn't angry or intensely political or overly socially conscious.

Up until the '80s the sources of African American creativity were usually thought to be either the Deep South (home to the blues, gospel, and the civil rights movement) or the big-city ghettos (spawning ground of R&B, bebop, nationalism, and basketball supremacy). Just as there was a celebrated black exodus from the South to the North in the early to middle part of the twentieth century, the '60s and '70s brought a steady movement of families from concrete streets to working-class suburbs. They were no longer in the big bad cities, but they weren't as far away from the urban centers as the majority of white suburban towns. For example, in the New York area, places like Mount Vernon, Queens, and Nassau County saw a growth in working-class and lower-middle-class black families. The town of Roosevelt, Long Island, in Nassau County, not very far from the Queens border, is one of those communities.

Like a great many crucial '80s icons (Spike Lee, Michael Jordan, Mike Tyson, Jean-Michel Basquiat), Murphy was born in Brooklyn. When he was a small child, Lillian and Vernon Murphy moved Eddie and his little brother Charlie out of Kings County and to Long Island, where they settled in a two-story suburban home.

In the '70s, "the Velt" produced one genius, Julius "Dr. J." Erving, perhaps the first great sepia hardwood star to call the suburbs home. In the '80s, the same general area of Long Island spawned a slew of rap stars (Public Enemy from Roosevelt, De La Soul from Wyandach, Rakim from Amityville, EMPM from Brentwood) as well as Murphy. There Murphy grew up wanting to be an entertainer, torn between being a pop singing star and a comic in the Richard Pryor tradition. As a teen he did stand-up on the Long Island comedy club circuit and later moved on to Manhattan venues like the Comic Strip, a largely white realm where Murphy's gift for impressions (James Brown, Little Richard, Bill Cosby) attracts the attention of managers and, ultimately, *Saturday Night Live* talent scouts.

On *SNL,* Eddie reveals himself to be a comic actor capable of an extraordinary range of personas and accents. Though Dan Ackroyd, Dana Carvey, Phil Hartman, and Mike Myers are remembered as the greatest chameleons in the show's long history, Murphy's catalogue of characters (Velvet Jones, Little Richard Simmons, Gumby, Mr. Robinson) is as impressive as anyone's. All are sharply observed, detailed, and drawn chiefly from television images. On a show that thrives on finding humor in the shared television experiences of its young viewers, Murphy brings some racial politics and his own personal take to bear on the material. By basing so much of his work around common pop culture, Murphy overcomes any racial barriers. Except for his color, Murphy had experienced America just like most of *SNL*'s viewers—via television from suburban homes.

What separates Murphy from the comic actors who excel at skits is that Eddie is funny as himself. He can don outrageous outfits and put on silly accents and be funny. Yet he can be both hilarious and rock-star charismatic just standing and telling jokes. This versatility is rare and allows Murphy to combine the best of the stand-up tradition with that of the sketch comic. Unlike John Belushi or Dan Ackroyd, Murphy is able to carry a movie without having to rely on being in character. Very few TV-bred stars have been able to do such stellar comic work on the small screen, yet have a persona big enough to dominate the large one.

Murphy is quite confident about his future. The twenty-year-old tells *New York Magazine,* "I don't think I'm gonna be as popular as Richard Pryor or Bill Cosby by the time I'm 22, but I hope I'm at the top by the time I'm 25."

SEPTEMBER 8-12 The Black Filmmaker Foundation holds a five-day conference at City University of New York's midtown campus. This conference introduces many festival programmers to the range of work being made outside Hollywood. Representatives from Amsterdam and Paris attend, which results in screenings of black indie films in Europe over the next two years. Several of the filmmakers (Charles Burnett, Charles Lane, Michelle Parkinson) are invited to attend the Berlin Film Festival.

The first day of the festival, BFF cofounder and filmmaker Warrington Hudlin is approached by an eager young man who is in his first year in NYU's film program. Though registration is closed, the young director pleads with Hudlin to be let in. Impressed by his intensity, Hudlin allows Shelton "Spike" Lee to register.

The BFF establishes a black film distribution service that serves as a clearinghouse for those interested in renting the work of its members. It is the first time the work of this non-Hollywood community is made accessible to the general public.

OCTOBER On the chilly streets of New York's SoHo and the Lower East Side, a self-conscious group of artists decides to make a movie about an arts scene that fuses punk, new wave, hip hop, and a contempt for uptown affluence into a worldview. The film doesn't appear for twenty years due to various technical snafus. There are glimpses of Blondie's Deborah Harry, Arto Lindsay, Fab Five Freddy, Lee Quinones, Kid Creole & the Coconuts, and others in *Downtown '81.*

The filmmakers, directed by photographer Edo Bertoglio, are prescient in their choice of protagonist, hiring a nineteen-year-old black graffiti artist from Brooklyn with the tag Samo as their star. Samo, a.k.a. Jean-Michel Basquiat, wanders around downtown, meeting people, picking up girls, and drawing on walls. The lofts where jazz is played and painters work, the dank clubs where punks roar and hipsters define their aesthetic provide the backdrop for Basquiat's sojourn. It is an amusing portrait of the artist as a young man.

OCTOBER 8 Prince's third album, *Dirty Mind,* and its provocative single, "Uptown," make it clear he is not just the soft-voiced Stevie Wonder wanna-be some have labeled him. "Uptown" is a multiracial anthem of fun, sex, and partying that garners much radio play. More problematic for programmers, but joyous for those seeking a new attitude in black pop, are "Head," a funky celebration of oral sex; the title cut, a fast-paced orgy on record; and "Sister," a disturbingly fun ditty about incest. Prince rips open the envelope on sexual frankness while widening the range of sounds available from a one-man band. His use of keyboards to re-create the feel of live horns is picked up by many other musicians. Prince backs this music up with a wicked live show. He performs in black bikini briefs, black knee-high boots, and a gray raincoat with a red bandanna around his neck. Backed by a visually arresting multiracial band, Prince announces that a new era is here and, without question, he's going to be one of the people running things in it.

Later in the fall Prince plays New York's Bottom Line, performing like the spawn of Hendrix and Sly. In *The Village Voice,* Pablo

Guzman wrote, "Not only does he rock, he does so with a style, a wit and a sound that places him at the cutting edge of whatever wave is now new." This is the show that turns rock critics from fans to fanatics, earning Prince unconditional love from the music press (though not from rock radio). Later he pens the sardonic "All the Critics Love U in New York," in response to the praise.

NOVEMBER Schoolboy basketball season is in full swing around the country. Down in Wilmington, North Carolina, a spirited game is under way between Williston Junior High and rival D.C. Virgo. A 5-foot, 9-inch ninth-grader on the D.C. squad steals the ball at midcourt and, to his surprise, dunks a ball for the first time. "It wasn't planned," he later recalled for *Sport Magazine*'s Paul Ladewski. "I didn't know that I had done it until after the fact. It was a surprise. I had tried it in practice, but I kept missing. I guess that I got caught up in the intensity of the game," says Michael Jeffrey Jordan.

DECEMBER 1 Democratic San Francisco legislator Willie Brown bests two white rivals to snare the powerful post of Speaker of the California State Assembly. A smallish, dapper, ambitious man, Brown had worked his way through college and law school as a night janitor in the late '50s and won an assembly seat in 1964 in an 80 percent white district, almost unheard of for a black politician at the time.

Despite some early run-ins with then-Speaker Jesse "Big Daddy" Unruh, Brown becomes a Democratic Party fixture. The self-described "Ayatollah of California" beats back rivals and dodges charges of corruption throughout the decade. He serves as national chairman of Jesse Jackson's Rainbow Coalition and becomes a potent Democratic fund-raiser. Brown is one product of the civil rights generation who successfully blends the idealism of his youth with the pragmatic politics of the '80s.

The end of the Atlanta child murder case?

1981

1981

Locals call him "the snatcher," as if he is some frightening mytho-
logical figure from a nasty bedtime story. To most of the nation he
is known as the Atlanta child murderer, a predator who, between
the summer of 1979 and his arrest on June 21, 1981, is thought to
have killed twenty-eight people between the ages of seven and
twenty-seven, all of whom are black. His mother, Faye, and father,
Homer, had named him Wayne B. Williams; he grew into a wan,
light-skinned twenty-three-year-old who hoped for a career in the
entertainment industry.

Williams is, if not the nation's first, then certainly its most famous black serial killer, though he is only actually charged with
the murders of Nathaniel Cater, twenty-seven, and Jimmy Ray
Payne, twenty-one, whose bodies are discovered floating in the
Chattahoochee River. Investigators for the 110-member special
task force created to capture the killer file an affidavit asserting
that Williams could have been linked to most of the other deaths,
but that these murders make the strongest case against him.
Williams is convicted of the deaths on February 27, 1982.

Few events in the '80s have an impact on a city quite like these
murders do on Atlanta, which has, since the early '70s, billed itself
as the capital of "the new South" and "the city too busy to hate."
For much of the previous two years, a 7 P.M. to 6 A.M. curfew has
been in effect, confirming the danger for a community of children
and parents traumatized by the news reports of the murders and
rampant rumors.

Stories that the killings are KKK- or white supremacist-
inspired swirl around Atlanta, feeding into deep-seated black

paranoia about white evil. To some, the killings are a kind of terror campaign against black advancement and power in the heart of the South. Some wonder whether Atlanta's first black mayor, Maynard Jackson, and his successor, Andy Young, stifle leads that would have uncovered such a racist conspiracy for fear of race riots.

When Williams is finally arrested, skepticism is widespread. Many think he is just a scapegoat and that the real murderer(s) remain at large. Camille Bell, mother of the nine-year-old Yusef Bell and founder of the vocal Committee to Stop Children's Murders, calls his trial "a kangaroo court." During the nine-week trial, prosecutors introduce evidence from ten cases to show a pattern that links Williams to twelve victims, primarily using tiny fibers and dog hairs plucked from the victims that match material from his home. In some cases there are eyewitnesses who saw Williams with some of the victims.

James Baldwin goes down to Atlanta to cover the trial for *Playboy* and turns the resulting essay into a book, *Evidence of Things Not Seen*. In it he writes, "The beleaguered, and, also, unhappily, divided defense could scarcely have avoided falling into the trap so carefully laid for them. Their legal obligation was to defend their client against a double murder charge. But the prosecution had absolutely no interest in this double murder, and it is doubtful, furthermore, that they had a case. Williams was on trial as a mass murderer, which charge, having no legal validity, could find no legal defense."

Williams's conviction gives Atlanta's largely black political establishment the sense of closure they sought. The city moves on to focus on completing the subway system, upgrading its massive airline terminals, and planning to host the Olympic games by the end of the century. Most of the victims' families are never totally convinced that Williams committed all the murders and Williams never admits any guilt. Enterprising Atlanta, a city with one of the most strongly entrenched black political machines in the nation,

Post-Soul
Nation
3 1

stays too busy moving forward to reflect too closely on the bloody loose ends of these murders.

Outside of Atlanta the biggest ongoing national story is the rapid reversal of the federal government's role as a prosecutor and advocate for civil rights. This year, President Reagan fires Arthur Flemming as chairman of the U.S. Commission on Civil Rights, naming black conservative Clarence Pendleton Jr. to replace him. Pendleton is one of many prominent black conservatives to emerge in the '80s who will play an increasing role in the national dialogue on race, becoming media darlings and appointed power brokers. Few, however, achieve elective office.

In keeping with the administration's conservative bias, numerous federal directives that affect minorities are rescinded during Reagan's first year in office. The U.S. Department of Labor announces the easing of affirmative action rules affecting contractors bidding on federal jobs. The U.S. Department of Justice announces it will no longer demand that employers maintain affirmative action programs or hire according to numerical quotas. The Department of Justice also announces it will no longer enforce busing as a means to counteract desegregation in public schools, labeling busing "ineffective and unfair."

JANUARY Beverly Johnson graces the cover of this month's *Vogue* magazine. Johnson is the fashion world's leading black model, having broken through the color barrier to become *Vogue*'s first black cover girl in 1974. The lean beauty also made the cover of *Glamour* in '75 and *Cosmopolitan* in '76.

FEBRUARY Max Robinson, one of three anchors of ABC's *World News Tonight,* makes news during a speech at New England's Smith College. Robinson complains about the "orgy of patriotism" that surrounded both Reagan's inauguration and the releases of the Iranian hostages, and charges that black reporters had intentionally been kept away from these stories. Robinson accuses the American media of viewing the world through "cracked glasses" and claims that ABC brass want him to speak "like any old white boy" and not incorporate his culture into his reporting. Mindful that his speech will be criticized and that he is taking a professional risk, Robinson argues that by speaking out against racism, "I will take myself out of the mean, racist trap all black Americans find themselves in."

Not surprisingly, Robinson's career doesn't prosper after this bold, biting-the-hand-that-feeds-him address. He is off network television by 1984. Sadly, the next time Max Robinson makes national news, it will be for something even more unexpected than his speech.

MARCH 28 The romance of downtown new wave/punk with uptown hip hop spawns Blondie's "Rapture," the first number-one pop single with rapping on it, which is certified a gold record with sales of 500,000 copies. Though Deborah Harry's flow is strictly amateur, the song serves to introduce many listeners to the sound. The video, which celebrates hip hop culture, includes cameos by Fab Five Freddy and Jean-Michel Basquiat.

MARCH 30 Indiana wins the NCAA championship with a score of 63 to 50 over North Carolina, a triumph for one of the great odd couples of American sport. During this season, the militaristic coaching style of Indiana's Bobby Knight meshes with the Chicago schoolyard flair of Isiah Thomas. Knight, a screaming, rigid product of old-school basketball who began his major college coaching career at West Point, has built a powerhouse program in basketball-mad Indiana. He is known to adoring Hoosier fans as "the General," a moniker he's earned for the infantry precision of his coaching style and his stern, often profane, displays of authority. Thomas is a baby-faced point guard from the ghetto streets of

Chicago who brings slick, city game ball handling and a sly inner-city flare to this Big Ten university.

In the '70s there had been an often bitter on-court aesthetic war between the more flamboyant "black" game and a more patterned "white" game. In the '80s these distinctions are blurred as white coaches become more flexible and the newer generation of black stars finds ways to work within systems. Thomas tones down his game for the Hoosiers, but once he leaves school after this season and joins the Detroit Pistons, this smiling assassin gets real funky.

MARCH 30 *Newsweek* publishes a cover story on Toni Morrison coinciding with the publication of *Tar Baby,* labeling her "the best of the black writers today." Throughout the '70s, Morrison, whose day job is editing for Random House, published prolifically and ambitiously (*The Bluest Eye, Sula, Song of Solomon*), creating a body of work that enthralled critics, college-educated females of all colors, and readers of all genders. Morrison's anointment signals mainstream awareness that black women writers—influenced by feminism, the spirit of Harlem Renaissance author Zora Neale Hurston, and a sense of grievance against white racism and black male chauvinism—are producing an assertive, exciting body of work.

APRIL David Bradley's *The Chaneysville Incident* is published to critical acclaim and later wins the PEN/Faulkner Award for best novel. *Chaneysville,* Bradley's second novel, takes place between March 3 and 12, 1979, but spans 250 years as its protagonist, John Washington, a Philadelphia historian, travels physically and mentally between the coastline and the Pennsylvania mountain range where he was reared. Though set in the present, Bradley's narrative is obsessed with the past as the thirty-one-year-old writer wrestles with balancing who Washington is with who he was. Like much black art of the early '80s, *Chaneys-*

ville meditates on the fallout as segregation fades and new opportunities emerge. Things should be so much better, and materially for many, they are. Yet the new post-soul reality creates as much unease as liberation.

APRIL Julie Dash, a Los Angeles–based indie filmmaker, makes an assured short film, *Illusions,* about a black woman passing for white at a Hollywood studio during World War II. Lonette McKee stars in the black-and-white work that (cinematically and metaphorically) illuminates the subversive strength of black women in a male-dominated, racist culture. Beautifully woven into the film is the bittersweet tale of a black singer who lip-syncs the voice of a white actress. This character is based on Anita Ellis, a singer who dubbed the vocals for Hollywood starlet Rita Hayworth in several movies.

APRIL 14 Tom Bradley wins his third term as mayor of Los Angeles in a landslide, garnering 64 percent of the vote versus his longtime political nemesis, former mayor Sam Yorty. It is the first time a Los Angeles mayor has won a third term without a runoff. A recent statewide poll gives Bradley the highest favorable rating in the state. When asked about rumors that he's planning to run for governor, Bradley replies, "Let me savor this for a few days."

MAY 22 Richard Pryor's first film release after his freebase sparked fire is Universal's *Bustin' Loose,* a comedy that unfortunately has a subplot involving a child arsonist, which draws titters from audiences. Cicely Tyson, the best black actress of the '70s (*The Autobiography of Miss Jane Pittman, A Woman Called Moses*), costars in this film by black director Oz Scott. In an interview around the time *Bustin' Loose* is released, Thom Mount, president of production at Universal, tells *Black Enterprise,* "Black films are not capable of making money. There's only one actor who's bankable, Richard Pryor, and one actress, Diana Ross, and we have Pryor under contract." The implication is, why make any black films if Pryor isn't in them?

Nineteen-year-old trumpeter Wynton Marsalis leaves Art Blakey's Jazz Messengers to join Miles Davis's early '60s rhythm section (pianist Herbie Hancock, bassist Ron Carter, drummer Tony Williams) on a Japanese tour. The New Orleans native has been a sensation in jazz circles since taking a leave of absence from the Juilliard School of Music at age eighteen to tour with the venerable drummer Blakey. Upon their return to the States, Marsalis and the Davis vets record *Herbie Hancock: Quarter,* a double album that makes young Marsalis a star.

CBS signs him to an unprecedented contract as both a jazz and classical artist. Marsalis's first self-titled jazz album is recorded before he even has a regular touring band. For the recording session he puts together a core group of drummer Jeff Watts, pianist Kenny Kirkland, and older brother tenor saxophonist Branford. This ensemble, labeled VSOP II and abetted by several different bass players, makes traditional acoustic jazz hip for a new generation of listeners.

The smooth-talking yet studious trumpeter attracts the attention of several sage jazz writers, among them Albert Murray (author of the classic *Stomping the Blues*) and Stanley Crouch (a contributor to *The Village Voice* and writer of liner notes), who become champions of and mentors to him.

Wynton, who at this point in his career is photographed only in suits, is the most debonair trumpet player since Miles in his 1950s *GQ* period. With his wire-framed glasses, studied Southern charm, and obvious smarts, Marsalis becomes a media darling jazz hasn't had in decades. His affable brother Branford (a year older) is quite witty as well. Together the Marsalis brothers, along with a generation of "young lions" like Terence Blanchard and Donald Harrison, make acoustic music relevant to the synthesizer generation.

JUNE Kathleen Collins goes into production on *Losing Ground*, which will be the first feature-length drama directed by a black woman. The eighty-six-minute film looks at the life of a black female college professor very much like Collins herself. Self-conscious and postmodern in its approach, *Losing Ground* shows viewers the making of the film as part of Collins's narrative strategy. This postmodern conceit limits the film's appeal, but doesn't minimize Collins's achievement in getting it completed in an environment hostile to fresh cinematic visions of black life.

JUNE 5 The *Morbidity and Mortality Weekly Report (MMWR)*, a journal of the Centers for Disease Control, features a story by doctors Michael S. Gottlieb and Wayne Shandera on the deaths of five gay men from what is diagnosed as Pneumocystis carinii pneumonia (PCP).

JULY 3 The *New York Times* publishes an article titled "Rare Cancer Seen in 41 Homosexuals."

JULY 18 Diana Ross and Lionel Ritchie's duet on the title song from the movie *Endless Love* tops the pop chart. The saccharine love song from a forgettable flick is part of a long run of hits penned by Ritchie that began in the mid-70s when, as a member of the Commodores, he wrote and sang "Zoom" and "This Is Your Life." As the decade progresses, Ritchie's songs become less R&B-based and more pop-friendly, as demonstrated by the country-flavored "Easy" and the piano-based "Still."

This duet with longtime Motown labelmate and fading pop diva Ross pairs old and new stars of Berry Gordy's legendary label. Ritchie, who will go solo next year, is the last huge pop star to be nurtured and promoted in the tradition of Motown. He developed his songwriting and vocal skills under the guidance of several Motown greats and his producer, even after he goes solo, is longtime staff producer-arranger James Carmichael.

Ritchie has hits with some up- and mid-tempo beats but his trademarks are sensitive ballads with one-name titles that rule pop radio. Ritchie, a skilled craftsman and emotive vocalist, creates his own "Motown sound" that polishes soul into shiny adult-contemporary fodder. Ritchie's hits are integral parts of the '80s and, ironically, are the kinds of records that fuel hip hop's rebel attitude. Despite his undeniable craftsmanship, Ritchie makes just the type of sweet, slick music a generation of rappers would deride in their boyish attempts to redefine black music and the image of black men.

JULY 29 A band from Minneapolis named The Time debuts with a slick, danceable self-titled album. Despite obviously being influenced by Prince, the band's singer, a comically suave Morris Day, denies his involvement. The album credits Jamie Starr as producer.

Only later is it revealed that Starr is, in fact, Prince, and that he wrote and played most of the music on this album. Jamie Starr is just one of several playful alter egos Prince will adopt (Alexander Nevermind, Christopher). As Jamie Starr he produces the debut of Vanity 6 (which he originally wanted to call Vagina), a sexy, multiracial female vocal trio that hits with the unself-consciously slutty "Nasty Girl."

AUGUST 1 The cable channel, Music Television, a.k.a. MTV, debuts with an airing of the Buggles's "Video Killed the Radio Star." The record is only somewhat prophetic. Radio remains central to how people use music (after all, you can't watch a video and drive). Video does change forever how music is marketed and how fans relate to music.

Prior to MTV's debut in America there had never been a consistent, easily accessible, mass market outlet for viewing specially prepared clips of artists performing their music. But TV shows that showcase these clips had been around for years in Europe, which is one reason that early MTV playlists are filled with British bands like the Buggles. It will take a year or more before the major American labels begin to finance a steady stream of music videos for domestic consumption.

In the original rotation of the on-air announcers known as VJs there is one black, J. J. Jackson, an old pop radio DJ with a very mainstream (non-black-sounding) style. Robert Pittman, the driving programming force behind MTV, says the format is aimed at replicating the rock radio experience. This is bad news for black performers, since rock radio in America in the '80s practices sonic apartheid, even for those who musically fit the format. MTV's reluctance to showcase black performers would be a bone of contention for both fans and makers of black music.

SEPTEMBER Linebacker Lawrence Taylor of the University of North Carolina, the second player taken in the National Football League draft, begins his career with the New York Giants. At the press conference held by the Giants to introduce him to the Big Apple, Taylor announces, "I like to eat quarterbacks in the backfield." Reporters laugh, but the six-foot three-inch, 240-pound man with the nasty scowl starts proving this fall that he wasn't joking.

Playing outside linebacker in a three lineman, four linebacker defense (the 3-4), Taylor revolutionizes his position with his speed, technique, and savagery. Sometimes he falls back in pass coverage. Sometimes he stays around the line of scrimmage waiting on runners. But he is most devastating when he attacks quarterbacks using a strip move that often jars the football free. He becomes notorious (and even more feared) a few years later when, during an ABC Monday Night game against Washington, he blitzes the Redskins QB Joe Theisman and twists him so far back that a bone snaps in the quarterback's leg. Taylor's propensity for awe-inspiring on-field mayhem gets him named to ten straight Pro Bowls and sparks the Giants to Super Bowl wins in '86 and '90.

Unfortunately LT's dynamic on-field exploits are matched by his off-the-field demons. He once said of his life, "Sunday is a different world. It's like a fantasy world which I'd rather live in. Then I go back to the rest of the world and that's when the trouble starts." Like several of the most prominent New York–based athletes of the '80s, Taylor eventually falls victim to crack cocaine. He enters drug detox programs in '86 and '88. After his 1993 retirement he is arrested twice for buying crack from undercover cops.

As one of the biggest stars in the world's brightest city, Taylor is an innovator and champion. Yet in the world of temptation and addiction the man is just another victim. In a way, addiction is a very democratic instinct. It puts all junkies—rich, poor, famous, or faceless—on equal footing.

SEPTEMBER 12   An NBC Saturday morning cartoon series debuts featuring cute little blue cartoon creatures from Belgium called Smurfs. While the network targets young children, the Smurfs' appeal crosses age and racial barriers and evolves into an urban craze that inspires a popular hip hop dance and scores of twelve-inch singles aimed at the youth market. Aggressive hip hop and dance labels jump all over the Smurfs, using different spellings of "smurf" in an attempt to avoid copyright infringement suits. Ghetto T-shirt vendors have a field day selling fake Smurf merchandise featuring "black" smurfs wearing gold chains, unlaced sneakers, beepers, and other b-boy attire. Well before sampling becomes a hip hop musical staple, the adaptation of the Smurfs by young blacks is an early fun example of their playful recontextualizing of mainstream artifacts. Bart Simpson, *Star Wars,* high-end clothing designers, and Buddhist monks are just a few of the other "found objects" that this post-mod sensibility will toy with in the coming years.

SEPTEMBER 25 Denzel Washington makes his big-screen debut in *Carbon Copy*, a comedy by Hollywood's most active black director, Michael Schultz. As the long-lost son of a white man played by George Segal, Denzel is miscast doing comedy (it is one theatrical arena he doesn't excel in), but it gets him in the Hollywood gate. The following year he gets a regular gig as Dr. Philip Chandler on the NBC drama *St. Elsewhere*, which plays to his leading man strengths.

For Schultz it's the latest competent job in a career that began with greater promise. He began directing in 1967 with the then-spanking-new Negro Ensemble Company. His work there wins him the job directing a play on Broadway, *Does a Tiger Wear a Necktie?*, in 1969. In 1972 the light-skinned, soft-spoken director supervised a ninety-minute PBS adaptation of Lorraine Hansberry's autobiography, *To Be Young, Gifted and Black*, with a fine cast (Ruby Dee, Roy Scheider, Al Freeman Jr.). That same year he shot an interracial romance, *Together for Days*, in Atlanta, that only saw limited release. After relocating to Los Angeles, Schultz got work on TV episodes (*The Rockford Files, Baretta, Starsky & Hutch*) and, for ABC, did a fine adaptation of a great play he'd originally directed at the NEC, Lonnie Elder III's *Ceremonies in Dark Old Men*.

Television led Schultz to his breakthrough film, *Cooley High*, in 1975. Based on a wonderful script by *Good Times* cocreator Eric Monte, the film captured the warmth and danger of mid-60s black Chicago, using great Motown music and heartwarming performances from a great crew of young stage-trained black actors like Glynn Turman and Lawrence Hilton-Jacobs.

Coming at the end of the blaxploitation era, *Cooley High* was the first major example of black nostalgia for the '60s. Its uncomplicated vision of the black community in the soul era struck a deep chord with a people suddenly confronted with the post-soul landscape. Though somewhat comparable to George Lucas's *American Graffiti* (1973), *Cooley High* had a grace and vigor all its own, and quickly became one of the most loved black films of all time.

NOVEMBER 10 The Negro Ensemble Company debuts Charles Fuller's *A Soldier's Play* at New York's Theater Four. The NEC is one of the great institutions of black theater. Founded in 1967 by actor Robert Hooks, playwright-director Douglas Turner Ward, and theater manager Gerald Krone, as a vehicle for the advancement of black people and their culture, the NEC survives into the '80s on the strength of powerful writing and the still relatively untapped community of black acting talent.

Playwrights like Lonnie Elder (*Ceremonies in Dark Old Men*), Joseph Walker (*The River Niger*), Leslie Lee (*The First Breeze of Summer*), and Sam Art Williams (*Home*) all receive national recognition while working at the NEC. So do two generations of superb actors (Glynn Turman, Gloria Foster, Phylicia Rashad, Sherman Helmsley, Louis Gossett, Adolph Caesar). All this bountiful talent ends up moving to Los Angeles seeking work in films, hour-long dramas, and with great regularity, situation comedies.

Charles Fuller is the last of the great playwrights to develop at the NEC. Through the late '70s, Fuller, a Philadelphia native, had written several fine dramas showcased at the NEC, including the critically acclaimed *Zooman and the Sign,* which starred a versatile young thespian named Giancarlo Esposito.

A Soldier's Play is, if not the greatest single piece of theater to emerge from the NEC, probably the most honored, winning the New York Drama Critics Award and the Pulitzer Prize in 1982, and being optioned by Hollywood (it is made into a movie titled *A Soldier's Story* in 1984). Fuller's play is a beautifully constructed mystery. It begins with the murder of a well-respected drill instructor, Sergeant Waters, on the eve of his all-black unit being shipped off from its Southern base camp to fight in World War II. The detective in this case, a polished, college-educated black captain from Washington named Davenport, initially suspects the obvious: that the murder was committed by a racist white officer.

But as the investigation unfolds, layers of racial self-hate and class discrimination are revealed. Fuller uses the "whodunit" structure to explore how racism has festered within the black community and puts it at war with itself. The idea that black art is not simply a vehicle for attacking racism or entertainment, but an instrument to articulate the class and color tensions inside the black community, is a recurring '80s theme.

Fuller's powerful craftsmanship is enhanced by a superb cast. Adolph Caesar's performance as the complex murder victim Sergeant Waters elevates him from an actor best known for doing voice-over work to the forefront of American acting. Unfortunately, he dies before reaching true stardom in film or TV.

Making a more enduring impression are two other actors: Denzel Washington, who plays the intense, intelligent Private Melvin Peterson in a brilliant performance; and Sam Jackson, in the smaller but sharply defined character role of Private Louis Henson. It is the first, but far from the last, stellar appearance for both.

Fuller, Washington, and Jackson represent the caliber of talent the NEC, and black theater in general, had been producing for generations. Sadly, *A Soldier's Play* would be one of the last great artistic explosions for black theater in the popular consciousness. As time progresses, younger talents, who a generation earlier would have toiled in these grassroots theaters, take advantage of the era's new opportunities. By the end of the decade, making a rap record will begin to replace black theater as a path to stardom.

DECEMBER President Reagan, as part of his effort to reduce government "waste," proposes large cuts in the federal budget for the Centers for Disease Control in Atlanta.

The musical *Dreamgirls* opens on Broadway to rave reviews for both Michael Bennett's stellar direction and its book written by Tom Egen, a clever reinvention of the mythology of Motown records with characters based loosely on Berry Gordy and Supremes members Diana Ross and Flo Ballard. Its plot hypothesizes the mysterious mid-1967 ousting of Ballard from the greatest girl group ever.

Thematically *Dreamgirls* is driven by a popular '80s argument: that in search of pop or "crossover" success (moving from black to white audiences), black performers sacrifice their connection to their "soul." As embodied in the heavyset, big-voiced Jennifer Holliday, the tragedy of soul is played out in Holliday's character's removal from the faux Supremes, the Dreams. Holliday's show-stopping "And I'm Telling You I'm Not Going" works as a metaphor for the loss of her lover (the Gordy character) and the loss of heart in black popular music.

The irony of *Dreamgirls'* argument about gritty soul music being discarded in favor of insubstantial musical styles is that Bennett's direction is as slick as a pair of spandex pants. His staging is very much a triumph of style over substance. The stage revolves from front to back, changing foreground and background as a movie would through edits. It is a showy, revolutionary style that makes people notice the direction as much as the tale being told. Bennett's staging, along with career-starting performances by Holliday, Sheryl Lee Ralph, Obba Babatunde, and Loretta Devine, makes *Dreamgirls* a Broadway landmark.

The musical also reflects the camp, surreal view of black divas that is a significant part of the gay aesthetic. Holliday's "And I'm Telling You" is a staple at drag shows for years. The show's biggest failing (and it is a huge one) is the music itself, which is literally a pale imitation of '60s soul.

Charismatic congresswoman Shirley Chisholm.

1982

1982

The going and coming of two incredibly different black politicians
reflect the tenor of Reaganite Washington. Seven-term congresswoman Shirley Chisholm of Brooklyn's Twelfth District announces
her retirement after fourteen years in office. Chisholm, a fiery and
compassionate woman, came to prominence in the late '60s and
was part of the wave of urban politicians to wrest power from
whites in areas once controlled by ethnic politicians.

The Crown Heights community Chisholm represents is a feisty,
occasionally combustible mix of blacks, Puerto Ricans, orthodox
Jews, and recently arrived Caribbean immigrants. But Chisholm, a
petite but fierce little woman with a memorable speaking voice, is
more than a match for her constituents, an inspiration to women
of all races, and is championed by both Democratic leaders and
feminists.

Chisholm was descended from West Indian immigrants herself
and spent eight years of her childhood in Barbados before returning to the United States to stay at age eleven. She attended public
schools before getting an undergraduate degree in sociology at
Brooklyn College and a master's in elementary education at Columbia. Like so many of New York's immigrant offspring, Chisholm
moved into civil service, working as a nursery school teacher, as
director of a day care center, and at the New York Department of
Social Services.

She ran for and won a state assembly seat in 1964 before easily
besting James Farmer, former president of the civil rights organization CORE, in a 1968 contest for a congressional seat created to
ensure a majority black voting block. As the first black woman in

the House of Representatives, she immediately became a national figure and she used this visibility to get on committees that dealt with education, labor, and urban issues.

Her high public profile was increased in 1972 when she announced her candidacy for the Democratic presidential nomination. Her goal, like Jesse Jackson's later effort, was to give voice to issues she feared white politicians were avoiding. Chisholm's poorly financed campaign never won more than 7 percent of the vote in any primary, and she came to the Democratic convention in Miami with only 152 delegate votes. Some have suggested she could have fared better if black male politicians hadn't been reluctant to support a woman.

For the next ten years Chisholm is a strident voice for liberalism who remains incredibly popular in her home district. But as the right wing grows stronger, Chisholm becomes more frustrated, often feeling like a voice in the wilderness. As a result, black America loses one of its most dynamic voices.

Just as this voice of the traditional civil rights agenda bows out, a new black conservative hero walks into the spotlight when President Reagan appoints Clarence Thomas chairperson of the Equal Employment Opportunity Commission. The thirty-four-year-old from Savannah, Georgia, came up under segregation and a black culture that ridiculed him for his dark skin and thick lips. He was the first black ever enrolled at the city's St. John Vianney Minor Seminary school and then headed north where, while attending Holy Cross College in Massachusetts in the late '60s, he was influenced by the call for black self-sufficiency in Malcolm X's speeches.

At Yale Law School he excelled in his studies, yet was irritated that he was often viewed by white students and teachers as an "affirmative action baby" who had been admitted to fill a quota. Moreover, it was at Yale that he formed the view that affirmative action was of benefit to the black middle class, but did nothing to aid the masses of poor people. Upon graduation he took a position in the office of Missouri's Republican state attorney general (and future senator) John Danforth, who became his mentor and sponsor. Three years later, in 1979, he moved to Washington with the newly elected senator and joined the GOP.

Thomas soon establishes himself as a principled opponent of affirmative action and an articulate spokesperson for conservative values. Being black and close to a popular heartland-state senator make Thomas a valuable asset for the GOP. When he accepts the EEOC appointment, Thomas becomes the second-ranked black in the Reagan administration, the top federal employee charged with curbing discrimination in the private sector, and the boss of 3,100 employees working out of forty-eight field offices as well as Washington. From this base of operation Thomas doesn't advocate for government policy—he makes it. (Not noted at the time, but of great import in the '90s, is the presence in the EEOC's D.C. headquarters of a bright, comely young staff member named Anita Hill.)

It seems inconceivable in 1982, but for all of Chisholm's accomplishments as a legislator and spokesperson, it's likely that Thomas's career will have a longer, deeper impact on American life.

JANUARY 4   Andrew Young becomes mayor of Atlanta, succeeding the city's first black mayor, Maynard Jackson. Young, who served as U.S. ambassador to the United Nations under President Carter, had been a close lieutenant to Dr. King during the height of the civil rights movement and is one of the many vets of that struggle to shift into electoral politics.

Atlanta, which was King's home base and that of his Southern Christian Leadership Conference, sees a number of civil rights activists run for office (Julian Bond, Hosea Williams, John Williams) as the leaders of that period wrestle with staying relevant in the post-soul era. Unlike Jackson, the city's first black mayor, who took an almost black nationalistic view of taking control of the city, Young is more conciliatory toward whites, leaning on his UN credentials to bring in business and make Atlanta "an international city."

Bryant Gumbel moves from sports reporter to coanchor of NBC's flagship morning broadcast, the *Today* show. There has never been a black presence quite like him on television before. Gumbel isn't funny, sweet, or ingratiating. Nor is he a stiff credit-to-his-race Negro. Instead the chunky, light-skinned Chicago native is sharp-tongued, smart, well-read, and comfortably cocky.

Gumbel toiled covering sports for years, editing the fine but short-lived *Black Sports* magazine in the early '70s and then graduating to hosting NBC's National Football League pregame show. In 1980 he begins doing sports reports on the *Today* show as the NBC brass groom him for a bigger job. Many don't think a black man from jock world can interview politicians and newsmakers. The doubters severely underestimate this man with the sharp elocution and crisp delivery. He handles Fidel Castro as expertly as he had head coaches.

Gumbel doesn't play the race card—he is often tougher on black guests than white—and apparently is as prickly with coworkers as with authors hyping books. This quick-witted television host is a supremely post-soul figure in that his intelligence and tartness make him not a role model, but a recognizable individual whose blackness happens to be just part of who he is.

FEBRUARY A study titled *Black-White Contact in Schools: Its Social and Academic Effects* is published by Purdue University sociologist Martin Patchen. In it he concludes, "Available evidence indicates that interracial contact in schools does not have consistent positive effects on students' racial attitudes and behavior or on the academic performance of minority students."

Quincy Jones wins five Grammys for his album *The Dude,* including producer of the year, at a ceremony in Los Angeles. Coming on the heels of his production of Michael Jackson's *Off the Wall,* the awards increase Jones's prestige as a maker of pop music.

For most of his career Jones was associated with bebop and big band music. His career began as a trumpeter, though he quickly established himself as a capable arranger. In 1961 he was hired by Mercury Records as head of A&R (artists and repertoire) and became the first black vice president at a major label in 1964. There he first displayed his pop chops, finding and producing hits for teenaged vocalist Leslie Gore ("It's My Party," "You Don't Own Me") as well as conducting a landmark collaboration between Frank Sinatra and the Count Basie Orchestra in 1965. Throughout the '60s Jones fought to break into the old boys' club of Hollywood film scoring. His first film was Sidney Lumet's *The Pawnbroker.* He'd go on to work steadily in film into the '60s and become one of the few behind-the-scenes blacks to have a profile in the industry.

In the '70s he began a lengthy association with A&M Records, where he made funky, jazz-tinged albums (*Mellow Madness, Body Heat*) that featured a medley of established blacks and newcomers, making his name a fixture on R&B radio. *The Dude* is Jones's last album for A&M as he moves to Warner Bros., where he sets up his own label, Qwest. Two singers showcased on *The Dude,* Patti Austin ("Baby, Come to Me") and James Ingram ("One Hundred Ways"), become staples of his new enterprise.

The move to Warner Bros. allows Jones to expand outside record production and scoring into film production. Now a hot pop culture figure, Jones begins searching around for a book to buy.

MARCH 4 The Centers for Disease Control lists four high-risk groups for AIDS infection, which become known as the four

H's—homosexuals, hemophiliacs, heroin addicts, and Haitians. The latter group is singled out because early studies suggest, wrongly, that the disease originated on that Caribbean island and spread to the States via tourists. This high-risk designation lasts until April 1985, but in the intervening years many Haitians are fired from jobs and isolated socially as hysteria over AIDS mounts. Meanwhile, native-born black Americans constitute 23 percent of initial cases reported, though they make up only 12 percent of the general population, an ominous ratio few are paying attention to.

While the early focus of American media coverage of AIDS is on vilifying promiscuous gays and Haitians, connections will soon be made to Africans and black Americans. There are unsubstantiated reports in medical journals and newspapers that the virus was born in Africa. In her 1988 essay "AIDS and Its Metaphors," Susan Sontag writes, ". . . illustrating the classic script for plague, AIDS is thought to have started in the 'dark continent,' then spread to Haiti then to the United States and to Europe. It is understood as a tropical disease: another infestation from the so-called Third World. . . . Africans who detect racist stereotypes in much of the speculation about the geographical origin of AIDS are not wrong. (Nor are they wrong in thinking that depictions of Africa as the cradle of AIDS must feed anti-African prejudices in Europe and Asia.) The subliminal connection made to notions about a primitive past and the many hypotheses that have been fielded about possible transmission from animals (a disease of green monkeys? African swine fever?) cannot help but activate a familiar set of stereotypes about animality, sexual license, and blacks."

One of the differences between the '80s and previous decades is that Africans have their own access to media. In reaction to finger-pointing from whites, a counter theory of AIDS' creation gains credence with blacks in Zaire and in Harlem. It is a theory based on a history of racism and abuse by predominantely white countries, particularly the technologically advanced and often insensitive United States. "Many doctors," Sontag writes, "academics, journalists, government officials, and other educated people believe that the virus was sent to Africa from the United States, an act of bacteriological warfare (whose aim was to decrease the African birth rate) which got out of hand and has returned to afflict its perpetrators."

This conspiracy-based view of AIDS creation spreads via newspapers, radio talk shows, and word of mouth. It cannot be proven any more than the theory of AIDS being the product of green monkeys in Central Africa. But both theories have passionate adherents because they conform to prejudices on both sides of the color line. Throughout the decade the blame game of AIDS distracts people and redirects energy away from the medical needs of millions.

MARCH 12 In his second brilliant concert film, *Richard Pryor Live on the Sunset Strip,* the comic once again demonstrates his remarkable gift for translating personal tragedy into art. By turns crude, tender, and blisteringly honest, Pryor holds the screen in this film with the command and complexity lacking in his narrative films. He does a long, masterful depiction of the attraction of freebase, which includes a talking crack pipe and a dead-on impersonation of Jim Brown.

Pryor also talks lovingly of a trip to Africa that leads him to renounce the use of the word "nigger," long a staple of his scatological stand-up. This announcement is hailed by black positive-image gatekeepers like *Ebony.* In a long interview with the magazine, Pryor asserts the word is "a devastating thing for the black psyche. . . . It's nothing positive. It's nothing to lay on our children. It can't make you feel good, because when the White man calls us that it hurts, no matter how strong we try to be about it." Some think Pryor's comments could be a benchmark in eliminating the word from black colloquial speech.

Ironically, Pryor also appears in one of his most successful and embarrassing films. In *The Toy* he plays a man who allows himself to be purchased by a rich father for the enjoyment of his spoiled son. Perhaps Pryor felt the film could be a barbed commentary on slavery and the role of black people in a capitalistic society. Whatever his intentions, *The Toy,* though a hit, makes his progressive black and white fans tremendously uncomfortable.

MARCH 18   Teddy Pendergrass is paralyzed in an auto accident in Philadelphia. This tragedy immobilizes the sex symbol from the neck down, effectively ending the career of one of the last rough, low-tenor vocalists in black music. Pendergrass, once a drummer and then a featured singer with Harold Melvin & The Blue Notes, made a place for himself in the strident tradition of Wilson Pickett, David Ruffin, and other tough, manly soul men. The tall, bearded Pendergrass is famous for his "Women Only" concerts packed with screaming female fans. Under the production guidance of the great producer-writers Kenny Gamble and Leon Huff, Pendergrass enjoys sexy hits like "Turn Off the Lights," "Love T.K.O.," and "I Don't Love You Anymore." After Pendergrass, the '80s are dominated by falsetto and high-tenor male singers lacking his voice testosterone.

MARCH 29   In the NCAA title game, the North Carolina Tar Heels prevail over the Georgetown Hoyas 63 to 62 before a crowd of 61,612 in the New Orleans Superdome. The game-winning play is a fifteen-foot jump shot released by a Tar Heel freshman named Michael Jordan. For many casual fans it is their first time watching number 23 in action.

APRIL   One of the most influential dance records of the decade is being played at clubs uptown and down, black, white, and gay. The Peech Boys' *Don't Make Me Wait* is a stripped-down, digital, hauntingly sexy jam cocreated by Paradise Garage DJ Larry Levan. Its spooky sensuality is an apt reflection of a night at the Garage. The atmospheric sound of Bernard Fowler's gospel-styled vocals will later lead other producers and DJs to create a dance music variation called garage.

Levan's taste has an impact on more than just the Garage regulars. One of his most devoted fans is Frankie "Hollywood" Crocker, the program director of WBLS, the number-one music station in New York. Crocker, a progressive musical thinker with one of the smoothest on-air deliveries in radio, regularly visits the Garage, where he watches what Levan mixes and cherry-picks choice cuts for WBLS. The story goes that the hot records Levan plays on Saturday night end up on the BLS playlist on Monday morning.

Out of this confluence of blackness, gay aesthetics, and dance music, Crocker transforms black-owned WBLS from a traditional black music station into what he terms "urban contemporary." By this phrase Crocker means to reflect the diversity of the New York area and not lock himself into a musical box. Crocker's vision keeps many significant black acts of the era (Millie Jackson, the Bar-Kays, Con Funk Shun) off a WBLS playlist that might include punk heroes the Clash and Euro-disco maven Cerrone. Though many of Crocker's musical choices don't travel outside New York, his philosophy of programming does.

The phrase "urban contemporary" spreads across the country. It is adopted for musical reasons (to expand playlists from traditional black music styles) and business reasons (to attract advertisers reluctant to be identified with a solely black environment). "Urban," used as a catchword for defining an audience interested in black culture but not necessarily all black itself, appears throughout corporate America. Soon urban divisions of companies pop up all over, selling everything from records to cars to cosmetics.

While the word "black" makes many white marketers uncomfortable, "urban" is vague enough to say what needs to be said with-out really saying it. To some degree "urban" replaces "soul" as a way of referring to black people without the overt racial dimension, and has the added benefit of including big-city white and Latino con-sumers as well. A discomfort with "black" as the exclusive term for people of African descent grows throughout the decade, as people of all colors often find it polarizing, a throwback to soul era agitation that irritates in the crossover '80s. For now, from the sweaty bisex-ual dance crowd at the inner-city Paradise Garage to the American suburbs, *urban* is a word.

APRIL Afrika Bambaataa & The Soul Sonic Force's *Looking for the Perfect Beat* is released by small indie label Tommy Boy. Produced by the Boston-based team of Arthur Baker and John Robie, the record has a spacy, synthesizer-driven track that is in-debted to the German computer innovators Kraftwerk. The eclec-tic taste of hip hoppers in rhythm is apparent in the instant embrace of this record by the core urban audience. *Perfect Beat* in fact is a signature record in a genre of dance music termed "elec-tro boogie" by its adherents.

Afrika Bambaataa is one of the creators of the hip hop DJ aes-thetic of using breaks and beats from a wide variety of musical sources. It's an approach that began in the streets and community center parties in the East Bronx, under the banner of the Zulu Na-tion, a collective of former gang members and music fans he orga-nized. *Perfect Beat* allows him to capitalize on a genre he helped create. Unlike many of hip hop's early innovators, Bambaataa is immediately recognized as an important figure in the culture's evolution and materially benefits from its growth.

Another beneficiary is Tommy Boy, one of the best of the rap-oriented independent labels. Of *Perfect Beat,* Tommy Boy president Tom Silverman told *Billboard* magazine, "Before I released high-energy disco records, but that market has really dried up in this country. The New York uptown sound, real beat records, is a growth field that still, to me, hasn't been fully tapped or appreciated."

Alice Walker's *The Color Purple* is published, garnering superb reviews, reaching best-seller status, and eventually winning the Pulitzer Prize in literature. Walker has been a fixture in the black literary world for many years, writing both well-regarded novels (*The Three Lives of Grange Copeland, Meridian*) and poetry collections (*You Can't Keep a Good Woman Down*).

Walker was born in the '40s in Eatonton, Georgia, the eighth and last child of sharecroppers. At age eight Walker lost sight in her right eye when one of her brothers accidentally shot her with a BB gun. Despite that injury she was a voracious reader, becoming valedictorian of her high school class and winning a scholarship that sent her to Atlanta's black women's college, Spelman. After two years at Spelman, Walker transferred to New York's Sarah Lawrence, and then spent her junior year as an exchange student in Uganda before graduating in 1965.

Walker spent most of the next ten years in Tougaloo, Mississippi, where she married, had a daughter, and began her evolution into a world-class writer. She began drawing on her diverse living experiences to inform her poetry and prose. Though most of her novels through *The Color Purple* were set in the South, the wider perspectives Walker's time in New York and Africa provided made her more than just a Southern writer. Her ability to place the Southern black experience in an international context would be essential to *The Color Purple*.

The Color Purple tells the story of Celie, a poor, uneducated black woman, through her letters to God and, later, to her sister Nettie, who goes to Africa to do missionary work. The novel begins when Celie is fourteen and has been sexually abused by her father, which is just the first of her many trials. Her two children are taken from her and she is married off to Mr. Albert, an angry, dissatisfied farmer who is in love with Shug Avery, a flamboyant, independent, bisexual blues singer whose love will help transform Celie's life.

The novel's frank depiction of black male subjugation of black women in the South irritates many black men, who feel Walker's tale plays into the hands of racism. These critics assert that the novel's commercial success derives from how it fulfills white stereotypes. But this view ignores the ample literary gifts Walker displays in creating powerful characters whose issues speak not only to black Americans, but to the human condition. *The Color Purple* succeeds not simply as an angry indictment of black American male behavior, but as a parable for the brutality inflicted on poor women all over the world.

The controversy over *The Color Purple* also resonates because many black male writers believe they're being overlooked by the publishing industry. This view sparks many angry exchanges at literary forums and talk shows throughout the '80s, with the novelist Ishmael Reed becoming a spokesman on the issue.

MAY 28 In *Rocky III,* Apollo Creed is no longer the Italian Stallion's nemesis but becomes his trainer to help best the brutal Clubber Lang, who is portrayed with streetwise boisterousness by former bodyguard Mr. T in his soon to be trademark heavy gold chains and Mohawk haircut. In his gruff way Mr. T points out the class and generational differences between him and the more refined Creed (Carl Weathers). In writing the characters, screenwriter Stallone actually anticipates the black cultural wars that shape much black pop culture for the next twenty years.

JUNE NYU student Spike Lee wins a student Academy Award for his *Joe's Bed-Stuy Barbershop: We Cut Heads,* about the uneasy relationship between a barber and a loan shark. The film is distinguished by its Brooklyn flavor, black cultural references, good humor, unusual character names, and ambiguous end-ing, all elements that will reappear in the young director's work.

JUNE 18 Congress votes to extend the 1965 Voting Rights Act despite a five-day filibuster by North Carolina's power-ful Senator Jesse Helms. The American Civil Liberties Union issues a report that despite the Voting Rights Act, Southern states still work to disenfranchise black voters.

JULY Grandmaster Flash & the Furious Five's *The Message* is released by Sugarhill Records. *The Source* magazine put the twelve-inch in perspective: "Despite its roots in the ghetto, how-ever, contemporary rap is, for the most part, hyperbolic braggado-cio with very little reference to the hardscrabble environment which inspires it. That is, until a new record from Grandmaster Flash & the Furious Five hits the airwaves. With lead MC Grandmaster Melle Mel and guest rapper Duke Bootee dropping nothing but color com-mentary on the world around them, the song goes on to create an entirely new genre that will influence the music for years to come."

With its stark production and memorable refrain ("Don't push me 'cus I'm close to the edge/ I'm trying not to lose my head"), *The Message* depicts the growing edge of paranoia in urban life. It is the record that rock critics, who have heretofore been cool to rap's "party hearty" chants, have to take seriously. *Rolling Stone* maga-zine, never a champion of hip hop culture, gives the record a five-star review. *The Message* is supported by a cheap music video shot on lo-cation in Harlem. Though the video is not of great quality, the song is so powerful that the video gets played at music video programs in the States and throughout the world, a first for any rap record.

JULY 9 The CDC's *MMWR* features a report titled "Opportunistic Infections and Kaposi's Sarcoma among Haitians in the United States."

JULY 27 The Centers for Disease Control adopts "Acquired Immune Deficiency Syndrome—AIDS" as the official name for the rapidly spreading new disease.

OCTOBER 27 Prince releases the double album *1999* and, for the first time since 1980, consents to do a series of interviews. Ten are scheduled but only one takes place. After speaking with the *Los Angeles Times*'s Robert Hilburn, Prince blows off the rest of the scheduled reporters (including me). In his talk Prince addresses some rumors: "One, my real name is Prince. It's not something I made up. My dad's stage name was Prince Rogers and he gave that to me: Prince Rogers Nelson. Two, I'm not gay. And three, I'm not Jamie Starr." About his musical direction, Prince explains to Hilburn, "The most important thing is to be true to yourself, but I also like danger. That's what is missing from pop music today. There's no excitement and mystery; people sneaking out and going to see these forbidden concerts by Elvis Presley or Jimi Hendrix. I'm not saying I'm better than anybody else, but I don't feel like there are a lot of people out there telling the truth in their music."

NOVEMBER 2 Tom Bradley loses his bid to become America's first elected black governor by 93,345 votes, or 1.2 percent of those cast in California. Two weeks before the election, Williams Roberts, campaign manager for the eventual winner, George Deukmejian, remarked that there was a hard core of voters, roughly 3 percent of the electorate or about 100,000, who he predicted would not vote for a black person no matter what they told pollsters.

Ron Brown of the National Democratic Committee said, "I'm very distressed. When a man like Bradley can't win in a state like California with 60 percent Democratic registration, what can blacks do?"

NOVEMBER 2 In the midterm elections the Republican Party offers up a number of black neo-con candidates for Congress, but none are elected. In fact, blacks nationally vote the straight Democratic ticket in higher numbers than usual in a rebuke of Reaganomics. Ronald McDuffie, executive director of the National Black Republican Council, comments, "We lost because we got a late start, and black people voted Democratic. We are committed to working for a black Republican Congress in 1984."

NOVEMBER 4 "Sugar Ray" Leonard retires from boxing after sustaining damage to his eye that results in a detached retina. This is a sad announcement since the handsome, charismatic welterweight, who has grossed around $30 million after winning a gold medal at the 1976 Olympics, brought a sex appeal to fighting not seen since Muhammad Ali's prime.

Leonard is a skilled and tactically brilliant fighter who can box, slug, or brawl, depending on what he needs for victory. Nicknamed after the great Hall of Fame boxer "Sugar Ray" Robinson, Leonard becomes a real media darling, and does many national commercials and endorses a slew of products, perks that elude most non-heavyweights.

In November 1979 he won the WBC welterweight crown from Wilfred Benitez in a brutal yet stylistically beautiful fight. He engaged in two memorable battles with lightweight legend Roberto Duran. In the first, Duran dethroned Leonard in a unanimous decision. In the second, Duran quit in the eighth round, saying "*no más,*" a phrase that entered boxing history. In '81, Leonard moves up in weight class to the junior middleweight division and knocks out champion Ayube Kalule. Then, in one of the greatest fights of the decade, Leonard wages a war with WBA champ Thomas Hearns. Hearns is ahead on all three of the judges' scorecards when Leonard puts together a lethal combination of punches and knocks Hearns out in the fourteenth round.

After two more fights, Leonard retires because of the eye injury. His record at this time is an impressive 32 and 1 with 23 knockouts. Leonard plans to stay at home with his wife and two young sons.

NOVEMBER 27 Over the Thanksgiving holiday, Marvin Gaye's "Sexual Healing" is the number-one black single according to *Billboard*. It is a major comeback for the soul great, whose work in the late '70s was marred by drug use, marital problems, and battles with Motown.

After a self-imposed exile in Europe, Gaye cleans up his life, regroups, and comes back with the *Midnight Love* album on Columbia Records. With "Sexual Healing," Gaye updates his sound with a softly sensual use of electronic keyboards and one of the sexiest vocal performances in a long career of romantic music. After his hiatus, Gaye sounds refreshed and seems poised to continue making great music.

DECEMBER 10 The CDC's *MMWR* issues a report titled "Possible Transfusion-Associated Acquired Immune Deficiency Syndrome (AIDS)—California."

DECEMBER 17 The CDC's *MMWR* issues a report titled "Unexplained Immunodeficiency and Opportunistic Infections in Infants."

DECEMBER 25 Just in time for Christmas, Michael Jackson's *Thriller*, the follow-up to *Off the Wall*, debuts on the *Billboard* chart, where it stays for thirty-seven weeks. While not as deep in great material as its predecessor, *Thriller* sells more than twenty million copies in the United States, eventually nearly 40 million worldwide, and spawns seven hit singles. The first, "Billie Jean," is already on its way to number one.

One of the keys to the success of *Thriller* is the state-of-the-art production by Quincy Jones that pushes the envelope for a black pop artist. The rock-flavored "Beat It," with a solo by guitarist Eddie Van Halen, and the campy, horror epic title song, with narration by Vincent Price, announce Jackson's and Jones's intention not to be pigeonholed by race or traditional genres. In addition, a palpable sense of paranoia and defensiveness to the songs written by Jackson ("Billie Jean," "Wanna Be Startin' Something") make the album less a pop product (though it truly is one) and more a personal statement. Jackson's ability to embed feelings of dread in great pop recordings is as central to his artistic vision as the videos that energize his historic sales.

DECEMBER 28 Rioting once again erupts in Miami. In the Overtown district a black man is killed by a Latino police officer. During the three-day riot, two other people are killed, twenty-seven others are injured, and scores of homes and businesses are damaged.

The late mayor of Chicago Harold Washington

1983

1983

Black power '80s style is in full effect in the city halls of two of America's biggest cities and at the Democratic presidential primaries. Harold Washington in Chicago and W. Wilson Goode in Philadelphia claim historic mayoral victories in cities where rising black populations, the erosion of the white working class, and the open minds of white swing voters bring them victory. Unfortunately, the administrations of both men are defined not by their civic accomplishments, but by the unprecedented psychodramas that consume them. Washington and Goode each find that capturing power is actually easier than implementing programs and making decisions.

Washington becomes the chief executive of a city closely identified with the black migration north and a vibrant black business community by winning close elections. In the February primary the congressman bested incumbent Mayor Jane Byrne and Richard M. Daley, son of four-term mayor Richard J. Daley, with 36 percent of the vote to Byrne's 34 percent and Daley's 30 percent. His margin of victory comes from the 79 percent of the black vote he garners. To gauge the impact of his campaign, consider that in the 1979 primary, with no black candidate, only 34 percent of registered Democrats turned out; but to support Washington, 64 percent of black registered Democrats pull levers.

In April's general election Washington runs against a previously unknown white Republican, Bernard Epton. Yet in a deeply Democratic city, 86 percent of white voters come out, most of them intent on preventing Washington's ascension to power. Counteracting Epton's "great white hope" appeal, blacks give 98 percent of their vote to Washington and Latinos give him 74 percent.

These racially polarized elections foreshadow Washington's contentious first term. The new mayor had served in various elective offices since 1965 and had been a fixture in local politics. If he'd been white, Washington would have been just another strong-willed Windy City politician. However, instead of supporting Washington, many in the local Democratic Party choose racial prejudice over party affiliation. Led by alderman and Cook County Democratic organization chairman Edward Vrdolyak, a hard core of between twenty-five and thirty white council members engage in vicious weekly battles with the new administration over issues big and small, from council chairmanships and municipal layoffs to the use of an empty room in City Hall.

At the end of this year the council passes an alternative to the mayor's budget, which gives more money to Washington's opponents and reduces salaries for some of his staff. This legislative combat only intensifies racial tensions in a city where race and ethnic identities have always been crucial, and that had never advertised itself as a melting pot. What is disturbing is how naked the racial nature of these debates is. Mid-'80s Chicago is a place where racial battle lines are drawn as harshly as at any time in its rugged history. The difference is that this time, whites aren't the only folks with bullets.

In contrast to the bitter Windy City, the City of Brotherly Love more or less lives up to its billing. In a heated, racially polarizing but ultimately calm campaign, W. Wilson Goode, age forty-five, enters Philadelphia's City Hall with 55 percent of the vote, easily defeating former mayor (and police chief) Frank Rizzo, an ex-Democrat who has converted to the GOP to exploit Reagan's popularity. Rizzo's problem is that Goode, the managing director of the City of Brotherly Love for the previous four years, has earned the support of the business community as well as blacks. While everyone acknowledges that Philadelphia has had some deep-seated problems (years of turmoil instigated by Rizzo's notoriously racist police policies; a sagging local economy; a high unemployment rate), Goode's positive profile and thoughtful, low-key style are viewed as cause for optimism. Unlike Washington, Goode takes his job with the goodwill of most of his city's citizens.

JANUARY 7 The CDC's *MMWR* features a report titled "Immunodeficiency Among Female Sexual Partners of Males with Acquired Immune Deficiency Syndrome (AIDS)—New York."

APRIL 11 Louis Gossett Jr. wins the supporting actor Oscar for his role as a demanding drill instructor in *An Officer and a Gentleman*. Gossett's performance is so indelible that the stern black supervisor (be he a soldier or cop) becomes a cinematic cliché. Unfortunately for Gossett, a peer of Poitier and a product of the black theater world, parts of similar quality elude him afterward.

APRIL 15 *Flashdance* is the first feature film to show the impact of MTV's montage editing to hype dance sequences. Star Jennifer Beales's mixed-race beauty gives the ludicrous story about a Pittsburgh welder and dancer an air of ambiguity and cross-racial box office appeal. The film climaxes with Beale (actually a stunt dancer) break dancing at a ballet company audition. There's also a brief cameo by real breakers, New York's Rock Steady Crew. The appearance of this street art in a mainstream youth hit sparks international interest in break dancing's proper execution and beginnings.

APRIL Arista Records president Clive Davis announces the signing of a sometime model to a recording contract.

The slim New Jersey native is the daughter of Cissy Houston, a former backup singer for Aretha Franklin and Elvis Presley, and the niece of pop star Dionne Warwick. This well-pedigreed vocalist has already recorded duets with a few artists, including Teddy Pendergrass. Her friends call her Nippy but in *Billboard* she is announced as Whitney Houston.

APRIL Yale scholar Henry Louis Gates Jr. authenticates for publication the 1859 manuscript *Our Nig; or, Sketches from the Life of a Free Black, in a Two Story White House, North: Showing That Slavery's Shadows Fall Even There,* by Harriet E. Wilson, as the first novel written by a black woman in the United States. Aside from adding more fuel to the fire of interest in black women writers, this literary archaeology catapults the ambitious Gates to prominence outside the academic world. The Piedmont, West Virginia, native, though an academic by training and profession, displays a very '80s ability to build a thriving enterprise by trafficking in ideas. Like many figures to emerge in this decade, Gates is as distinguished for his empire-building instincts as for his actual work.

MAY 7 Eddie Murphy, who's been doing a killer impression of Stevie Wonder on *Saturday Night Live* since his debut, meets his match when the real Stevie Wonder comes on as the musical guest and appears in several sketches. Murphy is in great form, playing the fey beautician Dion as well as Wonder himself in a singing contest with the Motown great.

MAY 16 Motown, a black-owned record label that provided the '60s with a vibrant soundtrack, celebrates its cultural importance with a prime-time NBC special titled *Motown 25: Yesterday, Today, and Forever,* taped at Pasadena's Civic Auditorium.

The lineup of Motown stars is amazing—a mellow Marvin Gaye, a playful Stevie Wonder, a spirited battle between the Temptations and the Four Tops.

But while the lineup salutes a soulful past, Michael Jackson puts his stamp on the present. After performing a medley of Jackson 5 hits with his brothers, Jackson sings the only non-Motown music of the night, the first single off his *Thriller* album, "Billie Jean." Taking moves from urban street dancers, he "moonwalks" a few graceful feet across the stage, electrifying America with his steps and creating a cultural moment on par with the Beatles' appearance on *The Ed Sullivan Show* two decades earlier.

From this springboard, Jackson, who was the last of Motown's production-line stars, reaches the kind of celebrity and sales founder Berry Gordy strove to achieve. Jackson embodies the integrationist ideas of the '60s but, in this new era, has a chance to extend his reach in ways inconceivable then. Jackson is one of the few artists who actually straddles the soul and post-soul worlds. While his concepts of showmanship date back to the chitlin' circuit, Jackson is brilliant at adapting new styles (for example, the moonwalk) to his needs. Straddling requires remarkable balance and the ability to adjust. On this night, Jackson certainly has both.

JUNE In the face of Pryor's abrasive style and Murphy's youthful energy, Bill Cosby keeps rolling on. By guest hosting for Johnny Carson and appearing in commercials and lucrative concert appearances, the old-fashioned clean comic has become a reassuring national presence. Perhaps that's why his obscenity- and controversy-free concert film, *Bill Cosby, Himself,* released this month, doesn't get the notice of Pryor's stand-up films or Murphy's HBO special.

Still, the film is a fascinating document of a black with power. As I write in *The Village Voice,* "Cosby voluntarily takes the role of the judgmental Boss who shakes his head at the vices of his underlings. This is an image of power that few comics . . . would embrace, feeling it builds a large wall between comic and audiences." Cosby's aura of authority is what makes him a credible salesman, and in the age of the faux father Reagan, that's a great skill to process.

JUNE Harvard undergraduate Reggie Hudlin directs a funny, fast-paced student short about a son who sneaks out to a party against his father's wishes. Unlike the serious political work of most independent black filmmakers, including Hudlin's older brother Warrington, *House Party* has a light, humorous tone grounded in the particulars of black culture, yet is still the story of any American teenager.

JUNE Using his own money, Spike Lee directs a video of Grandmaster Flash & The Furious Five's *White Lines* that features his Brooklyn neighbor, young actor Larry Fishburne (*Apocalypse Now, Cotton Club*). Spike wants to use this rough-cut video to break into the music video business, but Sugarhill Records doesn't give Spike the money to complete the video. However, without his permission, they sent out a copy of Spike's work to some local music video outlets where it receives some air time. Though frustrated by this turn of events, Spike continues to write scripts.

JUNE 6 Richard Pryor announces the formation of Indigo Productions, a company funded by Columbia Pictures to make black films. The new enterprise is given $40 million to make these films and the ability to green-light movies without having to ask Columbia's permission. It is an unprecedented deal that is based on Pryor's commercial track record and the apparent realization by Columbia of the commercial impact of black audiences on the bottom line. Pryor, looking serious and sober, announces that he's hired former football star and actor Jim Brown as president. People speculate hopefully that Indigo will become the Motown of black film.

Miles Davis and Wynton Marsalis, the past and future of jazz trumpet, perform on the same stage. The evening at Avery Fisher Hall is opened by the VSOP II Quintet, featuring Davis's mid-'60s rhythm section (pianist Herbie Hancock, bassist Ron Carter, drummer Tony Williams) backing saxophonist Branford and trumpeter Wynton Marsalis. Critic Robert Palmer praised Wynton's "sovereign command of his horn and apparently bottomless well of personality-inflected ideas."

The *New York Times* staffer is less than impressed by the headliner's band, saying this group "introduced two years and three albums ago" hadn't jelled. He notes that Davis's playing is "full of fire and brimming with personality, especially toward the end of the set. But the backing was cluttered, diffuse, constricted."

Richard Pryor and Eddie Murphy share the cover of *People* magazine and, at the magazine's request, spend three days together in Los Angeles with reporters and photographers following them around. Eddie, at twenty-two, has just helped push *Trading Places* to a $90 million box office gross, while Pryor, at forty-two, is simply the nation's best stand-up comic. He has also just been paid $4 million (the equivalent of $20 million twenty-first-century dollars) to add spice to *Superman III*.

It's clear that the two are pulling their punches when the tape recorders are on; or perhaps the editors at *People* magazine pull theirs in putting the story together. At one point the two go to the Comedy Store, where first Pryor and then Murphy go on stage, an amazing moment in comedy history, but little of the material is quoted. The piece ends with the comics talking about doing a movie together, though they prudently keep the concept to themselves.

SEPTEMBER 4 Oprah Winfrey, successful host of a Baltimore morning talk show, flies out for an audition to cohost *A.M. Chicago* for the local ABC affiliate. Winfrey, twenty-nine, wows the station management and signs a four-year deal worth $200,000 a year.

SEPTEMBER 16 Television can't get enough of sitcoms with black children being raised by white families. *Webster* debuts on NBC with the cuddly Emmanuel Lewis in the lead role. The show lasts three forgettable seasons. Lewis is now best remembered for being Michael Jackson's companion and mascot at award shows throughout '83 and '84.

Another new TV star is the *Rocky III* villain Mr. T (born Lawrence Tureaud). The burly ex-bodyguard from Chicago, who sports a haircut he claims came from Africa's Mandinka tribe and enough gold to bankrupt a pawnshop, is featured in a bad movie comedy, *D. C. Cab,* and in the NBC action series *The A-Team* as B. A. Baracus. With a gruff delivery and a Mohawk, Mr. T is a living, breathing action figure, clearly the '80s ancestor of the twenty-first-century pumped-up icon, the Rock.

OCTOBER White filmmaker Charlie Ahearn directs one of hip hop's most enduring films, *Wild Style,* in collaboration with Fab Five Freddy Brathwaite. The documentary-style film is filled with original uptown stars like Busy Bee, Grandmaster Flash, and Double Trouble, and is filmed in the clubs and parks that had nurtured rapping, breakin', graffiti, and DJ-ing since the mid-'70s. The film also sheds light on downtown hipsters such as art curator Patti Astor who were among the first whites to see true artistry in hip hop's expressions.

The Brooklyn-born painter-rapper-raconteur Fab Five Freddy is a crucial link between Bronx and Harlem hip hoppers on one hand, and East Village club promoters and gallery owners on the other. His ability to speak several languages (standard English, hip hop slang, art theory) makes him an indispensable figure.

OCTOBER 15 Eddie Murphy's *Delirious,* taped at Washington, D.C.'s Constitution Hall, airs on HBO. Murphy serves the adoring crowd with a medley of pop cultural references low-lighted by the image of Mr. T pleading for anal sex. Murphy's skills for mimicry and natural charisma are certainly on display, though there's a juvenile quality to much of the material. The most developed and heartfelt routine is about a family barbecue; in it, Murphy lovingly imitates his father, Vernon.

Murphy named his broadcast after a Prince song, which is appropriate since they are the most eligible young black stars of the time. (Michael Jackson doesn't hang out in nightclubs.) Significantly, both model themselves not on the standards of traditional R&B stars, but after rock icons like Elvis Presley and David Bowie. In his tight red leather suit and greasy, lightly curled hair, Murphy both reflects and influences black youth style.

Homosexuals react angrily to Murphy's many routines that involve (and ridicule) gay sex. Virginia Apuzzo, executive of the National Gay and Lesbian Task Force, reports, "We have gotten an enormous number of calls. It is a major source of concern." HBO also receives complaints about Murphy's gleefully profane language. The cable network's president, Michael Fuchs, tells *The New York Times,* "I am not looking for twelve more programs like this. No one likes to kick up a storm."

While admitting he is eager to do more business with Murphy, Fuchs adds, "We would have much more dialogue ahead of time." The idea of an HBO executive complaining about kicking up "a storm" with provocative programming is almost as funny as *Delirious* itself.

OCTOBER 25 President Reagan orders U.S. troops to invade the tiny Caribbean island of Grenada to "protect" nearly 800 U.S. medical students there. Twelve days prior, the Grenadian Army, controlled by former Deputy Prime Minister Bernard Coard, seized power of the island in a violent coup. Coard is a hard-line Marxist and ardent supporter of Cuba's Fidel Castro. The Reagan administration is obsessed with Marxist governments throughout Central America and the Caribbean, and seizes on this coup as an opportunity to eliminate one. (Clearly related to this U.S. military incursion is the October 23 Muslim suicide bomber attack that destroyed a Marine barracks in Beirut, killing 241 Marines. A show of force close to home was needed to balance that disaster for the administration.)

The initial assault consists of approximately 1,200 troops, who are met with heavy opposition from Grenadian forces. Quickly the U.S. force grows to 7,000 and the local army is overwhelmed. By December the troops are removed and a pro-American government is installed.

NOVEMBER 2 President Ronald Reagan signs the law designating the third Monday in January Martin Luther King Jr. Day.

DECEMBER Reverend Jesse Jackson announces his candidacy for the Democratic presidential nomination. Political pundits initially see him as a short-lived protest candidate, but to their surprise (and some dismay), Jackson will appeal to a great many liberal voters who are disappointed in the general direction of the party and nation.

Eventually Jackson captures two primaries (the District of Columbia and Louisiana) and accumulates over three million votes (about 18 percent of all Democratic primary voters) toward the Democratic nomination. His campaign stops and appearances increase his power in the party and activate many dormant, previously unmotivated black voters. Jackson's goal is to push the Democrats back toward their liberal roots, which many of the younger elected white officials in the party feel is a mistake. The future of the party, they argue, is a centrist middle ground far from Jackson's impassioned pleas for Great Society–styled social programs.

Jackson's campaign puts the tension between the new generation of white Democrats and the black agenda at center stage. Along with the victories of Harold Washington in Chicago and Wilson Goode in Philadelphia, Jackson's run identifies the Democrats with black voters more deeply than ever before. For white Democrats this is a double-edged sword; it solidifies this loyal base of support, which also makes them vulnerable to GOP charges that they cater to "special-interest groups" and to negative campaigns based on linking Democratic candidates to racist assumptions about blacks (for example, that blacks are welfare cheats). In addition, it gives credence to the arguments of black conservatives that the Democrats take black support for granted. This love-hate relationship between black voters and white Democrats unfortunately aids conservative strategies of divide and conquer throughout the '80s.

The idea of establishing an independent black political party that's been floating around since the '60s is never advocated by Jackson or other black elected officials. All in Jackson's camp are committed to coalition building, to crossing over to power within the Democratic Party, and not to exploring the more radical implications of black political power. Jackson and his crew long ago traded in their dashikis for business suits, and once you've worn Brooks Brothers, there's no going back.

As more blacks win prominent positions in the Democratic

Party, it becomes apparent even to the most optimistic souls that winning elections doesn't translate into fundamental social change. In fact, the more mainstream black politics becomes, the more its leaders are committed to a system that, at best, fights for incremental change. It is in this vacuum of truly oppositional voices that rappers, street activists, and other unlikely forces from outside the system emerge to play a political role.

DECEMBER 9   Brian DePalma's *Scarface,* written by aspiring director Oliver Stone, stars Al Pacino as Tony Montana, a vicious, ambitious Cuban refugee who finds in the Miami cocaine trade his bitter taste of the American Dream. In contrast to the stately *Godfather,* in which the Mafia is romanticized as a tragic national institution, *Scarface* depicts the paranoid, revenge-obsessed violence of '80s drug dealing. Despite his awful Spanish accent, Pacino plays Tony with unwavering gusto, establishing the character as the patron saint of crack dealers (the name is referenced in scores of rap records). Tony's coke-fueled death, whereby he introduces his "little friend" (a bullet-splattering automatic weapon), is a signature moment in pop culture. It makes some want to deal coke, others to rhyme about dealing coke, and many to make movies about dealing, with hip hop soundtracks.

DECEMBER 17   Richard Pryor holds a press conference to announce the firing of Jim Brown and the dismantling of Indigo. Pryor's reasons for this decision are vague. Some in Hollywood suggest that Columbia is uncomfortable being in business with Brown, a longtime activist for black empowerment. Whatever the reason, Pryor essentially gives back the $40 million invested by Columbia with his third concert film, *Here and Now,* the only project to be produced by Indigo. Many scripts that later get produced flowed through Indigo (including the biography of Charlie Parker, *Bird,* that Clint Eastwood later directs) and a number of talented young people (producer George Jackson, actor-director Robert Townsend) are affiliated with it. Still, the sudden disappearance of Indigo is a severe blow to those blacks working in Hollywood who are hoping for real black behind-the-scenes power in American movies. Murphy and Pryor notwithstanding, Hollywood is still clearly skeptical about the drawing power of black-themed films.

Ronnie, Michael, and Nancy in the White House Rose Garden.

1984

1984

In any epoch there are one or two years that define the time and the generation that lives through it. These years are so filled with incident—some immediately recognized as important, others that loom large in retrospect—that the mention of the date, say 1919 or 1945 or 1968, evokes sharply-etched memories and stinging emotion. One of those years is 1984, reverberating George Orwell's visionary, midcentury novel about a distant future world dominated by an oppressive government that utilizes mass media as a narcotic.

Well, Orwell certainly was right about the power of media to anesthetize the masses, though it is corporations using advertising who truly hold sway over the populace. But what the Englishman couldn't possibly have predicted is that so many of the personalities filling TV, radio, newspapers, and magazines are black.

Several key figures in twentieth-century pop culture reach their artistic, cultural, or financial zenith in '84. What no one could foresee is that, for several of them, the seeds of their decline are planted in this same rich soil. A lot of what happened was unpredictable—a black sports star emerging in Edmonton, Canada? And only a few trend-spotters bet money on hip hop's evolution from underground culture to mainstream phenomenon.

The importance of 1984 to America isn't defined simply by record sales or television ratings. From the margins of black culture, the values and desires of the disenfranchised find expression in a way that profoundly alters the nation. A new drug culture, one more virulent and vicious than the heroin influx of the '60s or the angel dust craze of the late '70s, takes hold. Just as this evil is unleashed, something powerfully positive appears. Activist politics, which has been moribund for years, is given new life by an anti-apartheid movement that sparks demonstrations around the country to protest South Africa's racist government and urge economic and cultural boycotts to topple it.

Unlike so many domestic issues, the antiapartheid movement has the sense of black goodness versus while villainy that energized the domestic civil rights battle. Being arrested at the gates of South Africa's embassy becomes a badge of honor. Black South African heroes (the imprisoned Nelson Mandela, the eloquent Bishop Desmond Tutu, the slain Stephen Biko) become international icons, their deification a stark contrast to the morally muddy perception of the new crop of elected black officials.

The U.S. antiapartheid activism is also a reflection of a vibrant, Africa-centered vision of black identity with adherents in academia, community activism, and education who support its political message and are appalled by a rising sense of materialism among the young. In 1984 the dark side of b-boy culture, as well as the bright side of black bohemia, comes into focus. Orwell was on the right track, but the year turns out to be much more racially complex than he imagined.

JANUARY The NBA borrows a tradition from its '70s rival, the American Basketball Association, and makes a slam-dunk competition part of its all-star weekend activities. On the day before the all-star game at Denver's McNichols Arena, an amazing array of players throws down for reputation and money: Julius "Dr. J." Erving (the ABA's last champ); Darrell "Dr. Dunkenstein" Griffith; Edgar "the Wild Helicopter" Jones; Clyde "the Glide" Drexler; Dominique "Human Highlight Film" Wilkins; Michael "Coop-a-Loop" Cooper; Larry "Fancy" Nance; Orlando "Oh! Oh!" Woolridge; and Ralph Sampson, who didn't have a nickname but at seven feet four inches didn't need one to be recognized. Nance wins the competition and the NBA scores big, too, as the slam-dunk competition highlights every subsequent all-star weekend and, more profoundly, helps "elevate" the dunk in the popular consciousness.

The slam dunk becomes as synonymous with '80s basketball as the pick-and-roll is with the more earthbound '70s. For basketball traditionalists, the prominence of the slam dunk epitomizes a diminution in skill they feel is permeating the game. That dunking is so associated with the "street" style of basketball brought into the professional ranks by the ABA is another reason they detest its celebration. Many coaches and sportswriters think the dunk represents a lack of respect for the game's fundamentals.

Yet it is precisely the flair and sheer macho grandeur of the slam dunk that helps the NBA. Dr. J., a man with amazing grace, huge hands (but no longer a huge Afro), and sex appeal, has brought the high-flying game into the older league and, along with Boston's Larry Bird and Los Angeles's Magic Johnson, rebuilt the profile of a league that suffered through a leaderless late '70s. Philadelphia's Erving and the two younger players bring a street aesthetic into harmony with basketball tradition. Between Erving, Johnson, and Bird, their teams win every NBA title from 1980 to 1988.

JANUARY 3 Reverend Jesse Jackson imposes himself on American foreign policy by securing the release of Navy pilot Robert Goodman from a Syrian prison after he is shot down over Damascus, providing Jackson a platform on which to appear heroic and patriotic, and inciting the ire of the GOP, which detests Jackson even more than Syria. Unspoken in all this is the quiet role Jackson supporter Louis Farrakhan plays in smoothing the reverend's negotiations with the Muslim nation.

JANUARY 4 Oprah Winfrey debuts as cohost of *A.M. Chicago*. The half-hour broadcast is scheduled opposite syndicated talk titan Phil Donahue. Within twelve weeks, Winfrey ends his sixteen-year reign as the Windy City's number-one talk show host by besting him in local ratings by an average of 265,000 viewers to his 147,230. This news sends ripples through the TV business.

FEBRUARY Run-D.M.C. releases their eponymous debut on the small Profile label. The album is composed of many twelve-inch singles released the year before, including the historic "It's Like That," with "Sucker MCs" on the B side. The breakout record is "Rock Box," a blend of aggressive rhyming and rock guitar that makes the reluctant MTV put the accompanying black-and-white video (shot at new-wave club Danceteria) in rotation. Throughout the mid-'80s, MTV mostly just dips a toe in hip hop, giving only Run-D.M.C.'s rock-edged rap regular exposure.

The first vehicle for exposing the low-budget rap videos from indie labels like Profile is Video Music Box, a local New York television program broadcast on city-owned WNYC, which debuts this year. Every afternoon after school and on Saturday mornings, the broadcast is hosted by Ralph McDaniels and, on occasion, his partner Lionel Martin, a.k.a. Vid Kid. It is the earliest outlet for the airing of rap videos and quickly becomes one of the most highly rated public TV programs ever.

Crucial to the program's appeal is that it's taped at black clubs all over the New York–New Jersey area and features "shout-outs," whereby party-goers send greetings to friends and lovers over the air. The shout-out, either on local video shows, on hip hop radio broadcasts, or on record, becomes a staple of hip hop media and is part of building a sense of community around the culture. As an offshoot of VMB, McDaniels and Martin form Classic Concepts, a music video production company, to make the kinds of videos the viewers are demanding. The average budget for a rap video in this era is $20,000; a big-budget rap video is $60,000; a major pop star gets a budget in the low six figures.

FEBRUARY 3 Whoopi Goldberg makes her New York City debut with *The Spook Show*. Her one-woman show receives great reviews and begins a love affair between the comedian-actor and white liberals that continues throughout her career. Whoopi, somewhat like Eddie Murphy, becomes a major star without having to cultivate a substantial black audience. Of course there is a crucial difference. Murphy became a star via a youth-oriented mass audience vehicle; Whoopi is supported by white tastemakers like Mike Nichols (and later Steven Spielberg) without having been previously embraced by large groups of consumers of any hue. This difference is manifest in their respective box office grosses throughout the decade.

FEBRUARY 13 Black *Washington Post* staffer Milton Coleman reports that in a private conversation, Jesse Jackson called New York "Hymietown" and Jews "Hymies." The references come in an off-the-record conversation that Jackson prefaces by saying, "Let's talk black talk." While acknowledging that fact, Coleman still passes the remarks on to his editors at the *Post*. The comments elicit a firestorm of criticism, first aimed at Jackson from Jews and his Democratic rivals Walter Mondale and Gary Hart, and then aimed at Coleman from black Americans.

FEBRUARY 26 After denying *The Washington Post*'s report for thirteen days, Jackson apologizes for his remarks, which does little to quell the debate about whether he (and by extension the black community) is secretly anti-Semitic. This event is a huge blow to Jackson's standing among progressive white voters. Moreover, it brings into the open the suspicions between blacks and Jews, once allies during the civil rights era, now wary of each other because of conflicts over the state of Israel's treatment of the Palestinians and affirmative action as a remedy for institutional racism.

Michael Jackson wins eight Grammys, including Record of the Year for "Beat It," and Quincy Jones is named producer of the year primarily for *Thriller*. Jackson is accompanied by teen model Brooke Shields and *Webster* star Emmanuel Lewis. That same night, Herbie Hancock & Grandmixer DST win a Grammy for "Rockit," a record that leads a generation of teenagers to ruin their family's stereo needles. Wynton Marsalis wins a Grammy for his second jazz album, *Think of One,* and for his first classical album, interpretations of trumpet concertos by Haydn, Hummel, and Mozart. No one in Grammy history has ever won a jazz and a classical award in the same year.

MARCH Louis Farrakhan, who has avoided overt involvement in electoral politics since he assumed the mantle of Nation of Islam leadership in 1978 (though he was certainly a behind-the-scenes influence in local politics), is excited enough by fellow Chicagoan Jesse Jackson's presidential run to throw his support behind the effort. Heretofore white Americans (and the vast majority of blacks) didn't care who he backed.

Farrakhan changes all that with one of his weekly radio broadcasts. In response to the *Washington Post* article, the minister says, "We're going to make an example of Milton Coleman. We're going to punish the traitor. One day soon we will punish you with death." In light of this comment other Farrakhan pronouncements surface in the mainstream media, including Farrakhan remarks that Nazi dictator Adolf Hitler was "a great man" and that Judaism was "a gutter religion."

The ripple effects of Farrakhan's introduction to mainstream America are multilayered and surprising. His support of Jackson becomes an issue that Jackson's opponents, and the enemies of progressive politics, use to put the civil rights leader on the defensive. As a result, Jackson spends much of '84 walking a rhetorical tightrope. "I disassociated myself from the message," he says at a May 2 Democratic debate in Texas, "but not from the messenger, and there is a distinct difference."

Conflicting agendas handcuff Jackson. To work in the mainstream he needs white liberal support, which very much includes Jews. Obviously he can't be in favor of Farrakhan's nastiest remarks. However, Jackson doesn't want to be viewed in the black community as turning his back on a black man because whites want him to, making him look like a puppet. So Jackson dances and, in the process, fails to fully satisfy either side.

As Farrakhan's visibility rises, the question of whether a black politician can publicly voice support for Farrakhan becomes a litmus test applied by whites. For example, a black Democratic congressman who needs liberal dollars for his campaign finds any statement about Farrakhan is rife with peril. Once an invisible man, the Nation of Islam leader becomes a media obsession. Every news show, all the news weeklies, and much of the increasingly powerful medium of talk radio focus on Farrakhan's words and history.

Born in the Bronx in 1934 and raised in Boston, Louis wanted to be an entertainer and sang calypso. As a young man he billed himself as "the Charmer" and "Calypso Gene" and made a number of records; the best (or most prescient) was "A White Man's Heaven Is a Black Man's Hell." In his late twenties he joined Elijah Muhammad's Nation of Islam and was renamed Louis X. As a young minister he was greatly influenced by Malcolm X's magnificent speaking style and studied him carefully. There are newsreels of Malcolm speaking at rallies in which Louis X can be seen on the dais smiling beatifically as his mentor speaks.

However, when Malcolm broke with the Nation of Islam in 1963, Farrakhan had no problem proclaiming him a traitor. For years critics felt Farrakhan's overheated attacks on Malcolm X contributed, either directly or covertly, to the leader's assassination in a Harlem ballroom, though Farrakhan vehemently denied any involvement.

After Elijah Muhammad's death in 1975, his son Wallace Deen decided to move his flock toward the traditional practice of Islam. Farrakhan and thousands of other members rebelled, took the Nation of Islam name, and kept faith with the vision of racial separation and black superiority the religion was founded upon. Though not the force it was in the '60s, the Nation continues throughout to do the work in the community (organizing in prisons, running small businesses, publishing a newspaper) that builds goodwill, while attacking white world supremacy. Supporting Jackson opens the closed world of the black Muslims to America.

So while whites are largely repulsed by Farrakhan, many blacks are more upset at the scrutiny aimed at him than at his inflammatory rhetoric. Even devout Christians feel the attacks on Farrakhan are overheated and racially biased. Moreover, it is upsetting to see black leaders, at the urging of whites, condemn him. Blacks now taking a calmer look at Farrakhan and the Nation are attracted by its discipline, its willingness to stand up to whites, its essentially conservative teachings, especially about schooling, man-woman relations, and the need for gainful employment, and its conservative dress (which is admired, though not necessarily emulated). The Honorable Minister Louis Farrakhan doesn't look at all like the boogeyman. The negative attention lavished on Farrakhan doesn't isolate him. It makes him and his followers, ironically, more accessible. Blacks begin to feel protective of the man and admire his unwillingness to compromise.

Nostalgia for strong, defiant black leadership is rife in black America. Jackson satisfies some of that yearning. Obviously Farrakhan does as well. But another figure begins to bubble up out of the collective consciousness, one who has never been a national hero and is unlikely ever to be one. Yet through taped speeches, posters, and books, especially his Alex Haley cowritten autobiography, Malcolm X is having a growing effect on black thought. And he's been dead for nineteen years.

In an extraordinary comeback, Tina Turner, the wild black chick of '60s rock & roll, remakes herself as a pop diva with a track that will go on to win the Grammy as record of the year, "What's Love Got to Do with It?" Turner, once the wife, muse, and property of bandleader Ike Turner, is adopted by a new generation as a venerable yet still hot symbol of female sexuality. Though she was nurtured by the old R&B chitlin' circuit, Turner is repackaged as a pop/rock goddess with a cutting-edge haircut and elaborate videos. This reinvention makes Turner (and her amazing legs) a rarity—an adult black female sex symbol for white men.

MARCH A pilot episode of a hip hop TV show titled *Graffiti Rock* is telecast on WPIX TV in New York. Hosted by downtown party promoter Michael Holman, the show has all the elements of hip hop represented and even ends with a furious MC battle between Run-D.M.C. and the Treacherous Three featuring Kool Moe Dee and Special K.

MARCH 31 In a historic NCAA semifinal game versus Kentucky, the Georgetown Hoyas force the Wildcats to shoot 9.1 percent in the second half. Kentucky, which stars several light-skinned black players (Kenny Walker, Sam Bowie), has been viewed by Hoya haters as a "semi-white hope" to stop the Hoyas' march to the title. Because of John Thompson, Georgetown's assertive, no-nonsense black coach; its intimidating center, Patrick Ewing; and its relentless defensive style, the Hoyas are the target of racist jeering throughout the season. The hulking Ewing, whom Thompson has kept away from the media, is ridiculed all season by fans at Big East schools carrying signs like "Ewing kan't reed dis!" Actually, Hoya style isn't epitomized by Ewing but by a bald-headed power forward named Michael Graham, who is one of the first players to bring b-boy nastiness to big-time ball.

The Georgetown Hoyas go on to take the NCAA championship,

beating the Houston Cougars and making John Thompson the first black coach to capture the college basketball title. This win validates Thompson's tough on- and off-court philosophy, which resentful sportswriters have labeled "Hoya paranoia." But Thompson, once a backup center to Celtic great Bill Russell and an intimidating six feet nine inches himself, feels limiting media access to his players is the best way to protect them.

This season Georgetown becomes black America's team and their gear, featuring a pit bull in a baseball cap, official urban wear. It is the first time that a college basketball team's uniform bears so much symbolic weight. It isn't the last.

The title game has additional significance because of the matchup in the pivot between Jamaican-born Patrick Ewing and Houston's Nigerian Hakeem Olajuwon. These two agile, young, foreign-born centers anticipate the influx of overseas players into the highest levels of this American sport. It is the start of a spirited rivalry between Ewing and Olajuwon that carries over into the NBA.

APRIL 1 Marvin Gaye is shot dead by his father at his Los Angeles home. Gaye's father, once a minister and an acknowledged transvestite, has always been a troubled man. The murder of his famous offspring brings their tortured relationship full circle.

Gaye, without a doubt, is one of the great artists to emerge from the soul explosion of the '60s. In the '70s he evolved from great production-line Motown hit-maker to a self-conscious artist capable of elaborate album-length masterworks like "What's Goin' On."

But it is his erotic honesty and vocal style that truly endure. With his "Let's Get It On" in 1973, Gaye began pushing the envelope in black pop on sexual frankness, a mission that continued with "Here, My Dear" and on his 1983 comeback smash, "Sexual Healing." Several generations of male vocalists, from Prince to Freddie Jackson right up to twenty-first-century stars like R. Kelly, are influenced by Gaye's subject matter and caressing mid-tempo vocals. Gaye's sensual sound endures while the more raw-sounding soul men Gaye once competed against are largely forgotten.

Until this year's Stanley Cup Final, there has never been a black player on a National Hockey League championship team. As the Edmonton Oilers end the New York Islanders' four-year domination of the NHL, their lead goaltender is a wheat-colored young man from Alberta named Grant Fuhr.

Fuhr is not the NHL's first black player. Willie O'Ree broke the color line with the Boston Bruins in 1958. In the late '70s the Washington Capitals had two blacks on the roster, Tony McKegney and Bill Riley. All those men were role players. Fuhr, however, is a crucial player on an Edmonton squad that is bursting with stars (Wayne Gretzky, Mark Messier, Paul Coffey). He is the primary goalie for the Oilers when they win Stanley Cups in '84, '85, '87, '88, and '90, and is an inspiration for the generation of youngsters who now have given twenty-first-century hockey a surprisingly dark tan.

A show of Jean-Michel Basquiat's work opens at the Mary Boone Gallery in SoHo. "With five New York solo shows to his credit and exposure in territories as remote from one another as Europe and Japan, California and the Bronx, Basquiat's success is as close to overnight as can be in the visual arts," writes Vivien Raynor in *The New York Times*. "His ascent is not without a touch of radical chic either, since technically he started out as a graffitist called Samo. But he is different from the defacers who, over the last decade, have moved from exhibitionism in the subways to exhibitions in galleries" because "his work is unquestionably art." Raynor ends her review on a cautionary note: "Right now, Basquiat is a very promising painter, who has a chance of becoming a very good one, as long as he can withstand the forces that would make him an art world mascot."

MAY 14 Michael Jackson visits the White House, where he is honored by President Reagan for donating "Beat It" to an anti-drunk driving campaign. Michael wears a blue military outfit and his trademark glove to the Rose Garden event. Some see his appearance as a tacit endorsement of the president, recalling embarrassing appearances by Sammy Davis Jr. and Elvis Presley with Richard Nixon.

JUNE The Fresh Fest Tour, which brings rappers and break-dancers on a twenty-seven-city tour, grosses an astounding $3.5 million. The lineup includes Run-D.M.C., Kurtis Blow, Whodini, the Fat Boys, Newcleus, and break-dance crews the Magnificent Force, Uptown Express, and the Dynamic Breakers. Because of this tour, sponsored by Swatch Watch, Run, Whodini, and the Fat Boys all achieve sales of 500,000 and introduce live audiences not just to the music but to the style and attitude of hip hop. For example, D.M.C. drinks the heinous malt liquor Olde English 800 onstage, influencing a generation of fans to indulge in "40s" (40-ounce bottles of beer). Throughout this decade malt liquor remains hip hop's official alcoholic beverage of choice.

Whodini's million-selling *Escape* is a prime example of how rap record making is evolving. Recorded in London under the guidance of former Run-D.M.C. coproducer Larry Smith, *Escape* is R & B-flavored hip hop that black radio embraces. The Jive Records release contains two hits that even adult rap haters love—"Friends" and "Freaks Come Out at Night." The acceptance of Whodini, who used a sound similar to Kurtis Blow (Smith wrote several of his early tracks), helps define radio-friendly, singles-oriented hip hop versus hard-core, more rhyme-centered rap. As the decade progresses, the divide between the two becomes more pronounced. Hard-core is taken more seriously by critics and collectors, while radio-friendly bands like Whodini help break down resistance at urban radio stations.

Aiding the acceptance of rap for black adults is its adoption by established R&B stars. One of the first is Chaka Khan, whose cover of Prince's "I Feel for You" is sprinkled with rhymes by Melle Mel. The promo clip is adapted from a Norma Kamali runway video (her line is very fashion-forward in embracing hip hop style) that includes breakin' by Shabba-Doo and Boogaloo Shrimp. The record and video's melding of R&B, fashion, and rap is revolutionary.

Another sign of hip hop's evolution is the debut this year of the country's first rap-only radio format at Los Angeles's KDAY. In the fractured L.A. radio market, it gives the weak signal of the AM station some distinction and automatically gives it a young, multiracial audience. In its early days, KDAY had an East Coast hip hop bias, but over time its championing of local acts helps foster a powerful local rap scene. Many key figures in the growth of Southern California hip hop are employed at KDAY, including a young DJ and mixer named Andre Young, a.k.a. Dr. Dre.

JUNE The Los Angeles Olympics is a showcase for black athletes and black style. Carl Lewis confirms his place as one of the greatest athletes of all time by capturing four gold medals. He also plays a role in popularizing the hi-top fade (a tall, black cone of hair on top and thinned out on the sides). In an impressive display of homegrown greatness, gold medals are won by several track and field veterans, including Evelyn Ashford in the 100-meter dash. Al Joyner in the triple jump, and Edwin Moses in the 400-meter hurdles.

At the games' closing ceremonies, one hundred break-dancers are on display. Breaking is, at this point, sort of the pet rock of hip hop—everybody likes it but few think of it as an art form. This same summer in San Bernardino, California, the city council bans breakin' because it interferes with shopping at a local mall, despite police reports that its popularity has helped decrease local youth gang violence.

Break dancing, however, isn't enough to tame the City of Angels. The Los Angeles Police Department's manpower deployment to protect the Olympic games is later cited as one reason its gang scene, fueled by sales of crack, grows in size and impact. Post-Pryor rock cocaine is quite visible in the city (in '82 Los Angeles hospital emergency rooms reported a 90 percent rise over the previous year, the nation's greatest increase in cocaine overdoses).

This summer South Central Los Angeles and the cities of Long Beach and Compton experience a tremendous rise in the availability of crack and the appearance of dozens of "rock houses." Officers reassigned from daily patrols to protect Olympic events throughout May and June give the area's biggest gangs, the Bloods and Crips, time to spread and multiply. DEA officer William Coonce tells *U.S. News & World Report,* "There was an awful lot of organizational focus on just keeping the city safe from terrorism. I think normal law enforcement took a backseat."

While this theory is difficult to substantiate, it's certainly true that after this summer, gang violence, instigated by turf battles over prime crack-dealing locations, grows noticeable even to those who only experience black and Hispanic L.A. via the Metro Section of the *Los Angeles Times.* Local gang leaders, fattened by crack profits, sent crews around the country in search of fresh new territories. From this summer on, references to gang culture begin to appear regularly in Los Angeles–based films. And, yes, in rap records, too.

JUNE 8 Stan Lathan, veteran black TV director, and singer-activist-producer Harry Belafonte bring *Beat Street* to the screen, which features a slew of great dancers and hip hop stars. As part of the hype, actor and dancer Robert Taylor busts a move on the cover of *Newsweek*. The soundtrack is a fine hip hop sampler with Afrika Bambaataa, Doug E. Fresh, and the Treacherous Three among the true school acts represented.

Not as real as *Beat Street* is *Breakin'*, a product of the exploitation film producers Menaham Golan and Yoram Globus, which contains some amazing poppin' and lockin' from Michael Boogaloo "Shrimp" Chambers and Adolfo "Shabba-Doo" Quinones, who appear in the "I Feel for You" video. But the plot, about a white classic dancer wanting to break dance, is an insult to hip hop.

JUNE 18   Jesse Jackson takes his presidential campaign to the United Nations, where he calls the Reagan administration's policy on South Africa "an act of barbarism" that permits American firms to exploit the black labor provided by the apartheid system. Jackson argues that "Ford, General Motors, Chrysler, IBM, Exxon, Control Data, and all others" must leave South Africa. Speaking before a special UN committee on apartheid, Jackson is greeted by a standing ovation and cries of "Run, Jesse, run" from the hundred-plus delegates.

JUNE 19   The Chicago Bulls select Michael Jordan third in the NBA draft, after Jordan forgoes his final year of college eligibility at North Carolina. Bulls general manager Rod Thorn loves Jordan but wishes he were seven feet tall, since the two players drafted before him were both centers, Hakeem Olajuwon of Houston and Sam Bowie of Kentucky. Prior to Jordan's arrival and despite the recent success of Magic Johnson and Larry Bird, the road to championships is still perceived to be paved by a dominating center. It is a view Jordan eventually changes. Jordan's annual salary is $600,000.

The Philadelphia 76ers later draft Charles Barkley, a burly, big-hipped power forward from Auburn University. The animated, cocky young man's aggressive on- and off-court style provides a huge contrast to the elegant Julius Erving. Over the next two years the team evolves from Dr. J.'s team to Barkley's, reflecting a generational and aesthetic shift in the sport. Where Grover Washington Jr. played brandy-smooth tenor sax for Erving, buck wild Barkley will be cited in many rap rhymes.

JUNE 22 The CDC reports that 4,918 AIDS cases have been reported to date. Of those cases 2,221 of the patients are dead.

JUNE 25 *Purple Rain* opens, transforming Prince from a musically ambitious, sexually and racially ambiguous cult icon into a mainstream superstar. Set in the exotic locale of Minneapolis, this high-energy musical film percolates with Prince compositions ("When Doves Cry," "Take Me with U," and the title song) and garners generally affectionate reviews. To the surprise of everyone, the Time's Morris Day and Jerome Benton nearly steal the movie as an '80s Abbott and Costello team.

Purple Rain sets a dynamic new standard for the marriage of contemporary pop and movies that so many ambitious musicians will fail to match—including Prince, who'll go on to make three more films. It inspires Warner Bros., at the urging of its record division, to finance a number of music-driven movies with cross-marketed soundtracks.

Prince's rise has been remarkably steady. With each album, he sells more records, plays at bigger venues, and receives more radio airplay. *Purple Rain* makes him a huge pop star in a league with Madonna, Bruce Springsteen, and Michael Jackson. Yet there is a part of this twenty-six-year-old musician that isn't comfortable with this audience. For all his gifts (there is no other performer of the period who excels at so many aspects of music making), Prince is an iconoclast at heart. The idea of being liked by so many doesn't necessarily suit him. After *Purple Rain,* Prince, driven by his love of danger and, likely, megalomania, makes many moves that undermine his mass acceptance.

Unlike his peers (Michael Jackson, Madonna, Bruce Spring-steen), who all seem to give great thought to career moves, Prince seems to work on instinct. He doesn't pick the obvious singles for records. He attempts to direct complicated projects. He signs non-singers to record deals. None of it is calculated. All of it has a will-ful, improvisational quality unusual in an era when the carefully orchestrated grand gesture is the norm.

In an event little noted in the year's Princemania, two of the Time's original members, bass player Terry Lewis and keyboardist Jimmy "Jam" Harris, are not in *Purple Rain,* having been "fired" by Prince prior to filming, after they were late coming back from a pro-ducing gig. Prince's loss is their gain as the duo embark on a hugely successful producing career, building their own Minneapolis empire.

JULY *A.M. Chicago* with Oprah Winfrey expands to a full hour. Writing in the *Chicago Tribune,* Jon Anderson notes, "On and off screen, her presence is undeniable, despite her short Chicago track record. She is greeted by strangers on the street, rec-ognized in restaurants and once was driven to work by a Chicago policeman when she was late and couldn't get a cab."

JULY 6 The Jacksons' Victory Tour opens in Kansas City's Arrowhead Stadium after a hectic spring of speculation and behind-the-scenes battling over who controls it. *Newsweek* re-ports, "For months the story of the tour had been punctuated with question marks. When would it start? Where would it play? Would it happen at all?" Two nonmusic promoters, boxing's Don King and football's Chuck Sullivan, initially institute a cumbersome system that requires fans to buy tickets in blocks of four at $30 each. At a press conference the day before the concert, Michael announces a less rigid system to mend fences with the public.

The tour itself, though lucrative, is somewhat anticlimactic. For those who witnessed the Jacksons' last tour, the staging and set structure is remarkably similar. Several huge *Thriller* hits are included, as is a short set of songs by brother Jermaine, who returns to the fold for this tour. There is a warmed-over quality to the presentation.

The controversy over the tour (*Newsweek*'s cover story was labeled "The Tour, The Hype, The Hysteria") is Michael's first truly negative press of the *Thriller* era. Michael's judgment and his personal habits, treated with kid gloves for years, now increasingly become the focus of media coverage. Again from *Newsweek:* "Ever since the heyday of Presley, people have questioned the virility of certain rock stars. But never before have such questions been aired so widely, persistently and explicitly, in the face of continued denials."

JULY 17 Jesse Jackson makes an electrifying address at the Democratic National Convention in San Francisco. That speech, which easily overshadows nominee Walter Mondale's acceptance speech, is the apex of Jackson's political career. After being showered with applause at the podium, Jackson appears to have overcome the taint of Hymietown. The truth is, in Democratic circles, he would never receive this undiluted admiration again.

JULY 19 *Penthouse* magazine announces that nude photos of the first black Miss America, Vanessa Williams, appearing in the September issue will show her being "intimate" with another woman. Pageant officials ask her to resign, but Williams refuses.

JULY 21 *Billboard* magazine's issue carries a huge tribute titled "The Saga of Michael Jackson." The magazine is filled with pages of pictures, ads, and Jackson-approved editorial copy. In a wonderful bit of gamesmanship, Warner Bros. buys the back page of the issue and prints a foldout that contains a poster-size ad for *Purple Rain*. It carries the tag line "The Rain Has Just Begun."

JULY 23 Ten months after winning the crown, Vanessa Williams resigns as Miss America and Suzette Charles, Miss New Jersey, takes over, becoming the second black Miss America in the process.

JULY 28 Sade's "Hang On to Your Love," a huge UK hit, introduces the integrated Brit-soul band here and makes its Nigerian-British lead singer a multi-culti fashion trendsetter. While many black British soul artists attempt to break through here (Loose Ends, Soul II Soul, and Billy Ocean all had some success), Sade becomes a staple of black radio by celebrating black pop's more sophisticated traditions.

SEPTEMBER Euzhan Palcy directs *Sugar Cane Alley,* a coming-of-age tale set on the French-speaking island of Martinique in the 1930s. This is a supple, insightful picture of class and color conflicts within an insular black community. Palcy's very confident direction and foreign location get *Sugar Cane Alley* a good art-house release, making her one of the few women directors (much less black) to get a film into American theaters.

SEPTEMBER The issue of *Penthouse* magazine that contains the nude pictures of Vanessa Williams is the biggest-selling issue in its fifteen-year history. Williams says she is devastated, while *Penthouse* publisher Bob Guccione is unmoved, claiming in *People* magazine, "It made her by far the most famous Miss America that ever lived."

SEPTEMBER Paula Giddings publishes *When and Where I Enter: The Impact of Black Women on Race and Sex in America,* an ambitious narrative that chronicles all the crucial figures (Ida B. Wells, Mary McLeod Bethune, Ella Baker), critiques the assumptions of black male scholars (E. Franklin Frazier, Robert Staples), and paints a keen portrait of black women vis-à-vis black and white men. Giddings, a Howard University grad and book editor, covers some of the same terrain as Michelle Wallace's *Black Macho* but does so with a more modulated, less accusatory tone.

SEPTEMBER 11   In his *Village Voice* article, "Stagolee Versus the Proper Negro: The Treacherous Three Cross Over—Prince, Wynton Marsalis and Eddie Murphy," critic Greg Tate sums up '84, noting that "right now black America's got more crossover acts happening than it's had since the '60s, and the funny thing is they're all taking Babylon by storm in an era noticeably absent of agitation from the streets."

Tate wonders, ". . . has Massa granted us equality without us eben knowing it?" He thinks not, suggesting instead that "all the aforementioned are yer super-blacks, Biggers so baad they can't help but outshine (no pun intended) the honkie competition." Of the trio of Prince, Marsalis, and Murphy, he is impressed by "the degree to which they seem to be in manly control of their respective images." In summation he notices that each has a very direct antecedent (Richard Pryor, Miles Davis, Jimi Hendrix), yet that "they've managed, unlike their forefathers, to make it in the mainstream without compromising their edge."

SEPTMBER 14   *A Soldier's Story* opens. Playwright Charles Fuller adapts his play into a movie directed by Canadian Norman Jewison (who handled the Sidney Poitier vehicle *In the Heat of the Night* in 1967). Howard Rollins tries to channel Sir Sid, but it is the intensity of two actors reprising their onstage roles, Adolph Caesar and Denzel Washington, that gives the film its moral complexity. Comic actor Robert Townsend has a small role as an enlisted man.

He borrows film ends from the production to work on a project about the sad state of black actors in Hollywood.

SEPTEMBER 20 *The Cosby Show* debuts on NBC. It quickly becomes the most watched show in America, with an average of 30 million people tuning in each week, numbers that pull the NBC network up from third to second in the ratings race. It is Bill Cosby's first network show in eight years and the culmination of his success as a commercial pitchman in the '80s. The show is proudly bourgeois and acts as a powerful antidote to sitcoms like *Webster* and *Gimme a Break*. Dr. Cliff Huxtable, his lovely wife, Clair, and their five well-mannered kids are the pages of *Black Enterprise* and *Essence* readers come to life. The parents are professionals, their offspring are college-bound, and they reside in a roomy brownstone in pricey Brooklyn Heights.

Cosby is the program's artistic conscience and, by definition, the nation's, as he shapes each half-hour show to reflect his views of what black life in America is (at least in many houses) or should be. For those who believe pathology is the race's only reality, the show is science fiction. There are no victims on-screen. There is no crack. There is no overt agitation. There is old-fashioned morality. Because of this approach some blacks argue that the very idea of a successful, non-dysfunctional, basically happy black middle-class family on national TV makes it harder to agitate for social change. In an era of neoconservative power, some think *The Cosby Show* gives comfort to the enemy.

Cosby, a confident man who has supported black causes since the days of the Freedom Marches, brushes aside these claims and stays true to his vision. Supported by the advice of consultant Dr. Alvin Poussaint of Harvard, the forty-seven-year-old humorist makes his show a source of humor and tranquillity for viewers white and black.

About the critics, Cosby tells *Ebony,* "Why do they want to deny me the pleasure of being an American and just enjoying life? Why must I make all the Black social statements? My family here is not going to sit around for half an hour and do Black versus White versus Asian jokes so people can say, 'This is a Black show.'" Continuing, he asserts, "I'm here because I'm a human being and I want to have fun. I want to show the happiness within our people. I want to show that we have the same kinds of wants and needs as other American families."

Like Ronald Reagan, Bill Cosby's Cliff Huxtable serves as a surrogate father for America—warm, though, inviting, stern, and consistent. Moreover, wherever you stand in the debate about the message of *The Cosby Show,* there is no question the program gives the veteran comic his best platform since his landmark comedy recordings of the '60s.

Lisa Bonet, playing daughter Denise, becomes America's first black bohemian pinup girl. This character, with her unconventional attitudes, who resists the careerism of the black middle class, is one of the show's sharpest creations. Also smart is having the Huxtable kids come in many hues, a range of color that accurately depicts the diversity of color within so many black families. There is a wonderful sense of sexual play between Cosby and wife Clair, played by Phylicia Allen, that is unusual between two blacks on network TV (and that explains their large family).

Unlike most other classic sitcoms that are peopled with many comic types, *The Cosby Show*'s other actors are basically straight men for Cosby, who skillfully carries the comic weight for thirty minutes. Cosby's comic viewpoint is so strong it feels like one giant monologue. Rarely is a single star's life philosophy so carefully woven into the usually rigid sitcom format. In that respect, *Roseanne, Martin,* and *Seinfeld* are among the later sitcoms that owe a debt to *The Cosby Show.*

OCTOBER   Hip hop's kinship to the wild days of early rock & roll is well illustrated by the saga of "Roxanne, Roxanne." UTFO's nasty take on a young woman named Roxanne results in an "answer" record by a fourteen-year-old named Roxanne Shante (Lolita Gooden), who disses back with "Roxanne's Revenge." UTFO's producers, Full Force, then recruit a Puerto Rican cutie who replies with "The Real Roxanne."

The Roxanne records appear throughout the summer as the acts continue to dis each other in rhymes that recall the dozens of MC battles in the parks of New York. Underneath the playful banter is a rather nasty, distrustful view of young women that's becoming a recurring theme in rap music.

OCTOBER 8   Struggling Brooklyn filmmaker Spike Lee makes a note in his diary about a screenplay called *She's Gotta Have It.* He writes, "Have a person, a beautiful Black woman who loves sex, she's not a whore, nothing like that, she just loves sex and she can love more than one man at a time. That's the premise."

OCTOBER 11   *Ma Rainey's Black Bottom* opens on Broadway at the Cort Theater, introducing August Wilson's unique blend of mysticism, elegance, and streetcorner poetry to the American theater. Yale graduate and ex-con Charles Dutton begins his starring career with the role of Leeve, a frustrated 1920s trumpet player who wants to record his own compositions. Theresa Merritt, a fine singer and actor who spent much of the '70s in black-oriented sitcoms like *That's My Mama,* cuts loose as the regal and strong-willed Ma Rainey.

Wilson is obsessed with the blues as the central voice of the black experience in America and claims to have been inspired to write the play after repeatedly listening to an old 78-rpm record. He was born and raised in the same Pittsburgh neighborhood that nurtured John Edgar Wideman. During the '60s young Wilson was involved with many black arts organizations. He focused primarily on poetry before turning his talents to the theater, and captures the rhythms and cadences of black urban speech in his dialogue.

Veteran director Lloyd Richards, who guided the original production of Lorraine Hansberry's *A Raisin in the Sun,* adds to his legacy by nurturing Wilson's talent while running the prestigious Yale drama department. Wilson's plays serve as a showcase for an impressive roster of Yale Drama School grads, of which Dutton is but the first.

NOVEMBER In the Winter issue of the *Black American Literature Forum,* Calvin Hernton publishes "The Sexual Mountain and Black Women Writers." Years earlier, Hernton had written a pioneering article called "Black Male Writers and the Sexual Mountain." This new look at a rich topic is equally well developed and analytical. "Because much of the writing of contemporary black women is critical of black men, both in the literary sphere and in real life, the men find it unpalatable," Hernton writes. "But black writing owes its very nature to the oppressive conditions under which blacks were and are subjected in America. . . . It is altogether consistent with the heritage of black writing that black women write about the meanness they have experienced and still experience at the hands of black men as well as white men. It is inescapable that women writers seek to illuminate and elevate the condition of black women, their whole condition."

NOVEMBER President Ronald Reagan and Vice President George Bush are reelected by one of the biggest electoral margins in history, 59 percent to 41 percent, over Walter Mondale and Geraldine Ferraro (though with only half the electorate exercising their franchise, only 29 percent of the eligible voters actually pulled the lever for Reagan), insuring that neoconservatism grows stronger through the rest of the decade and continues to reshape the federal government's relationship to blacks by turning many Great Society social policies on their ear. In contrast to the great strides blacks make in pop culture, the political flow in this country does them no favors. Moreover, this electoral debacle and the contradictory impact of Reverend Jackson's campaign (he activates black voters, but also steels the resolve of white moderate swing voters against progressive liberalism) affect the strategic thinking of many Democrats, including the ambitious young governor of Arkansas, William Jefferson Clinton.

NOVEMBER John Edgar Wideman's breakthrough book *Brothers and Keepers* is not one of his several polished, nuanced works of fiction but a memoir that contrasts the writer's relatively privileged life in academia with the troubles of his brother Robby, who's serving a life sentence for murder. The juxtaposition of John Edgar's bookish lifestyle and Robby's in the poor black Pittsburgh 'hood of Homewood is presented in the book's three sections. The power of Wideman's narrative emanates from his struggle to bridge the emotional and psychological divide between the two brothers and their fates. Wideman poignantly depicts the struggle of blacks who've escaped the limitations of race to stay connected with those still trapped by race, in a sad, thoughtful report from inside one of the race's great internal challenges.

Wideman has long been mining the tensions in his relationship with Robby, as can be seen in some of the stories in his collections *Hiding Place* (1981) and *Damballah* (1981). The commercial success of *Brothers and Keepers* is aided greatly by a *60 Minutes* episode on the two brothers. *Brothers and Keepers* is the latest contribution to a long literary tradition of black autobiographies of lives tainted by racism that have appealed to American readers. Unlike narratives such as Booker T. Washington's *Up from Slavery: An Autobiography* or Richard Wright's *Black Boy* that tend to be aspirational, up-by-your-own-bootstraps sagas, there's a painful ambiguity to Wideman's prose that complicates expectations even as it breaks your heart.

DECEMBER Tipper Gore, wife of Tennessee senator Al Gore, purchases the *Purple Rain* album for her eleven-year-old daughter, then listens to the sexually explicit "Darlin' Nikki," and decides America needs to be warned when such unbridled carnality is put on vinyl. Along with the wives of several other senators and D.C. political figures, Gore founds the PMRC (Parents Music Resource Center), which presses for and wins a series of concessions from the record industry regarding its marketing to minors. Because of the PMRC's efforts, recordings are stickered with warning labels addressing their lyrical content. Eventually artists, mostly from rap and heavy metal, have to make "clean" versions of their recordings to accommodate mall retail outlets who won't stock the stickered versions. All major labels institute screening committees that go through the lyrics of records in search of questionable rhyming couplets. All this is sparked by a ditty about a girl who sat in hotel lobbies and masturbated with a magazine.

DECEMBER 3 *Business Week* publishes an article about Michael Jordan, calling him "the most exciting player to hit the NBA in years." In his first four weeks with Chicago, the Bulls are selling an extra fifty season tickets a day. After he scores forty-five points in a victory over San Antonio on November 13, the Bulls have consecutive sellouts at the Chicago Stadium for the first time in three years. The periodical notes Jordan "is becoming one of the hottest endorsements in professional sports."

DECEMBER 5 Eddie Murphy's star status is confirmed by *Beverly Hills Cop.* Unlike his previous hit, *48 Hours,* in which he costarred with white actor Nick Nolte, Eddie carries this film by himself with no white costar (but a solid white supporting cast).

Cop grosses $58 million in its first month of release and goes over $100 million by the end of its run.

For a period in the middle of the decade, Murphy reigns as Hollywood's biggest box office attraction, the first black person to hold that position since Sidney Poitier in 1968. Unlike Richard Pryor, whose non-concert film persona is that of a jittery, scared everyman, Murphy is cocksure, fast-talking, and always on top. He personifies an aggression that, despite being comic, is actually less cartoonish than that of the blaxploitation heroes, since it is Murphy's wit, not his exaggerated swagger, that makes him so potent.

As he announces in his career-defining scene in *48 Hours,* "There's a new sheriff in town." By that Murphy isn't just poking fun at country-and-western macho (though he is also doing that), but making it clear this is a very different kind of black man that American moviegoers are about to experience. In *Beverly Hills Cop,* Murphy, the funnyman with a gun, a cop who ignores the rules, a black man working easily in a white world where race is never mentioned, establishes a template that a generation of black actors and Hollywood screenwriters follow religiously.

DECEMBER 10 Anglican bishop and eloquent spokesman for the antiapartheid movement, South African Desmond Tutu is awarded the Nobel Peace Prize. Tutu's award is part of the growing international resistance to apartheid.

DECEMBER 14 EEOC chairman Clarence Thomas, in Congressional testimony, uses the fact that Georgetown University's number-one ranked basketball team is all black, though it represents a predominately white school, as an argument against statistics as a measurement of racism. "You could conclude from the results of a study of the Georgetown basketball team that statistically you have to be black," Thomas remarked, "or you could also conclude, if you did not use race-conscious statistics, that you have to know how to play basketball. Now, what does that mean in Georgetown's case? Obviously you need to be taller than five-foot-eight; you probably have to be aggressive on defense, and with Coach John Thompson's system, you probably have to be disciplined and a good student, because if you are simply a good basketball player, you cannot play for him. So there's a whole range of considerations other than race."

The Democrats Thomas testifies before are not impressed by his basketball metaphor, but the neo-cons are undaunted. In fact, throughout this fall Thomas gives many combative public statements. In October he comments about the election campaign. "What black leaders have successfully done is they have essentially disenfranchised blacks. Blacks don't have clout in the Democratic Party. . . . Look what happened to Jesse Jackson. And the black leaders have alienated blacks so badly from Reagan and the Republican Party—made him into an evil person—that there is no chance at this point for blacks to discuss the Republicans as an alternative to the Democratic Party." To illustrate the good works of the Reagan administration, Thomas reports that the EEOC has enjoyed three successive budget increases and has increased the number of cases it handles. "When I hear them say the president has a bad civil rights record," said Thomas, "I think that's me and my agency and we have a very good record."

Thomas, along with Clarence M. Pendleton Jr., chairman of the Civil Rights Commission, and Stephen Rhodes, assistant to Vice President Bush for domestic policy, criticizes U.S. blacks for focusing on antiapartheid activities. These men, three of the highest-ranking blacks in the Reagan administration, say they oppose apartheid but give full support to the government's policy of "constructive engagement" with South Africa. "All of us who have lived under segregation, a mild form of apartheid, are concerned," says Thomas. "But in terms of the immediate, in terms of priorities, I think we should focus more on what is happening here. If these were protests about the quality of education black kids in the United States receive or about the high crime in black neighborhoods . . . I would be right out front in that kind of march."

DECEMBER 22   Bernard Goetz, a white man traveling alone on a New York subway train, is approached by four black male teens. He claims they threatened him—they say they just asked for $5 to play video games. Either way, Goetz feels threatened. In response, Goetz pulls out a 38-caliber revolver and shoots all four, including Darrell Cabey, who is paralyzed by a bullet. Goetz becomes a national figure (and hero to many) who is hailed as the "subway vigilante," like the character in the Charles Bronson film *Death Wish*. Instead of showing any concern for his victims, Goetz asserts, "If you're injured, paralyzed, or whatever while committing a violent crime against me, that's not my fault."

After much delay and many lawsuits, Goetz is acquitted of attempted murder and assault. He is convicted of criminal possession of an unlicensed weapon and serves 250 days in jail. In the '90s, Cabey sues Goetz for his injury and a Bronx jury awards the black youth $43 million in damages. The polarizing reaction to the Goetz shooting is one of the many stark racial incidents that marks New York in the '80s and resonates nationally. Fear of black teens, already high, is increased, as well as white resentment of them. The idea that black youth are an "endangered species" pops up in the speeches of black leaders and on T-shirts sold in black 'hoods.

DECEMBER 31   Garry Trudeau illustrates the cover of *Newsweek* for a story titled "Year of the Yuppie." Both the story and Trudeau's picture nail the stereotype of the young urban professional that defines the decade's concept of upward mobility. The term "buppie" or "bumpy" (depending on your taste) comes into vogue to describe the yuppies' sepia counterparts.

The honorable (and infamous) Louis Farrakhan.

1985

1985

One quandary of the post-soul era is the question of black political leadership. Who is a black leader? How is it defined? Who has the right to define it? And what should they be leading toward? Is it about tangibly uplifting the race? Is it spiritual inspiration or, perhaps, reflecting a reality most people want to ignore? In this year various modes of leadership are on display that speak to a diverse (and fractured) black consciousness. The example that dominates the media is provided by the Honorable Minister Louis Farrakhan, who embarks on a national speaking tour that rivals the Jacksons' Victory tour for hype.

Starting in Detroit in January, Farrakhan speaks in most major American cities, attracting 10,000 in Washington, D.C., 15,000 in Los Angeles, and 25,000 at his concluding gig at Madison Square Garden. "Two years ago, Louis Farrakhan couldn't fill a church in Chicago," observed Chicago political consultant Don Rose of the once-obscure figure, now regular front-page fodder.

Farrakhan's tour puts particular pressure on black mayors to denounce the minister's anti-Semitism. In Chicago, Farrakhan is used as yet another weapon to attack Mayor Harold Washington during his embattled first term. In L.A., Tom Bradley, long a favorite of the Jewish community, has his loyalty questioned for not speaking out fast enough against Farrakhan. In contrast, white pols jump on the minister with both feet.

In New York, Mayor Ed Koch calls Farrakhan "a Nazi in clerical garb" and Governor Cuomo says his ideas are "ugly and divisive." Harlem congressman Charles Rangel points out how dramatic a white loyalty test Farrakhan has become for black pols. Comparing the situation to South Africa, where blacks must carry passbooks, Rangel quips, "I just hope this is not coming to the point where . . . black Americans have to carry their last statement refuting Farrakhan."

By year's end the Jewish community is so spooked by Farrakhan that the Simon Wiesenthal Center, an L.A.-based organization for the study of the Holocaust, polls black Americans to see who they'd cite as their leader. Surely to the pollsters' relief, Jesse Jackson emerges in unprompted responses as the only widely recognized spokesman for blacks by 59 percent of respondents. Farrakhan only comes in sixth (behind the late Dr. King and his widow, Coretta), being named a black leader by only 7 percent of those questioned. Seemingly the Christian-church-centered model of black leadership is intact. But, crucially, Farrakhan is rated most favorably by those with the least formal education and the lowest incomes, symbolic of how far from the black mainstream many of the race's poorest find themselves.

Rappers, heretofore seen primarily as feisty entertainers with street credibility, begin to expand on their role, with some presenting themselves as truth-tellers, articulating an underclass reality that Farrakhan, for example, sees his Nation of Islam as the solution to. But even that eloquent religious leader is no match for the nihilism of the culture's newest wave.

Far from the radar screen of mainstream black radio and white media, Boogie Down Productions, the brain child of former homeless teen KRS-One, a.k.a. Kris Parker, and shelter counselor DJ Scott LaRock, a.k.a. Scott Sterling, release *Criminal Minded* on small B-Boy Records. This collection of beats and rhymes is a seminal document of mid-'80s street culture that describes automatic weapons fire, drug dealing, and poverty with none of the sentiment or sanctimony of R&B. This is black music with no illusions and precious little contemplation of hope.

Typical of the album is "9mm Goes Bang." In this tale, KRS-One and his posse are attacked by a drug dealer named Peter. KRS-One pulls out his gatt and handles his business in a cold-blooded narrative. According to KRS-One, the lawless environment of homeless shelters, home to so many poor black families, is his inspiration: "You had gangsters and criminals, murderers, drug dealers, and their idea of survival was just that: knock off the next man, sell your drugs over here, steal, gunpoint robberies." To paraphrase two later BDP album titles, *Criminal Minded* is truly ghetto music and a blueprint for much of hip hop.

The self-taught and intellectually curious Parker reveals himself to be one of the more complicated thinkers in all of American popular culture, analyzing violence, religion, and capitalism, on and off vinyl, with such acuity he ends up a regular on the lecture and concert circuit. Parker, in fact, is one of the MCs who affects the thinking of black academics as they wrestle with the nuances of the '80s.

But while most black academics made their mark via scholarship, one proved a genius at manifesting black culture into a quasi-educational, quasi-political power base. In this year Professor Henry Louis Gates, editor of *Our Nig* and the collection *Black Literature and Literary Theory,* moves from Yale to Cornell. Gates proves a peripatetic scholar who later shifts to Duke (in 1990) and then Harvard (in 1991). At each stop along the way Gates edits books, collects scholarly disciples, and builds a black academic empire. Just as in music, television, and politics, there's black expansion in higher education in the '80s that spawns a generation of academic stars like Cornell West and Bell Hooks. These professor-writer-commentators, through writings in the popular press, TV appearances, and lectures, develop a high public profile.

But no one is as canny at marshaling this high profile into power than this West Virginian known to pals as Skip. Gates doesn't simply win grants and appointments, but gains such access to power that he becomes an academic kingmaker in the white university world like no black person before him, spawning acolytes and enemies with letters of recommendation. Gates's path to power is as unprecedented as is the coverage of Farrakhan's tour or the street visions of Kris Parker. All are leaders of very distinct, if sometimes overlapping, often oppositional communities.

JANUARY 28 The day after the American Music Awards broadcast in Los Angeles, a recording session is organized to raise money and awareness to combat a famine in Africa. The session is led by black pop heavyweights, with Quincy Jones producing "We Are the World," a song penned by Michael Jackson and Lionel Ritchie. It is testimony to the clout of that trio that almost every major American pop star of the day—including Bruce Springsteen, Cindy Lauper, and Kenny Rogers—gathers to sing the words of and take direction from these black men. The record itself is a soaring bit of sentimental self-congratulation that becomes the biggest-selling single of all time and raises millions for famine relief.

JANUARY 29 Oprah Winfrey makes her first national television appearance with a slot on *The Tonight Show,* guest hosted by Joan Rivers. Soon her Chi-town rival Phil Donahue pulls out of Chicago and relocates his show to New York, explaining that he wants to be closer to his wife, Marlo Thomas, who's working there. Cynics think Winfrey's rise forced him to reposition his show.

Either way, after one year in Chicago, Winfrey is the city's dominant television presence. Quincy Jones, in town to testify in a specious lawsuit over the copyright of a Michael Jackson song, notices her and becomes convinced she is right for the part of Sofia in the film adaptation of *The Color Purple.*

FEBRUARY Gloria Naylor publishes the follow-up to *The Women of Brewster Place.* The novel, *Linden Hills,* is a surreal take on the compromises blacks make moving on up in America. The thirty-five-year-old novelist creates an upper-middle-class black community built on a plot of land owned by the Nedeed family, who've controlled this property since 1820. Founded to be "a beautiful, black wad of spit right in the white eye of America," Linden Hills contains a dark, Satanic secret about the costs of that achievement that parodies Dante's *Inferno*. Naylor's metaphor is bold, though the novel's plotting is a bit schematic and much of the dialogue overly didactic. Still, *Linden Hills* testifies to Naylor's ambition and artistic seriousness, solidifying her place as an author interested in redefining black America's goals.

FEBRUARY Whitney Houston's debut album, *Whitney,* is a canny synthesis of the pop-soul tradition of her aunt, Dionne Warwick, and the adult contemporary schlock of earlier Arista hitmakers Barry Manilow and Air Supply. A team of the day's top pop producers and songwriters (Kashif, Narada Michael Walden, Michael Masser) are guided by Arista president Clive Davis to create hooky ballads and mid-tempo singles that fit on black and pop radio.

Houston's voice is a versatile instrument capable of Aretha-style belting and elevator-friendly balladry. This former model from Newark, New Jersey, is a slender beauty whose image is so traditional it's almost quaint in comparison to her chief competitor, the sluttish provocateur Madonna.

Houston gives few in-depth interviews, and her real personality is carefully protected by Arista. Unlike Madonna, Michael Jackson, Prince, and others, it is her music and looks alone that carry her to stardom. This formula is supremely successful, making *Whitney* the all-time biggest-selling album by a woman, a status the album would maintain into the '90s.

MARCH 6 Mike Tyson, product of Brooklyn's rugged Brownsville 'hood, arrested thirty-eight times before his current age of eighteen and eventually mentored by boxing guru Cus D'Amato, turns pro. Tyson has shown promise as an amateur but doesn't truly blossom until he begins getting paid for his work. D'Amato, who trained Floyd Patterson and Jose Torres, does a brilliant job, and his protégé wins his first fifteen professional bouts by knockouts.

Though he's just a youngster, *Sports Illustrated* calls Tyson "the most devastating puncher in boxing, a remorseless attacker," and within a year "Iron Mike" moves from unknown to near legend. His path to the title seems clear. Many in boxing predict Tyson will one day be compared with the greatest heavyweights of all time—Jack Dempsey, Joe Louis, Muhammad Ali.

APRIL The New York Mets open the season with two of baseball's most highly touted young talents on the roster: Darryl Strawberry, twenty-three, a tall, lanky slugger from Los Angeles with amazing bat speed, is projected as a Hall of Fame outfielder after being named National League rookie of the year in '83; right-hander Dwight "Doc" Gooden, twenty, rookie of the year in '84, is seen as a future Cy Young winner. And, in fact, the Florida native wins twenty-four games this season, making him the youngest twenty-game winner of the century. Strawberry and Gooden, along with colorful, feisty teammates, make the Mets the sport's most exciting team. Every start of "Doc" Gooden is an event because of his blazing speed and supple curveball, while Strawberry's at bats always send ripples of excitement through the stands because any of his long, looping swings could result in a tape measure home run. In 1986 this dynamic duo sparks the Mets to a 108-win season and a World Series title. There is talk of a dynasty around Shea Stadium. It doesn't happen. The early success is accompanied by an insecurity and weakness that makes both players stars in a very sad soap opera. The number of run-ins both of them have with drugs comprises a list of time and opportunities squandered. They begin in the off-season following the '86 Series victory, when Gooden is arrested for brawling with Tampa police. Later, Strawberry is ordered to stay away from his wife, Lisa, after breaking her nose with a punch. They seem like unfortunate incidents at the time, but they are really early warning signs.

Throughout the '80s, Gooden and Strawberry both spend time for cocaine and alcohol abuse at New York's Smithers Alcohol and Treatment Center and the Betty Ford Center in Rancho Mirage, California. Along the way their immense gifts slowly wither away, appearing in maddening flashes but never for more than a year at a time before they fall victim, yet again, to addiction. Ironically, the two don't get high together. "I never partied with Doc," Strawberry later tells *Sports Illustrated.*

Both stay in the majors well into the '90s and collect world championship rings with the Yankees, but we never watch them play without wondering what might have been.

MAY The black women's magazine *Essence* celebrates its fifteenth anniversary with Lena Horne on the cover and its fattest advertising issue ever. *Essence* has a circulation of 800,000 and a readership of 3.7 million. The magazine has also spun off a syndicated TV show broadcast on forty-nine stations. Editor-in-chief Susan Taylor notes that much of the magazine's focus is on black male-female relationships: "You can't really look at the problems that divide black men and black women without looking at how a larger society impacts on black relationships. Black men have been raised to believe, like all other men, that they should be in charge of their lives and ours too. Unlike white men, black men don't have an opportunity to flex their muscles in corporate America. This puts an incredible burden on black men to look for other sources of empowerment. For black women, when you're unable to feed and clothe your children and keep a roof over their heads, it's real hard to be loving and supportive of your man's efforts."

MAY 5 After a fifteen-month, $10 million renovation, Harlem's Apollo Theater reopens under black ownership. A crowd of 1,500 attend an event hosted by Bill Cosby to celebrate a venue that had showcased generations of black talent, from Ella Fitzgerald to Stevie Wonder to Luther Vandross. The Apollo is still too small to compete for big stars, but younger black acts, particularly in hip hop, book it regularly. The famous Wednesday Amateur Night competition is revived, attracting performers from all over the country. Eventually a syndicated TV show, *Showtime at the Apollo,* is developed and becomes a staple of fringe time in America and around the globe. The theater becomes a regular stop on tours of New York, combined with a dinner at the nearby soul-food institution Sylvia's.

MAY 10   The CDC's *MMWR* announces the diagnosis of the ten-thousandth AIDS case. It took three years for the first 5,000 cases to be reported and twelve months for the second 5,000.

MAY 13   The city of Philadelphia, in an attempt to evict members of the radical group MOVE from a home in a black residential neighborhood, drops a bomb on its rooftop bunker that kills eleven people (five of them children), burns down the building, and ultimately destroys sixty-one other row houses at a loss estimated at $8 million. Two and a half city blocks are burned bare in the wake of the bombing. That this debacle happens under the watch of a black mayor, Wilson Goode, just compounds the tragedy.

MOVE is a communal organization that blends black nationalist rhetoric, a back-to-Africa orientation, and their own personal twists on '70s radical thought (all the members are given the last name Africa) into a presence that irritates their largely middle-class neighbors. The building and its dreadlocked, unkempt residents are long a source of trouble and even intimidation on the block. For the Philadelphia police, they are the enemy, especially after a nasty 1978 confrontation that resulted in the shooting death of one officer and the conviction and imprisonment of nine MOVE members.

During the winter, tensions between MOVE, their neighbors, and police boil over. MOVE is officially evicted from their home by the city but refuses to leave. Over the years, MOVE has fortified the building until it looks more like a fortress than a home. Arguing that any police action could involve shooting and potential loss of life, Police Commissioner Gregore Sambor devises a plan that is presented to Mayor Goode. Everyone agrees that such a meeting occurred.

However, everything else that happens on this day is the subject of debate. Goode claims he was misled by both Sambor and City Managing Director Leo A. Brooks about the details of the bombing as well as the reasons the fire department doesn't step in to put out the rapidly spreading blaze. Both men contradict the mayor's story. Birdie Africa, the only adult survivor of the attack, claims police gunfire keeps MOVE members penned inside the house during the fire; firemen charge that shots from inside the house keep them from putting out the inferno.

A key police justification for using the bomb is an arsenal of weapons reportedly stockpiled in the basement, yet in the fire's aftermath only a few weapons are discovered. Lawsuits ensue and recriminations abound. What is unassailable is that Goode provided ineffective leadership. One reason blacks looked forward to taking over City Halls was to preclude excessive use of force by local police departments. Yet in one of the nation's biggest cities, a black mayor allows a black community to be destroyed. The MOVE bombing becomes a national symbol of inept big-city leadership.

JUNE *Black Enterprise* reports that the last year was "good" for the top one hundred black-owned businesses. These enterprises registered sales of $2.6 billion. But not all are impressed by this number. Writing in the *Los Angeles Times,* Earl Ofari notes that the bottom company in the *Fortune* 500, a Coatesville, Pennsylvania, machinery company named Lukens, had sales of $416 million, a number that "far exceeded the combined sales of the top three black companies ($380 million)."

"The sad fact," Ofari writes, "is that black business is still nothing more than a promise failed." He notes that "under Reagan their share of federal procurement dollars has shrunk" as black vendors received only 4 percent of government contracts in 1984. The Small Business Administration has been under attack from a predominantly white trade group about its minority set-aside program. That pressure forces the SBA to put a five-year limit on the period in which companies can participate, resulting in the removal of 180 minority firms from the program. Ofari concludes, "Black business cannot be a substitute for corporate and government action to fund and expand programs for jobs, education and social services."

JULY 13 A survey conducted in New York City using the recently developed HIV antibody test finds that of frequent drug users tested, 87 percent carried the infection. The majority of the addicts sampled were black and Hispanic.

SEPTEMBER King World Productions, owned by the brothers Roger and Michael King, who handled the successful *Wheel of Fortune* and *Jeopardy,* makes a deal with Oprah to syndicate her show nationally. World domination is imminent.

SEPTEMBER Wynton Marsalis's *Black Codes (From the Underground)* is receiving fine reviews when the jazz world is shocked by the news that two members of his exciting band, saxophonist Branford (his brother) and keyboardist Kenny Kirkland, are exiting to record and tour with pop star Sting, who has split from his own band, the Police. In search of a new musical direction, Sting successfully woos these two young, adventurous jazzmen into his fold.

Already scornful in interviews about the direction of popular music, Wynton is particularly pissed at his brother (who goes on to build a multifaceted career that embraces hip hop, acting, and television) and grows more conservative in his pronouncements, evolving from jazz's Pied Piper to an articulate critic of non-jazz black music.

SEPTEMBER Jean-Michel Basquiat and Andy Warhol collaborate on a gallery show at Tony Shafrazi's SoHo gallery that mates new graffiti glamour with old pop-art hype. It elevates Basquiat's public profile while making him seem Warhol's protégé in the eyes of the uninitiated. Art pros are blown away that Warhol, the master of latching on to new talent and ideas and then claiming ownership, agrees to share billing with this young black painter. It is the only collaboration of this kind in Warhol's long career, and some suggest that Warhol, like so many in the art world, is simply in love with Basquiat.

New York Times critic Vivien Raynor, however, is not among the smitten. "Last year, I wrote of Jean-Michel Basquiat that he had a chance of becoming a very good painter providing he didn't succumb to the forces that would make him an art world mascot. This year, it appears that those forces have prevailed." Raynor is not very impressed by the sixteen works, all titled "Untitled," which she describes as "large, bright, messy, full of private jokes and inconclusive."

She writes in summation, "The collaboration looks like one of Warhol's manipulations, which increasingly seem based on the Mencken theory about nobody going broke underestimating the public's intelligence. Basquiat, meanwhile, comes across as the all too willing accessory."

SEPTEMBER 13 A group of New York musicians and artists come together to start the Black Rock Coalition, an organization whose purpose is to reconnect rock music with the black community. Or, as they write in their manifesto, "Rock and roll is Black music and we are its heirs." Among its founders are artist-manager Konda Mason, guitarist Vernon Reid, and *Village Voice* critic Greg Tate. Reid is an adventurous player who's worked the jazz fusion fringe with Ronald Shannon Jackson's Decoding Society and done gigs backing R&B singers. But Reid, like his fellow founders, feels that the disconnect between rock and black music, which has occurred because of segregated radio formats and ignorance of their musical history among blacks, must be bridged. The BRC bands are not doctrinaire in their approach to rock. They look at it as a legacy, not a blueprint. Over the next few years the BRC will give showcase gigs around New York that attract media, music lovers, and A&R staff. Eventually, for some BRC members, the manifesto becomes a prophecy.

Meanwhile, out of California's San Fernando Valley arrives Fishbone, a gaggle of young black suburban rebels reared on punk, ska, reggae, and funk, who bring forth music with a joyful anarchy. They come out of the same Los Angeles rock scene as the Red Hot Chili Peppers and bask in a similar desire to rip up musical orthodoxy and concert stages. The BRC and Fishbone reinvigorate the black presence in rock music.

OCTOBER 21 In a Monday Night Football game versus the Green Bay Packers, the Chicago Bears put 310-pound tackle William "the Refrigerator" Perry in the backfield to block in a goal line situation. Twice he leads Walter Payton to touchdowns. In a third goal line situation, coach Mike Ditka has quarterback Jim McMahon hand off the ball to Perry, who plunges across the goal line for a touchdown. With this exposure (and the fact that the dominating Bears will win the Super Bowl), Perry becomes a hulking, grinning endorsement machine.

The colorful, media-friendly Bears go on to make another contribution to pop culture. Much of the team gets together to record "The Super Bowl," an awful rap record that sells well and continues the process of familiarizing mall America with music approximating the sound of rap.

OCTOBER 25 *Krush Groove* opens at 515 theaters and takes in $3 million, which makes it the number-one movie in America this weekend. The film, a softhearted treatment of a tough street culture, is a bit of a comeback for Michael Schultz.

The film was finally green-lit with some prodding from Warner Bros. Records, an example of the synergy between film and music that Warner's previously exploited with *Purple Rain.* Some of Schultz's collaborators have active cinematic futures ahead of them: cinematographer Ernest Dickerson, leading man Blair Underwood, and producer Doug McHenry. In the short run, however, the future belongs to the rappers, as Run-D.M.C., the Fat Boys, and Kurtis Blow all profit from the film.

Krush Groove grosses one million dollars in the New York metropolitan area alone, an achievement that is overshadowed by violence at several area screenings. This combination of large rap-based youth gatherings and criminal activity becomes a sad running theme through the second half of this decade.

NOVEMBER L.L. Cool J's *Radio* is the first album released by Def Jam Records under a distribution deal with CBS subsidiary Columbia. Besides introducing the teenaged rapper to America, the album begins a business relationship that changes hip hop. Despite the huge crossover acceptance of Run-D.M.C., this is the first time a label makes a commitment to this insurgent culture.

Def Jam heads, black manager and promoter Russell Simmons and white record producer Rick Rubin, gain access to radio promotions, in-store displays, and shelf space none of the rap-oriented indies can provide. L.L.'s album, "reduced" by Rubin, has a hard metallic sheen that backs the youthful arrogance of L.L., a.k.a. Todd Smith, and contains one certifiable hip hop classic ("Rock the Bells") and a couple nearly as good.

The marriage isn't smooth—Simmons and Rubin often bump heads with staff at CBS's Black Rock offices in midtown Manhattan. Still, *Radio* goes gold and serves notice that the stakes in the rap game just got higher.

DECEMBER Wynton Marsalis goes into the studio to record with a vibrant group—bassist Robert Hurst, drummer Jeff "Tain" Watts, and a recent addition to the band, the blind pianist Marcus Roberts, whose presence seems to light a fire under his sometimes too studied leader. In *Jazz: The Modern Resurgence,* Stuart Nicholson argues "that this is his best ensemble of the decade; making brilliant use of shifting meters, Marsalis demonstrated lyrical, harmonic and rhythmic ingenuity, employing a subtle variety of tonal variations."

DECEMBER The Equal Employment Opportunity Commission, chaired by Clarence Thomas, mounts a publicity campaign to combat charges that it is turning back the clock on antidiscrimination laws. In a report, the EEOC notes it has filed 411 court cases in fiscal year 1985, including a record ninety-six cases of age discrimination that recovered $54 million for its victims. Thomas commented that the agency's enforcement of laws was "tough and thorough."

Most of the criticism comes from speculation that the Reagan administration seeks to weaken the 1965 Executive Order 11246, requiring federal contractors to take affirmative action to hire women and minority members. Douglas G. Glasgow, a National Urban League vice president, charges that the EEOC has regularly failed to go to court to protect the rights of workers and has refused to provide statistics on its enforcement efforts. Prior to

Reagan, the EEOC used goals and timetables for the hiring and promoting of minority workers to decide whether court action was necessary. It also frequently filed class action suits.

Under Thomas these approaches are reversed or ignored. He believes quotas both represent reverse discrimination and suggest blacks and women can't succeed on their own. He calls class action suits a "giveaway." When asked by the *Los Angeles Times* about his critics, Thomas replies, "I don't give a golden damn what they say."

DECEMBER 18 Spike Lee catches the first showing of *The Color Purple* at a Times Square Theater. Spike is unimpressed, while professional critics are split. Some think this will be Steven Spielberg's first commercially successful adult film; others think he sugarcoats the grit in Alice Walker's novel. The film is a financial success, earning $94 million and eleven Academy Award nominations (though it wins none). "Mr. Spielberg's curious achievement is not in making a movie of any original artistic merit, but a movie that's satisfying just because of his mastery of clichés," writes Vincent Canby in *The New York Times.*

Black male *Daily News* columnist Earl Caldwell comments, "*The Color Purple* can make you see red. That's especially true if you are a man and happen to be black. There is not much in the movie you wanna see."

The Color Purple makes Whoopi Goldberg a movie star, though much of the goodwill generated by her performance as Celie, a woman who triumphs over ignorance, poverty, and a loveless marriage, is squandered in humor-free comedies like *Jumpin' Jack Flash* and *Burglar.* Oprah is the film's biggest winner, earning an Academy Award nomination in the supporting actress category and hyping her already hot talk show. Her satisfying experience whets Winfrey's appetite for greater involvement in film production.

Just one of Oprah's many triumphs.

1986

1986

Black advancement has traditionally been predicated on education, particularly mastering the ability to read. Kept from slaves throughout the long years of slavery and given grudgingly in the separate-but-equal schools of the Jim Crow past, the quest for quality education was a fundamental goal of the civil rights movement. Almost all the major early battles of the South pivoted around integrating schools, from *Brown v. Board of Education of Topeka, Kansas,* to federal marshals on the Ole Miss campus. The ongoing legislative and legal wrangling over affirmative action always comes back to issues of access to higher education.

So what does it mean when the American Council on Education reports that the number of black men enrolled in colleges and universities has declined in the last ten years, from 470,000 in 1976 to 436,000, while the number of black women enrolled during that time span rose from 563,000 to 645,000? Quite simply, a change in priorities has been undertaken among the black poor and working class.

Some of this disparity can be traced to age-old problems— negative racist expectations of black male academic achievement and the lure of the criminal culture lurking outside the schoolyard. The appeal of crack, as a business opportunity and an addiction, exacerbates the latter tendency tenfold. In conjunction with this nasty trend is the maturation of a generation of young men impatient with the gradual progress education implies and, most profoundly, holding precious little faith that hard work in school actually pays off.

In the decade of *Dynasty*, Wall Street "paper" millionaires, and conspicuous consumption not seen, perhaps, since the 1920s, an increasing number of young black men don't think aspiring to manage a McDonald's is a worthwhile goal. Phrases like "cold gettin' paid" and "clockin' major figures" are part of the seductive language of ghetto capitalism. Gordon Gekko's "Greed is good" from Oliver Stone's *Wall Street* resonates both on the street corner and in the boardroom. Imbedded in those college enrollment numbers is a generation gap that crack exploits and hip hop articulates.

The much more positive female numbers reflect that many women from these same backgrounds aren't as easily seduced by the romance of quick money and have more patience with gradual individual progress. The progress of black women in higher education translates into a wave of educated, ambitious folks moving into the white-collar workforce and establishing themselves as a potent consumer market whose tastes affect the sale of everything from cosmetics to home furnishings, from periodicals to literature.

But these statistics also reflect a deep social problem that affects blacks' mating rituals. These college-educated women find themselves in increasingly fierce competition for a mate among the shrinking group of white-collar black men. The phenomenon of the white-collar black single mom becomes a commonplace. Women willing to mate with men making less money face challenges as well. Tension between these women and their less upwardly mobile men over money, sex, and romance is manifest throughout the community. This economic disparity is a central theme of much black popular culture, articulated for women through high- and low-brow literature (as it has been at least since Shange's *For Colored Girls*), while finding a new male-centered point of view in rap records that speak to the resentments of young men. Sometimes numbers lie. These statistics, alas, contain too much truth.

Prior to the release of *Control,* Janet Jackson is just one of the many unfortunate Jackson family siblings who are not Michael. She'd made some impression as Penny on *Good Times* as a youngster, but no one expected much from Janet as a singer. A previous solo effort had been way too cute and easily forgotten.

But a match made in Minnesota becomes one of the most enduring singer-producer collaborations in pop. Former Time members Jimmy "Jam" Harris and Terry Lewis turn *Control* into a bold declaration of independence from both childhood and being Michael's little sister. "What Have You Done for Me Lately?" is an instant dance anthem and the video, choreographed by an ex-Laker Girl named Paula Abdul, becomes an MTV staple and popularizes the snake dance.

Though she lacks Michael's vocal richness, Janet's good looks, pedigree, and adventurousness, combined with the crafty producing and writing of Jam and Lewis, make her a major star. While Michael's ongoing theme is paranoia, Janet's is overdue sexual awakening and exploration.

JANUARY 3-19 The Whitney Museum of American Art hosts a series titled "The L.A. Rebellion: A Turning Point in Black Cinema," which focuses on the work of a collective of filmmakers who attended UCLA's film school in the '70s. Among the important filmmakers who went through UCLA and have work screened at the Whitney are Haile Gerima, a determined political man who teaches for many years at Howard University, Julie Dash, Charles Burnett, Alile Sharon Larkin, and Larry Clark.

In his gallery talk, film scholar Clyde Taylor asserts, "By the turn of the next century, film historians will recognize that a decisive turning point in the development of black cinema took place at UCLA in the early 1970s. By then persuasive definitions of black cinema will revolve around images encoded not by Hollywood,

but within the self-understanding of the African American population. . . . The films in this exhibition form the core of a declaration of independence, but they are by no means its only
manifestation. The ethos that arose in Los Angeles extends to other
films by black UCLA students and to diverse efforts to build a black
cinema culture."

The Whitney program illustrates the gap between the world of
Eddie Murphy and black indie films. At this point the films with
blacks are either popular entertainment manufactured by white
entertainment companies and made for the mall, or smart, politi-
cized black films controlled by black auteurs and not widely seen
outside of festivals or museums. Is there a way to be entertaining
with political content and be widely seen? At the midpoint of the
decade the question lingers: Can entertaining black films with political content ever receive wide distribution?

FEBRUARY 1 The Black Rock Coalition holds its first major
event, an antiapartheid concert at New York's leading avant-garde
showcase, the Kitchen. At one point, twenty-six musicians are onstage jammin' on classic rock and funk tunes. In a sense this is a
coming-out party for the community of non–hip hop musicians in
the city. It puts a focus on black acts who play guitar-centered music and influences the later signing of several black rock bands to
major labels.

APRIL Ishmael Reed's satirical *Reckless Eyeballing* is
published as the veteran author's broadside against feminism.
Reed, who has written seven previous novels, including the 1972
masterpiece *Mumbo Jumbo,* uses the comic misadventures of playwright Ian Ball as a window into how black culture is being manip-
ulated by critics and thinkers outside of it. After Ball's successful
debut, *Suzanna,* is heavily panned by feminist critics, he has doubts
about the direction of his second play, *Reckless Eyeballing* (the

title refers to the crime of looking at a white woman, which got scores of black men lynched).

Reed's high comic style is well suited to poking fun at black nationalists, self-conscious artists, and condescending liberals. The novel is the forty-eight-year-old writer's amusing yet pointed attack on what he feels ails black art, especially literature, at this time. Some feel the book is just sour grapes from a bitter male writer overshadowed by his female peers. If Reed is driven by resentment, then this is jealousy rich in humor.

When asked about the movie *The Color Purple* by *Essence* magazine, Reed doesn't bite his tongue: "I think there is a great deal of animosity aimed at Black men by the feminist movement, Black and white. The feminist movement would not be the first to make the Black man the scapegoat when in crisis. When I saw the ad line for the film *Come Join the Celebration,* I thought I was being invited to a public lynching and I was . . . *The Color Purple* borrows imagery from 18th century pro-slavery notions. If you look at *The Color Purple* and look at *The Birth of a Nation,* you see some of the same camera angles and some of the same direction."

APRIL   In the spring issue of the black literary journal *Callaloo,* author Sherley Anne Williams writes an essay titled "Some Implications of Womanist Theory." Using "womanist," a term coined by Alice Walker, is a way to distinguish writings from "feminist" thought, in which Williams sees "separatism: its tendency to see not only a distinct black female culture but to see that culture as a separate cultural form having more in common with white female experience than with the facticity of Afro-American life."

For Williams, womanism "assumes that it can talk both effectively and productively about men. This is a necessary assumption because the negative, stereotyped images of black women are only a part of the problem of phallocentric writings by black males. In order to understand that problem more fully, we must turn to what black men have written about themselves."

Williams believes, "Black women as readers and writers have been kept out of literary endeavor, so we had, and have, a lot to say. But to focus solely on ourselves is to fall into the same hole The Brother has dug for himself—narcissism, isolation, inarticulation, obscurity."

Among black female writers, "womanist" becomes an increasingly popular term, since it implies a racial identification with black men, although that identification has a strong critical perspective. In short, womanism becomes a way for black women to create a space independent of white women, while remaining critical of black machismo.

APRIL 20 The legend of Michael Jordan grows. On this spring afternoon in Boston, Jordan scores sixty-three points on Larry Bird, Dennis Johnson, and the rest of the Celtics' stellar roster during a first-round playoff game. The Celtics win the game, sweep the Bulls in three games, and will later take the NBA title. But Jordan and Nike win big as well, as his nationally televised scoring binge sells hundreds of thousands of pairs of Air Jordans.

APRIL 25 Quincy Jones hosts a birthday party for son Quincy Jones III, a.k.a. Snoopy, at Canestelle's, a restaurant on Park Avenue South near the offices of Russell Simmons's Rush Management. Snoopy (who will become a fairly successful rap producer in the '90s using the moniker QD III) wants to meet his East Coast rap heroes and Quincy, who knows Simmons, asks the rap impresario to put it together. Guests include the Fat Boys and the Beastie Boys. The Beasties are a little obnoxious, as they tend to be, but overall the event goes off smoothly (though many of Canestelle's other clients seem put off by the hip hop contingent).

This event has two long-term consequences. It makes Jones, who sees a kinship between the MCs and his bebop youth, a strident supporter of hip hop. His *Back on the Block* album in the early '90s would be heavily influenced by hip hop. Jones's relationship with Simmons is strengthened and later the two partner in the development of *Vibe* magazine. (Simmons eventually pulls out.) Quincy's support of hip hop, along with that of great bebop drummer Max Roach, gives some old-school credibility to the culture.

MAY 5 *Adweek* publishes a special report titled "Bad Times for Black Businesses." The subhead declares, "Growing competition from mainstream firms is spelling trouble for many minority companies." As an example *Adweek* reports that the market for black health and beauty products is $2.5 billion and "steadily increasing," which is why companies like Alberto-Culver, Clairol, and Revlon are moving in. And that is why the black-owned Chicago-based company Johnson Products has seen sales decrease from $46 million in 1981 to $37 million last year.

Adweek lists several areas of weakness for black businesses: they tend to be small and undercapitalized; most are located in the Rustbelt in low-income neighborhoods; and white businesses are now competing in areas they once left to blacks (cosmetics, newspapers and magazines, insurance, undertaking). The $180 billion black consumer market has been put in play by the long-term effects of desegregation.

MAY 21 *Jo Jo Dancer, Your Life Is Calling,* directed and cowritten by Richard Pryor, is as close as black cinema has come, at this point, to the self-conscious autobiographical aesthetic of auteur filmmaking. The flawed yet ambitious biopic of a comic much like Pryor chronicles his rearing in a brothel, his rising career, his mixed-race marriages, and the infamous freebase fire that nearly kills him. The most touching moments center on his early days performing stand-up at a strip club. Supported by a wonderfully world-weary Paula Kelly and Billy Eckstine, Pryor captures the beauty and sleaze that characterize the chitlin' circuit on which he cut his teeth. Aside from his own concert films, *Jo Jo Dancer* is one of Pryor's few narrative films with artistic ambition.

MAY 30 Outfielder Barry Bonds begins his major league baseball career with the Pittsburgh Pirates. The left-handed hitter is the son of Bobby Bonds, a brilliant, oft-traded player who put up impressive numbers but was never loved by fans. His son has a similar unapproachable quality and never warms up to the press. The Pirates' management doesn't care because Bonds wins rookie of the year and quickly makes Pittsburgh a championship contender.

JUNE 19 The evil consequences of smoked cocaine are tragically illustrated by the death of Maryland University basketball star Len Bias. Selected in the first round of the NBA draft by the Boston Celtics, the twenty-two-year-old is immediately hailed as the successor to Larry Bird in the franchise's hallowed history. The day following his selection, Bias is partying big-time, overdoses on cocaine, and dies on the spot.

The Bias tragedy sends ripples through the world of sports, resulting in increased drug testing for athletes (and student athletes) at every level of American sport. Bias, however, isn't the only drug victim in the '86 draft. Roy Tarpley, skilled power forward from Michigan, is drafted number one by the Dallas Mavericks, seems poised to be a dominant player in the league, but will be repeatedly caught in drug tests abusing cocaine. Eventually Tarpley is banned from the NBA. William Bedford, number-one draft choice of the Phoenix Suns from Memphis State, admits to cocaine use during his rookie season, is suspended for thirty-eight games, and is traded at season's end. Chris Washburn, drafted by

Golden State, is accused of stealing at North Carolina State and has drug problems in the pros. Portland's Walter Berry is never linked with drug use in the pros or at St. John's. However, he is called before a grand jury to talk about possible links to a local drug dealer.

Bias, Tarpley, and Bedford are high-profile examples of how smoked cocaine can ruin the most promising lives. Those with less money and smaller dreams are falling victim to this white plague all over the country. It's a truism that drug abusers say that any drug strong enough to cause an OD is a drug they want to try. Bias's death, like Pryor's accident, only increases demand for this intense high.

JUNE 25   Anita Baker headlines an Avery Fisher Hall concert at New York's Lincoln Center on the heels of her second album, *Rapture.* In an extraordinary outpouring of affection, Baker receives standing ovations after her third, seventh, and tenth songs. *Rapture,* Baker's first on Elektra after a previous album (*The Songstress,* in 1983) on indie Beverly Glenn, is similarly embraced by radio. The diminutive Detroit singer's album is on its way to selling four million records, bucking trends with her husky, mature vocal style.

While many contemporary singers owe their allegiance to Aretha Franklin's gospel soul, Baker taps into the blues of Dinah Washington mixed with the soaring style of Chaka Khan. Unlike most female singers, whose musical personas are designed by male A&R executives or producers, Baker is executive producer of *Rapture* and has the final say on songs and their arrangements. The enthusiasm of the New York crowd speaks to a desire for an emotional intimacy, a personal touch, that black singers once routinely communicated. Now, with the exception of Baker and Luther Vandross, most ballad singers sing rigidly chromatic songs or lack the depth to move listeners. Baker isn't a "soul" singer in the traditional sense but a singer with a mountain of soul in her small, swaying body.

JULY 19 Run-D.M.C. sells out Madison Square Garden and plays a triumphant show. Executives from Germany's sportswear company, Adidas, are in the house, attracted by the band's hit single "My Adidas." During the show, Run has the house lights raised and asks everyone wearing Adidas sneakers to raise them in the air. A sea of white three-striped athletic shoes appears, a show of strength that leads to a multimillion-dollar endorsement deal that includes jerseys, sweat suits, and more.

This match of a leisure-wear clothing manufacturer and a rap act illustrates how interconnected hip hop style and brand consciousness are. It is an organic relationship that will no longer be ignored by marketers or artists. It's ironic that the band that once rapped "I don't wear no one's label on my behind" in fact becomes a wearable brand themselves. But then the theme of Run-D.M.C.'s career from the start has been the institutionalization of hip hop as a commercial and cultural force. This is just another step on that journey for the band and the culture.

JULY 19 New York mayor Ed Koch calls for a meeting of U.S. mayors to discuss the "epidemic" of crack addiction. In this calendar year there are 67,677 drug arrests in the city, a 14 percent increase in murders (1,582), and overall crime is up to 5 percent, the first rise since 1981. Koch is so worried about crack's toll he suggests the government end the use of $100 bills because of their prevalence in drug transactions.

AUGUST Paul Simon, a very successful folk-based singer-songwriter, releases the revolutionary and highly controversial *Graceland,* his interpretation of South Africa's vibrant musical culture, and runs afoul of the international cultural boycott of that country. Simon has quietly been traveling to South Africa to work with instrumentalists and singers, then bringing the tracks back to the States to compose melodies and lyrics. Paying the South African musicians three times the union scale wages and introducing the world to some amazing talent (the vocal group Ladysmith Black Mambazo, guitarist Ray Phiri), Simon uses this rich musical base to jump-start a slumping career. The recording goes on to win the Grammy for album of the year and to make the music of Africa "cool" for an audience that begins buying the real thing under the marketing moniker "world music."

Throughout '86, proponents of the cultural boycott (like singer and activist Harry Belafonte and TransAfrica's Randall Robinson) remain skeptical of Simon's motivations and worry that *Graceland* undermines the cultural boycott. Some of the South African musicians involved, including Ray Phiri, are criticized back home for their involvement with *Graceland.*

Eventually, several prominent South African musicians, including exiled stars Hugh Masekela and Miriam Makeba, voice support for Simon's project. Despite the misgivings of many, *Graceland* proves a great tool for making otherwise uninterested Americans aware of apartheid in Southern Africa.

AUGUST 7 The Senate Labor Committee votes 14 to 2 to approve Clarence Thomas for a second four-year term as chairman of the Equal Employment Opportunity Commission.

AUGUST 8 *She's Gotta Have It* opens at the Cinema Studio on Broadway and Sixty-sixth Street. Perhaps the smartest review of the film that begins the auteur era in black feature filmmaking is by *The Village Voice*'s David Edelstein. Headlining his piece "Birth of a Salesman," Edelstein cites many problems with the film (the underdevelopment of sex object and central character boho Nola Darling; and the smarmy trio of brothers who pursue her—b-boy Mars Blackmon, bap Greer Childs, buppie Jamie Overstreet). This is by no means a ringing endorsement.

Yet Ernest Dickerson's cinematography, father Bill Lee's score, and the fluidity of Spike's filmmaking pull him in. And ultimately he can't resist Spike Lee as actor, director, and hustler. Of the unique trailer, Edelstein comments, "You see the director on a street corner, hawking tube socks three for five dollars. He turns to the camera; introduces himself; explains that because he's so poor, he has to sell socks to make movies . . . Audiences go crazy for this preview, and so did I—despite the fact that Lee has a three picture deal with Island and is not exactly hurting for work. But that's part of the charm—you're not supposed to believe him. As far as I'm concerned Eddie Murphy has a new kid brother; *She's Gotta Have It* marks the birth of a salesman. Attention will be paid."

Attention is paid. Spike's low-budget wonder is one of those crucial films that inspires a generation. All over black America, nerdy, glasses-wearing boys don baseball jackets and caps with the name of their new production company stitched on (for reference, check out early publicity photos of directors John Singleton and Matty Rich). Now the black nerd has a role model. You, too, can be skinny, small, and on the cutting edge of the culture. Wearing unlaced Adidas or a red leather jacket is no longer the only way.

Between the release of *She's Gotta Have It* and his next film, *School Daze* in 1988, Spike works at a hectic pace that will become typical for him, directing music videos for Miles Davis ("Tutu") and Anita Baker ("No Where in the World"), some shorts for *Saturday Night Live* (one features Branford Marsalis), and two historic black-and-white ads for Nike with Michael Jordan and Spike in full Mars Blackmon gear. Spike will not become simply the most visible black director in American history, but one of the most entrepreneurial black artists ever.

Spike, though a sometimes reticent interview subject, warms

quickly to controversy. He blasts Whoopi Goldberg for wearing blue contact lenses; he attacks Spielberg for *The Color Purple*; he thinks Eddie Murphy should do more for blacks in Hollywood. The list of people who get sliced by his tongue is long. He makes enemies—a great many of them his black entertainment industry colleagues. Spike seemingly doesn't care. He bulls forward, writing screenplays, directing commercials, and building the name "Spike Lee" into one of the most identifiable brands in the nation. Way before Puffy, Spike is a "won't stop, can't stop" brother.

She's Gotta Have It, largely shot around Spike's Brooklyn 'hood in Fort Greene, draws attention to an area defined by roomy brownstones, a large park, and a prolific community of artists. Aside from Spike, musicians Branford and Wynton Marsalis, Vernon Reid, Terrance Blanchard, Donald Harrison, Cecil Taylor, and Lester Bowie; actors Wesley Snipes and Laurence Fishburne; writers Thulani Davis and Nelson George; as well as designers, graphic artists, and cartoonists reside in its roomy, relatively cheap housing. Articles begin appearing in *The New York Times* and elsewhere about Fort Greene as a black cultural mecca. That's all well and good, but there won't be a decent supermarket in Fort Greene until damn near the twenty-first century.

Playing at that same Lincoln Center theater as *She's Gotta Have It* is *Mona Lisa,* a stylish British film noir with one of the decade's few meaty roles for a black actress. Kathy Tyson, a twenty-year-old product of Northern England, plays Simone, a prostitute with a problematic present, a dubious future, and a mysterious past. The incandescent Bob Hoskins is given the job as her driver, eventually falling sadly in love with this cold, obsessed young woman.

Written and directed by the promising Neil Jordan, *Mona Lisa* taps into the levels of self-deception love can lead one to. Tyson gives a wonderfully multilayered performance as Simone. Unfortunately, she isn't seen much in the States after this (except in Wes

Craven's Haitian voodoo flick, *The Serpent & the Rainbow*) but builds a UK career. Like *She's Gotta Have It, Mona Lisa* is distributed by Chris Blackwell's Island Pictures, a fine independent company that, along with other similar indies, won't survive despite a catalogue of quality films.

AUGUST 16 Run-D.M.C.'s collaboration with Aerosmith on the rock anthem "Walk This Way" is the number-one single in the country, the high point of an incredible year for the Hollis, Queens, trio. It pushed the band's *Raising Hell* album to sales of three million copies on the small Profile label and lands them an appearance on the cover of *Rolling Stone,* the first rap act so recognized.

This summer, Run-D.M.C. headlines a tour with another band managed by Russell Simmons, the Beastie Boys, a white rap trio that records for Def Jam. What took Run-D.M.C. five years to accomplish, the Beasties manage in about a year. *Licensed to Ill,* produced by Simmons's partner Rick Rubin, garners amazing critical acclaim and goes on to sell four million copies, setting a new sales plateau for rappers. Their rock-based single "Fight for Your Right" made them instant MTV icons, though they are a band as disliked (by many white rock and black rap fans) as they are loved. Later, opening for Madonna on a late fall national tour, they often have to duck beer bottles hurled from hostile fans.

What Run-D.M.C. and the Beastie Boys share is hard-edged production by Rubin, shrewd marketing by manager Simmons, and a yelling rap style. The summer tour of Run-D.M.C. and the Beastie Boys, which also includes L.L. Cool J and Whodini, is a landmark event. Rap crowds, which had once been predominantly black, are now, depending on the city and venue, becoming 50 to 60 percent white. Despite ongoing concern about violence at the concerts, arena rap shows are regular parts of the summer concert scene. And most of the biggest tours are controlled by Simmons's Rush Management.

SEPTEMBER 8   *The Oprah Winfrey Show* is on 181 stations, covering every major television market, and now begins a direct showdown with Phil Donahue for supremacy in daytime talk TV, a confrontation that's been building all decade. Winfrey's show on this day is "How to Marry the Man or Woman of Your Choice," while Donahue centers his broadcast around the infamous Mayflower Madam and her Manhattan call girl ring.

On day one Donahue gets a 26 percent rating and Oprah 23 percent. On September 9, Oprah gets a 30 percent and Donahue an 18 percent rating. On the third day of the battle, September 10, Oprah gets 29 percent to his 22 percent. Once the tide turns toward Oprah, *The Phil Donahue Show* never turns it around.

SEPTEMBER 10   A party for the movie *Soul Man* is thrown at the Hard Rock Café. In this reactionary Reaganite comedy on affirmative action, brat-packer C. Thomas Howell wears blackface makeup to gain a minority scholarship to Harvard University. This film, not surprisingly, enrages many blacks and, unfortunately, makes a lot of money.

One of the chief beneficiaries of the film's success is Rae Dawn Chong, a multiracial beauty who becomes another poster girl for mixed sexuality in a previously "She's either black or white" movie world. Her first major break came in *Quest for Fire* in 1981, a film about man's primitive beginnings in which she spends most of the film running nude around frigid Canada and tropical Kenya. Following that part, Chong works steadily, appearing in *Choose Me, Beat Street, The Color Purple,* and notably as Arnold Schwarzenegger's reluctant helper in *Commando,* the Joel Silver–produced action flick.

The daughter of doper comic Tommy Chong (of Cheech &

Chong fame), Rae Dawn's café au lait looks and acting chops keep her busy, though she never lands a juicy on-screen drama. Her career, like those of so many women of color in Hollywood, is about injecting some personality into cardboard "girlfriend" parts. Chong and Howell get married, albeit briefly, after *Soul Man* is released.

SEPTEMBER 28   *X: The Life and Times of Malcolm X,* an opera composed by Anthony Davis with a libretto by Thulani Davis, debuts at the New York City Opera, an important moment in the mythologizing of Malcolm X's legacy. Though it occurs in the rarefied world of opera, this piece again affirms the central place the slain leader occupies in the psyches of blacks. Malcolm as icon, prophetic and ever-evolving brotherman, is in the minds of the race across class and intellectual lines. It feels like his journey from street thug to race man to spiritual being mirrors the struggle of so many to find a clear path through the post-soul world.

OCTOBER 17   It's rare that an actor can make a lasting impression in just one scene, but Forest Whitaker manages the trick in a bit part in Martin Scorsese's Tom Cruise and Paul Newman pool hustler vehicle *The Color of Money*. Newman, as an aging pool shark, engages the lumpy, naïve-seeming Whitaker in a money game. But in a reversal, Whitaker hustles Newman and, with a sly smile, lets him know it. Whitaker, who was only on the set of *The Color of Money* for two days, uses this role as a stepping-stone to even more memorable acting roles. The actor's large body disguises a charming yet lethal quality that quickly makes him one of the most respected character actors in American movies.

OCTOBER 18   After the departure of Eddie Murphy for Hollywood in 1983, *Saturday Night Live* lost its brief cachet in the black community. But the increasing white acceptance of black pop stars even touches Lorne Michaels, not known for his sensitivity to black pop culture (none of the black cast members hired under his tenure has ever been showcased like Murphy). *The Cosby Show*'s Malcolm-Jamal Warner hosts a show that features musical performances by Run-D.M.C. and an appearance by Spike Lee as his *She's Gotta Have It* character, Mars Blackmon.

NOVEMBER 6 After winning twenty-seven consecutive fights and enduring the death of his mentor Cus D'Amato a year earlier, twenty-year-old Mike Tyson beats Trevor Berbick and claims the World Boxing Council's heavyweight belt. D'Amato had predicted he'd win a title by age nineteen. Not a perfect prophet but certainly a great trainer, D'Amato leaves his legacy via one of the most fearsome fighters of all time.

This bout with Berbick is typical of Tyson at his peak. He wears black trunks, socks, and shoes. He enters the ring to the beat of a rap song. He glowers at his opponent. The bell rings and, literally in a matter of minutes, the fight is over. In this bout Berbick lasts under six minutes before he needs a doctor. In several other fights Tyson disposes of challengers in less than a round. Many of the fighters seem scared to enter the ring, as if the outcome is preordained. During the '80s Tyson rarely goes the full twelve rounds in any fight. Not only does he go undefeated in this decade; Tyson is, in fact, rarely challenged in the ring. "I took boxing back to its raw form," he tells *Playboy*. "The winner gets it all. That's what people want. And they paid me for it."

During these years Tyson embodies the myth of the ultraviolent, street-hardened urban male as a survivor (though he can actually be quite soft-spoken and studious about the fight game). Like no other athlete, the dominant heavyweight champ of any era defines the masculine idea. In Tyson's case, he is truly representative of his generation's desire for instant gratification (the quick knockout) and unself-conscious boasting (what rappers claim to do with their rhymes, Tyson did with his fists). And Tyson was "paid in full" ($20 million for knocking out Michael Spinks in ninety-one seconds in '88).

Mike loves clubs, loud music, and women (and not in that order). Aided by some old friends from the 'Ville and a posse of hangers-on, Tyson's nights are an ongoing bacchanal of sex. Tyson is not one of the many '80s athletes felled by crack. Sex is what knocks this champ out.

NOVEMBER 7   George Wolfe's play *The Colored Museum,* a humorous critique of black cultural truisms that reflects a new mood of self-examination among the black intelligentsia, premieres at Joe Papp's Public Theater to rave reviews. The five-actor play centers around eleven "exhibits," each a satirical look at some aspect of black life or its projection via the media.

One brilliant bit of satire is "The Last Mama-on-the-Couch Play," in which Wolfe ridicules two of the most important black plays to reach Broadway, *A Raisin in the Sun* and *For Colored Girls Who Have Considered Suicide When the Rainbow Is Enuf,* by tossing them into the blender of his wit and dicing their weaknesses for the audience's edification. By fearlessly taking on sacred cows like Lorraine Hansberry and Ntozake Shange, Wolfe—along with Spike Lee, Chuck D, and others—confirms that self-criticism is a major thread in the tapestry of late '80s black art.

The Colored Museum also establishes Wolfe as one of the rising stars of American theater. Though he is not credited as director, Wolfe's play has very precise and distinctive stage directions, suggesting that this Frankfort, Kentucky, native has a great gift for theater. At the time of *The Colored Museum*'s New York debut, Wolfe is working on an ambitious musical about the life of New Orleans jazz great Jelly Roll Morton, which he will both write and direct, called *Jelly's Last Jam.*

DECEMBER The phrase "brat pack," referring to a loose collection of white actors who appeared in some films together *(St. Elmo's Fire, The Breakfast Club),* has already entered the lexicon. Eddie Murphy jokingly refers to the "black pack" at a press conference for the otherwise forgettable *The Golden Child.* People take Murphy more seriously than he intends, but the comic-writer-directors he mentions (Arsenio Hall, Robert Townsend, Keenan Ivory Wayans, Paul Mooney) all stand on the verge of getting it on.

DECEMBER Greg Tate publishes "Cult-Nats Meet Freaky-Deke" in *The Village Voice.* The visionary article looks at the roots of an emerging black aesthetic built on the ideas of the '70s cultural nationalists but informed by the new post-soul access. Tate writes, "Though nobody's sent out any announcements yet, the '80s are witnessing the maturation of a postnationalist black arts movement, one more Afrocentric and cosmopolitan than anything that's come before." Tate later notes, "These are artists for whom black consciousness and artistic freedom are not mutually exclusive but complementary, for whom 'black culture' signifies a multicultural tradition of expressive practices; they feel secure enough about black culture to claim art produced by nonblacks as part of their inheritance."

DECEMBER 14 As a sign of her now generally acknowledged cultural triumph, Oprah Winfrey is profiled by Mike Wallace on *60 Minutes.*

The chief by-product of America's ad hoc urban enterprise zones.

1987

1987

On Wall Street and in the Sun Belt states, prosperity and economic growth are a given. If you are participating in the junk bond market or the housing and energy industries, life is good. After all, isn't it still "morning in America"? But what if you don't have the money to play the market? In fact, what if you barely have the cash to buy milk and bread at an ill-stocked, overpriced inner-city supermarket? What if you are among the one in three black Americans existing on a wage below the government's own poverty line? If you are an adult, it is tough. But it is even more difficult if you are among the 46 percent of black children living below the poverty line, the highest percentage since the mid-60s when President Lyndon Johnson began the Great Society programs that the GOP is now happily dismantling.

These numbers, from a report published by the Center on Budget and Policy Priorities, based in Washington, D.C., reflect the failure of trickle-down economics. For a Reaganite subscriber to the administration's economic policies, the glass is mostly full and, in some cases, overflowing. For a working-class black person, there is often barely a glass.

One of President Reagan's few domestic policies aimed at inner-city poverty is the concept of enterprise zones. Instead of spending money to employ or train the poor, Republicans argue that the way to help these people is to bring jobs to them. Areas in poverty-wracked urban communities are designated for tax abatements and other financial incentives to lure businesses. These businesses then train and hire locals. It is a nice idea that does bring in some low-skill businesses to impoverished communities like New York's South Bronx.

However, in practice, too few enterprise zones bring in too few businesses that employ too few local residents for the concept to have more than a piecemeal impact. Any real change requires a massive investment in education and redirection of economic policy that the Reagan administration has zero interest in. But where there is a vacuum, a force usually fills that space.

In mid-'80s America a new grassroots economic force emerges and employs thousands of working-class people all across the country, inspiring a new wave of business development that empowers citizens of all hues. All they have to do is be willing to pay the price for participation in this new economy—that price being possible incarceration, addiction, or death by overdose or murder.

The crack economy creates urban enterprise zones all over this post-soul nation. The product is so addictive and sells so quickly that it creates a class of criminal as reckless and notorious as the bank robbers of the Depression. And, just as in the '30s, many of these outlaws are immortalized in Warner Bros. movies. For example, what the Mafia is to Italians, the Shower Posse is to Jamaicans because of their crack-slinging violence. Its founders, Vivian Blake, based in Miami, and Lester Coke, in Jamaica, had been dealing marijuana for three years before deciding to tap into the burgeoning crack market. At its mid-'80s peak the Shower Posse reportedly has a membership of 5,400 people in more than a dozen cities, including New York, Rochester, Washington, D.C., and Toronto.

The name Shower comes from its members' penchant for "showering" rivals with automatic weapon fire. In a shoot-out at a New Jersey picnic, Shower members reportedly let fly more than 700 rounds of ammunition. In 1987 an FBI investigation is under way that will eventually lead to grand jury indictments of thirty-four members of the Posse, including Blake and Coke.

The Shower Posse leaves a legacy in popular culture. In Hollywood action movies of the late '80s and early '90s, Jamaican drug dealers join the Mafia, Nazis, communist spies, and Arab terrorists in Hollywood's rotation of cardboard villains. A prime example is the 1990 film *Marked for Death,* which pits martial arts expert Steven Seagal against a Jamaican drug kingpin armed with occult powers. Sadly, the real dealers are more versed in the art of the Uzi.

While the Shower Posse raises havoc on the East Coast, another vicious crack empire thrives in Detroit, Michigan. Billy Joe and Larry Chambers, arrivals in the Motor City from the small town of Marianna, Arkansas, bring a cruel efficiency to the city's crack economy, building a drug operation that, at its late '80s peak, operates 200 crack houses and employs approximately 500 people. The Chambers have workers sell in twelve-hour shifts and adhere to rules posted on crack house walls: crack and money are not to be carried at the same time; no speeding while driving; no expensive cars are to be used for business. There is even a quality control team, "the wrecking crew," who toss sloppy employees out of open windows.

To understand the scope of crack's impact and that of the Chambers brothers on the Motor City, note that in 1983 about 100 patients were admitted to local drug treatment centers. In this year that figure soars to 4,500. Cocaine-related emergency room admissions in '83 were 450. Now that number balloons to 3,811. When the Chambers are finally brought to justice in 1988, Billy Joe receives a twenty-nine-year sentence and Larry gets life for running a criminal enterprise, and the legacy of their crimes lingers in the streets of a city that became the nation's murder capital during their reign of terror.

One of the definitive pieces of journalism of the era is Barry Michael Cooper's cover story for *The Village Voice,* "New Jack City Eats Its Young," about the crack-fueled consumerist teen culture of Detroit, Michigan. The purchase of jeeps, gold chains, and designer brands of these "new jacks," street slang for the young and fly, speaks to how the Wall Street ethos of reckless capitalism has trickled down to the street. Well-organized crack operations, like the one run by the Chambers brothers, fill the employment gap in Detroit, creating violent urban enterprise zones that elected officials like Mayor Coleman Young seem helpless to combat.

Cooper, a Harlem native who has been writing excellent pieces on hip hop throughout the decade, coins the phrase "New Jack City" to describe Detroit and, by implication, all the areas of this nation that have fallen under the sway of crack culture. This piece will later be the inspiration for Cooper's screenplay for the 1991 black gangsta epic *New Jack City*.

While American movies eventually reflect the harsh economic reality of crack, rap music begins delivering instant messages about and for the streets transformed by the drug. The anger, social criticism, and break beat intensity of the music rises in response to the decay rappers observe. The rising aggression in rap has its roots in the nation's economic disparity. As much as Afrika Bambaataa and Kool Here begin hip hop's musical aesthetic, Ronald Reagan's America inspires the coming wave of harsher-toned rhymes.

For some MCs, the culture of crack just gives them a much-needed topic to mix in between raps about girls and parties. For the more socially conscious artists, crack's ubiquity precipitates a search for a philosophy that counteracts its nasty values. An idea called Afrocentricity rises to prominence, while Malcolm X and the Nation of Islam grow in importance. "Black consciousness," a phrase that went out of wide use in the mid-'70s, makes a comeback along with many of its associations.

"Afrocentricity," writes the concept's creator, Temple University professor Molefi Kete Asante, in his 1987 book *The Afrocentric Idea*, "means literally placing African ideals at the center of any analysis that involves African culture and behavior." He later explains, "[just] as fifteenth-century Europeans could not cease believing that the earth was the center of the universe, many today find it difficult to cease viewing European culture as the center of the social universe. Thus, the work they produce seldom considers the possibilities of other realities or, indeed, shared realities."

Though Asante's critique primarily centers around lapses in critical thinking in the works of scholars, his concepts find wider applications. Gary Byrd's popular radio call-in show at New York's WLIB-AM is titled "Afrocentricity: The Global Black Experience" and becomes a powerful clearinghouse for news, analysis, and activism. From aspiring mayoral candidate David Dinkins, to street activist Al Sharpton, to TransAfrica's Randall Robinson, to black scholars explaining the sweep of African slavery, Byrd's show provides a forum where ideas and people who would receive a hostile reception on white stations feel right at home. Similarly, the influence of Asante's Afrocentricity is felt in a sudden vogue for the multicolored Ghanian fabric called Kente, which is weaved into scarves, tuxedos, and hats. No photograph of any significant black gathering of the next few years (weddings, banquets, graduations) is taken without at least one person in the shot wearing some piece of Kente. Less upscale but almost as ubiquitous are African medallions, which show up in street fairs, swap meets, and countless music videos.

So in '87 the person seen reading *The Autobiography of Malcolm X* might also be reading Elijah Muhammad's *Message to the Blackman in America* or the ghettocentric work of Holloway House authors Iceberg Slim and Donald Goines. People wearing the popular "Black by Popular Demand" and "It's a Black Thing, You Wouldn't Understand" T-shirts might also be watching '70s blaxploitation flicks *The Mack* and *Superfly* on the VCRs becoming more common in black households. Eventually the tensions between these outlooks put them into conflict, but not in '87. Not yet.

The Miami Hurricanes are named the national champions of college football for the second time in the decade. They are awarded the title again in '89, making them the college football program of the decade.

But the 'Canes are famous for more than just football. Under coach Jimmy Johnson this team becomes known for being loud, confrontational, and bad sportsmen. There is a ghetto swagger to this program that aggravates opponents and NCAA officials. Epitomizing this attitude is wide receiver Michael Irvin, a trash-talking, strutting peacock of a player who proves difficult to cover and, thus, impossible to shut up. (Along with coach Johnson, Irvin builds a '90s pro football dynasty in Dallas and gets arrested for some nasty sexual hijinks.)

The 'Canes, in a way, come to represent the aspects of Miami that *Miami Vice* left out, the teeming black ghettos in Dade and Broward counties that experience more riots than any other urban area in the '80s, the part of Miami that supports the intense "Miami pumping bass" scene, a fast-paced version of hip hop that emphasizes rapidly undulating booties. Luther Campbell, leader of the notorious 2 Live Crew and owner of a local label, becomes a vocal booster of the 'Canes, even getting involved in the recruitment of players.

As a result of this strutting success, gear bearing the Miami Hurricanes' orange and green logo joins Georgetown's as essential urban survival wear.

JANUARY PBS begins airing the six-part series *Eyes on the Prize,* a detailed documentary chronicling the civil rights movement. Produced by Henry Hampton's Boston-based company, Blackside, *Eyes* celebrates the heroes and curses the villains of a struggle that makes the current post-soul landscape possible.

The last program, "Back to the Movement, 1979-85," is a melancholy affair—heroes are scarce and villains are not as obvious. Moreover, the story lacks the momentum of history. Compared to the early heroic chapters, part six is unsettling in its ambiguity.

JANUARY Terry McMillan publishes her first novel, *Mama*, the highly autobiographical story of the life of Mildred Peacock, a working-class woman, as she tries to keep her family together in a dying Michigan city. This mother of five kids struggles to raise her brood during the '60s and '70s, working on the assembly line and even as a prostitute. The story starts in Port Huron, shifts to Los Angeles, and then ends back in Michigan when Mildred, though never able to fulfill her material dreams for her children, takes quiet satisfaction in how they turn out.

The book is distinguished by McMillan's feisty, funny, and earthy dialogue. Unlike the reigning queens of black lit, Morrison and Walker, McMillan writes in a prose style that is very direct and full of contemporary references and pop culture. If Walker and Morrison write with the agility of a jazz singer, this thirty-six-year-old writer has the style of a salty, down-home soul woman. While Morrison and Walker influence many writers, McMillan ultimately inspires an entire literary genre.

FEBRUARY Fair-skinned black model Louise Vyent appears on the cover of *Vogue*. This follows an appearance by Karen Alexander in the December 1986 issue of *Elle* magazine. Later in the year Katie Ford, vice president of Ford Models, Inc., remarks, "Black models are starting to be used again." She continues, "In the early '70s black models were used a lot. Then we went to a really low point."

A slew of young beauties, like Vyent, Alexander, Kirsti Bowser, Gail O'Neill, and Veronica Webb, have been making waves on runways as well as in editorial layouts and some advertising. French-owned *Elle* magazine has been particularly aggressive in showcasing black women in photo spreads.

Bethann Hardison, president of Bethann Management and, along with Beverly Johnson and Iman, part of the '70s wave of black models, suggests, "Today's black models are 'safe.' They have white features. They're acceptable to the white eye." Hardison has a point in that most of the models in this wave range in skin tone from light brown to yellow. Still, this generation makes major strides in increasing the visibility of black women as symbols of beauty.

FEBRUARY 4 Against the advice of many doctors and boxing pros, "Sugar Ray" Leonard doesn't simply return to the ring but, in what is called the "upset of the decade," he out-points "Marvelous" Marvin Hagler to win the middleweight title, the third different championship belt of his career.

FEBRUARY 9 "I am worried about the destruction of the nuclear family among black people, particularly in a population where more than half the families are headed by women." Dr. Beny J. Primm, the executive director of a drug treatment program in Brooklyn, tells *The New York Times*. "It is such a devastating addiction that these people are willing to abandon food and water and child to take care of their crack habit."

Phoenix House, the largest operator of residential drug treatment programs in New York, reports that the number of women seeking treatment rose from 774 in '85 to 1,349 in '87. Babies born addicted to crack are swamping hospital pediatric wards. The nasty phrase "crackhead ho," a girl who will do anything sexually to earn money for crack, has become a commonplace, entering the rap lexicon and day-to-day conversation.

FEBRUARY 9 In one of her most famous broadcasts, Oprah Winfrey tapes a show in Forsythe County, Georgia, a community that hasn't allowed black people to live there since 1912.

FEBRUARY 22 Simply Red's Mick Hucknall and Lamont Dozier do a series of interviews together in Los Angeles the day before the Grammys. Hucknall, the lead singer and chief creative force behind this British soul band, collaborated with the longtime Motown songwriter-producer because of his respect for Dozier's work with the Supremes, the Four Tops, and others. This speaks to the esteem UK acts have for traditional R&B musical values. (Dozier will also collaborate with Phil Collins and have a hit with "Two Hearts.") In contrast, few younger black artists in the States are interested in working with Dozier or the talents of the '60s, illustrating the generation gap in black music (and culture).

FEBRUARY 23 *Ethnic Notions,* a documentary directed by San Francisco–based filmmaker Marlon Riggs, who studies institutionalized racism in American popular culture using evidence as far afield as cartoons, household implements, and cigar and washing powder boxes, is released. The film presents images that disturb viewers as well as possible funding sources. Riggs, who studied American history at Harvard and journalism at Berkeley, asserts that the film documents "how the culture subconsciously, perniciously shapes and mirrors and stigmatizes groups such as blacks in America today." It is the first of many unflinching views of the black image Riggs will direct, including the controversial *Tongues Untied,* about black gay men, in 1991.

MARCH The Beastie Boys' *Licensed to Ill* reaches number one on the *Billboard* chart.

MARCH Longtime black theater fixture Morgan Freeman receives an Academy Award nomination as best supporting actor for the role of a vicious pimp in *Street Smart*. After years of fine theater work and some television exposure, Freeman is put on the map with this part. This same year, Freeman wins an Obie for his work as a chauffeur in *Driving Miss Daisy*, a harbinger of his cinematic future. Critic Pauline Kael opens her review of *Street Smart* by asking, "Is Morgan Freeman the greatest American actor?"

MARCH The members of Public Enemy, their Bomb Squad production team, and various pals meet the press through a month of interviews held at Def Jam's East Village offices in support of their debut of *Yo! Bum Rush the Show*. Flavor Flav (Rico Drayton) misses many of the interviews, but lead MC Chuck D (Chuck Ridenhour) is always there, often accompanied by producer Hank Shocklee (a.k.a. Boxley), his brother Keith, Def Jam executive producer Bill Stephney, Bomb Squad member Eric "Vietnam" Sadler, and writer and friend Harry Allen.

Calling themselves "the Black Panthers of rap," Public Enemy assails crackheads, "cold gettin' dumb" rappers, and black America's current political lethargy. They also take time to rhyme the praises of Oldsmobiles. The balance between Chuck's baritone declaiming and Flavor Flav's silly asides is captivating, like hearing Muhammad Ali and his cornerman Bundini Brown at a prefight press conference.

Public Enemy is proudly from Long Island and articulates a suburban hip hop aesthetic. Chuck D explains: "Hip hop may have started in the inner city but it took people on Long Island and Queens to take hip hop and look at it differently—they dissected it and built it up again. Meanwhile the people who were so close to the original scene, they didn't know the difference between good and bad. They just knew how to do it. But life isn't like that. Life has to be planned. Life has to have a structure and the Long Island and Hollis guys put structure to it."

The core of this rap posse came together at Long Island's Adelphi University, where they congregated around the campus radio station WBAU. There "Chucky D," "Mr. Bill," and others either worked on air as DJs or provided theme music. This collective also congregated at Hempstead, Long Island's Spectrum City studio where, along with non–college buddy Flav Flav, they cut tracks (as did their neighbor Eddie Murphy, who aspired to make rock & roll records).

MARCH 6 *Lethal Weapon* is released, establishing Mel Gibson and Danny Glover as the most commercially successful interracial duo in cinema history. Glover, like most black actors of his generation, developed his craft through black theater, slowly working his way up via small television and film roles. He made a strong impression a few years earlier as the villain in the Harrison Ford vehicle *Witness*.

In *Lethal Weapon*, Glover plays Sergeant Roger Murtaugh, the sane, stable family man, to Gibson's buckwild Sergeant Martin Riggs. In contrast to earlier black-white buddy flicks that feature either two comedians (Richard Pryor and Gene Wilder in *Stir Crazy*) or a black comic with a white straight man (Pryor and Christopher Reeve in *Superman III*, Murphy and Nick Nolte in *48 Hours*), Gibson carries the humor and most of the action in this film. However, Glover isn't a traditional second banana, since his personal life and values anchor this film (and the ensuing sequels).

For producer Joel Silver, this is yet another vote in his one-man campaign to include black heroes in the action genre. Unlike many in Hollywood, Silver recognizes the role black audiences play in making actions films work, and he caters to them in numerous films, hiring Murphy, Glover, Damon Wayans, Rae Dawn Chong, Chris Rock, Halle Berry, DMX, and others in key roles.

Glover, who emerges as the most politically active black star of the era, uses his *Lethal Weapon* box office clout to produce (and star in) low-budget independent films that wouldn't exist without him (for example, 1991's *To Sleep with Anger*, directed by Charles Burnett).

A screening of Robert Townsend's *Hollywood Shuffle* at the Embassy Theater in Times Square is followed by a party at B. Smith's. Townsend's funny, heartfelt look at the compromises black actors have to make in American films is the second big break for black indie films, after *She's Gotta Have It*. Townsend, a charming man with a trademark fedora, beguiles listeners with his tale of financing *Shuffle* with credit cards. Cowritten with "black pack" buddy Keenan Ivory Wayans (who makes a hilarious appearance as the evil "Jheri Curl"), *Hollywood Shuffle* is a product of the frustrations Townsend and other blacks feel working within the limitations of Hollywood.

Unlike Spike, whose voice is that of a testy social critic, Townsend makes a plea for inclusion in his film (and attitude). So although it's made outside the Hollywood system, this film fits smoothly into the old-school integrationist agenda of the NAACP. Where Spike represents the long-ignored black indie film underground, Townsend is a pal of Eddie Murphy and a working movie actor; where Spike wants to work on his own terms, Townsend just wants to work. In the next few years these two different viewpoints on film yield two diverging kinds of black-directed films—gritty dramas and humorous entertainments.

The afterparty at black-owned B. Smith's restaurant is a warm, loving affair. More low-key than Spike's Puck Building events, this party is energized by the sense of possibility that *Hollywood Shuffle* presents. Members of the hip hop community mingle with older members of the black theater world and younger wanna-be filmmakers—all of whom will get their moment in the next few years.

Prince releases the double album *Sign O' the Times*. Though *Purple Rain* made him a superstar, this double album absolutely confirms his greatness. The range of approaches, topics, and styles Prince employs to paint a picture of the world circa '87 defines the world "eclectic." The slow-tempo funk of the socially conscious title track, the guitar-heavy stomp of the religious "Cross," the funk dance jam "Housequake," the quirky, poignant, Beatle-like "Starfish and Coffee," the perverse R&B of "If I Was Your Girlfriend," and the graceful ballad "Adore" attest to Prince's mastery of pop music idioms. Typical of his late '80s decision making, Prince releases the wrong singles ("Girlfriend" when radio is clamoring for "Housequake") and doesn't seem to care that he alienates his label and many radio programmers. Since *Purple Rain,* the Minneapolis native has made many bad moves (such as the film *Under the Cherry Moon*), but his music endures despite his missteps.

APRIL Lisa Bonet continues to refine her non–*Cosby Show* persona by appearing topless in this month's issue of *Interview* magazine. This photo follows her sexy role in the R-rated film *Angel Heart.* Cosby's take: "It's a movie made by white America that cast a black girl, gave her voodoo things to do and have sex." Bonet's view: "My obligation wasn't to Denise. I felt obligated to myself and my career." Meanwhile, NBC and the actors prepare for the fall launch of *A Different World,* a series starring Bonet set at a fictional black women's college called Hillman (a.k.a. Spelman).

APRIL With the new baseball season begins one of the briefest yet most amazing careers in the history of professional sport. Bo Jackson begins his first full season in the major leagues. Later in the year he'll play running back for the Oakland Raiders, becoming the first two-sport star since the '20s. With athletes incredibly well paid and professional seasons so long they all overlap, it appears no athlete will have the desire, skill, and stamina to compete in more than one of America's big-four sports.

Yet Bo Jackson, a star running back at Auburn University, earns a spot on the Kansas City Royals as an outfielder while signed with the NFL's Oakland Raiders as a running back. For the next four years, Jackson tests his body's ability to withstand stress and strain by playing major league baseball and pro football at the position where you take the most hits.

As a baseball player, Jackson has prodigious power and often hits balls over 400 feet. He not only makes the baseball all-star game in '89, but also is named the game's most valuable player. In a 1990 contest against the New York Yankees, he clouts three homers. Later that year, in a game broadcast on ABC's *Monday Night Football*, Jackson runs for 221 yards, a testament to his stamina and tenacity on the gridiron.

Jackson has a severe stutter, which he works successfully to control, but that doesn't prevent him from starring in a memorable ad campaign. Before Gatorade's "Be Like Mike" and Nike's "Just Do It," the greatest sport-related ad line of the '80s was probably "Bo Knows." In a series of ads based around Jackson's multisport career, Nike uses the "Bo Knows" line to photograph him in a wide array of unlikely scenarios that exploit his versatility while requiring him to do very little speaking. The "Bo Knows" line is quoted in rap records, comedy routines, and general conversations all over the country.

Jackson's career ends, as many commentators expect, with a football injury. In a 1991 game against the Cincinnati Bengals, Jackson receives a hip injury from a tackle that makes him quit football and hinders his ability to play baseball as well, ending his athletic career in 1994. In a decade of remarkable athletes like Jackie Joyner-Kersee, Carl Lewis, and Magic Johnson, no one knew (or could do) what Bo did.

MAY 30 The Boston Celtics have just defeated the Detroit Pistons in game seven of the Eastern Conference finals in the Boston Garden. In the cramped visiting team locker room, Dennis Rodman, then just an aggressive young player and not yet a national symbol of outrageousness, tells reporters that Larry Bird, who's won the MVP award three years running, receives this acclaim "because he's white." Another reporter approaches the team's star, guard Isiah Thomas, who replies, "I think Larry Bird is a very good basketball player. But I have to agree with Rodman. If he were black, he'd be just another good player."

The comments set off a firestorm of public indignation. The media feeding frenzy against Thomas is only calmed when Bird himself appears with Thomas and chalks it up to a misunderstanding. Thomas's career survives. Bird continues to be loved in Boston and elsewhere. Everyone forgives Rodman, thinking his comment is just a rookie transgression and not the first sign of a perpetually rebellious persona.

JUNE With the major labels chasing rap acts, MCA makes a deal with Andre Harrell, ex-rapper and former vice president at Rush Management, that will result in Uptown Records. Harrell's vision is that hip hop records can appeal to the same audience as R&B dance music. Whereas Def Jam positions hip hop as rock & roll, Uptown's philosophy is to make hip hop that is a slightly more aggressive version of R&B.

Harrell's first major artist is Heavy D, a heavyset MC from the New York bedroom community of Mount Vernon, a suburban area that, like Roosevelt, Long Island, spawns many important hip hop figures. Heavy has a booming voice and a snazzy flow and dances gracefully for a big man. Rejected by Def Jam, Heavy comes to epitomize Uptown (in the '90s he even becomes the label's president). Much of his debut album, *Big Tyme,* is produced by a teenaged producer-writer-keyboardist from Harlem named Teddy Riley.

Harrell also hires Warrington and Reggie Hudlin, stalwarts of the black independent film scene, to direct his first two videos: Warrington handles the label's introductory video, "Uptown's Kicking It" (which features a cameo by Nelson George), and Reggie does Heavy D's first single, "Mr. Big Stuff."

JUNE 30 Oprah Winfrey beats twenty-year talk show vet Phil Donahue at the Daytime Emmys in the categories of best talk show and best talk show host. At one point during the ceremonies, Donahue walks over to Winfrey's table, kisses her on the cheek, and tells her, "Congratulations, you deserve it." Winfrey's response is, "Ain't this a year I'm having." Because of her deal with King World Productions, Winfrey is expected to gross $30 million within the next year.

AUGUST 1 Mike Tyson defeats Tony Tucker in a twelve-round unanimous decision to win the IBF championship. Tyson already owns the WBA and WBC belts, making him the first undisputed heavyweight titlist since Larry Holmes.

AUGUST 1 San Francisco mayor Dianne Feinstein announces the formation of a task force to deal with the rise of crack sales in her city. The task force targets five public housing projects in the city. Like many other American mayors, Feinstein tries to sound tough and in control ("I would like to issue one warning to drug peddlers: Get out while you can"), yet the $836,000 budgeted for this task force is just a finger in the dike.

AUGUST 17 Blacks and Hispanics are twice as likely as whites to contract AIDS, reports *U.S. News & World Report*. At a conference on AIDS and minorities, it is announced that for the first time money ($7 million) is being earmarked for minority organizations to use in prevention and education. In New York City the percentage of homosexuals infected with the disease has dropped from 70 percent to about 50 percent, while drug abusers now make up one third of all AIDS cases and 54 percent of all cases are black and Hispanic.

AUGUST 20 While visiting a "notorious Northeast drug market," D.C. mayor Marion Barry announces that the city's Operation Clean Sweep, a citywide drug crackdown, has resulted in 23,000 arrests (55 percent for drug-related offenses) as well as $5.6 million in police overtime and court costs. A resolute Barry explains, "The costs are worth it. We're suffering from a drug epidemic. . . . This mayor and this police department's tired of it, and we're not going to take it any more."

AUGUST 26 DJ Scott LaRock of Boogie Down Productions is shot outside the Highbridge Gardens Homes in the South Bronx. LaRock, a.k.a. Scott Sterling, who dies the next day, has traveled up to this housing project hoping to squash a dispute involving BDP member D-Nice and another man over a woman. As LaRock and his posse exit their jeep, a shot rings out that hits LaRock in the kind of senseless murder that is sweeping black America. Because LaRock is a semi-celebrity, the murder is well documented. Yet in its arbitrary nature this shooting is sadly representative of a growing disrespect for human life.

As a result of LaRock's murder, Boogie Down Productions' next album, *By All Means Necessary,* is a project weighty with significance and symbols. Since the release of *Criminal Minded,* the group has signed with Jive Records, an early supporter of rap that is now upping its commitment to the music. Death hangs over the project. On the cover, lead MC KRS-One poses with an Israeli-made Uzi automatic weapon, an homage to a famous photo of Malcolm X with a rifle taken after his Queens home was firebombed. References to crack-related violence abound. But in the urban landscape that KRS-One depicts, death can come in unexpected ways: in "Jimmy," he rhymes about the need to wear condoms to protect yourself in the age of AIDS, one of the first and smartest safe sex records ever made.

The video for the single "My Philosophy" is a crucial hip hop document. Directed by Fab Five Freddy, again in the role of cultural interpreter, the video begins with KRS-One rhyming a cappella in a customized track suit in front of that new "official" urban ride, the jeep. Much of the video is shot on location in the beaten down yet strangely beautiful South Bronx with a posse of b-boys supporting KRS-One, a combination of MC 'hood and posse that becomes standard in rap videos. In a club setting, huge pictures of Bob Marley, Malcolm X, and others are hung as symbols of empowerment. Scott LaRock's child is also seen in the video, increasing the sense that this album, the music, and the culture are involved in a drama with very high stakes. This riveting black-and-white video, in support of a landmark album, along with its memorable cover photo, sets a new, high standard for hip hop visuals.

AUGUST 31   *Bad,* the third and final collaboration between Michael Jackson and Quincy Jones, doesn't have the freshness of *Off the Wall* nor does it become a phenomenon like *Thriller.* But vocally it may be Jackson's best work; in songs like "Smooth Criminal" and "Man in the Mirror," his singing is more vigorous and precise than ever.

There's something humorous about Jackson trying to out-"bad" L.L. Cool J in proclaiming his toughness. Jackson, clearly wanting to somehow compete with the street edge rap is bringing to pop culture, hires Martin Scorsese to direct an elaborate video that depicts Jackson as a high school student riding the New York subway before bursting into a *West Side Story* dance number in a station. Jackson's attempt to mix his big-budget, state-of-the-art sensibility with "street" elements is a joke, but a joke that speaks to the unease established black culture has with hip hop. While many of his peers ignore rap or detest it, Jackson, like all great pop stars, attempts to bend this new element of black culture to his will. It doesn't work, but at least Jackson is willing to engage in a dialogue.

In the *Bad* video, Jackson has a showdown with a dark-skinned tough guy. The actor isn't well known, but Wesley Snipes's face will become very familiar in a few years.

SEPTEMBER Toni Morrison publishes her masterpiece, *Beloved,* which wins the Pulitzer Prize and confirms what was already obvious—that she is not simply the nation's most celebrated black novelist, but that she may be America's most accomplished novelist. Morrison's fifth novel is set in the Reconstruction era and is based on the true story of a runaway slave who kills her daughter rather than allow her return to slavery. In Morrison's telling, the runaway slave, Sethe, is ostracized by both whites and blacks. The novel obviously explores the nature of mother love, but is also concerned with ownership (of other people, of land, of souls) as a reflection of American identity. Morrison's prose is a mystical, dense, and even as frightening as her tale. It is because of the themes and execution of *Beloved* that Morrison becomes a Nobel Prize contender.

Another example of literary excellence is Rita Dove's book-length poem *Thomas and Beulah.* This is the thirty-six-year-old poet's third collection. In narrative verse, Dove writes a loose biography of her maternal grandparents, Thomas and Beulah Hord, who lived in Dove's native Akron, Ohio. The volume is divided into two sections: "Mandolin," twenty-three poems told from Thomas's perspective, and "Canary in Bloom," twenty-one poems told from Beulah's point of view. Along with the actual poems, Dove provides a chronology of her family's history. This unique blend of biography and verse makes her the first black poet since Gwendolyn Brooks (in 1950) to win the Pulitzer Prize. In the '90s Dove becomes the first African American to be named poet laureate of the United States.

Ice-T, a.k.a. Tracy Morrow, a Newark, New Jersey, native who relocated to Los Angeles as an adolescent, debuts with *Rhyme Pays,* a collection of raps influenced by his criminal past, L.A.'s burgeoning gang culture, and the ghettocentric fiction of Iceberg Slim and Donald Goines published by Holloway House. His "6'N the Morning," a successful underground twelve-inch released before the album, has the storytelling style of a jailhouse rhyme and is one of the first recordings made in Los Angeles in the gangsta rap style.

SEPTEMBER 20 "It's the most revolutionary thing that's happening in the black fashion market," beauty consultant Audrey Smaltz tells the *Los Angeles Times.* The item in question is colored contact lenses that turn brown eyes blue or green or hazel. Whoopi Goldberg is the most prominent black celebrity to sport blue eyes but, as Smaltz suggests, she is far from the only black person with them. Wesley-Jessen's DuraSoft Colors is the market leader, with retail sales of over $100 million in the first half of this year. These lenses, introduced to consumers last fall, are the first to work in changing the color of dark eyes.

SEPTEMBER 24 *Rolling Stone* runs a feature on the Black Rock Coalition that focuses on Vernon Reid and his band, Living Colour. Mick Jagger sees the band at CBGB's and is so impressed he produces and pays for two demos. This heat leads Living Colour to be signed by Epic records. Other BRC bands—I&I and 24/7 Spyz—also win label deals.

OCTOBER In the subset of black artists working to escape the orthodoxy of black musical tradition, none is more idiosyncratic or gifted than Terrence Trent D'Arby. Though he was born in Florida, D'Arby, like Jimi Hendrix, makes his mark first in

England, where his church preacher vocals, penchant for rock guitar, and male model looks make him a sensation.

D'Arby is reminiscent of Prince in his ability to draw on various pop and soul traditions in his music. The difference is that while Prince is a master of accessible song structures, D'Arby never met a chord change he doesn't like, filling his songs with individual moments of great sonic excitement that can sound like clutter. In the long run, D'Arby's challenging music and edgy personality (he seems to carry a huge chip on his shoulder that is ever ready for tossing) make him a cult star, but not the superstar Columbia Records hoped for. D'Arby epitomizes the comedy world phrase "Too hip for the room."

Yet his *Introducing the Hardline According to Terrence Trent D'Arby* is an often inspired record filled with neo-soul ("If You Let Me Stay"), dance music ("Wishing Well"), and tender love songs ("Sign Your Name"). His cover of the Smokey Robinson classic "Who's Lovin' You" distills decades of soul vocalizing into a single performance. Of all the black artists who push the envelope on black music in the '80s, D'Arby is one of the most musically talented and willful, a combination that makes for a long and checkered career.

D'Arby is also a voracious reader and one of his favorite books is *Black Athena,* by white Oxford scholar Martin Bernal. The scholar argues that Egypt, not Greece, is the cradle of Western Civilization and documents the obfuscation of the Afro-Asiatic roots of world culture by white historians beginning in the eighteenth century, arguing that these historians couldn't stand the idea that their beloved Greece had been made "impure" by African technology, philosophy, and political theory. Black scholars such as Ivan Van Sertima and John Henrik Clarke have made this claim for years, but Bernal's Oxford pedigree gives the idea some credence in white academic circles. Still, most dismiss Bernal even as the Afrocentric ideas he references find more adherents in black America.

HBO, the cable channel best known for showing Hollywood movies and star-driven comedy performances, discovers the black audience when it broadcasts the Eddie Murphy-produced *Comedy Express*. Taped at an old South Central Los Angeles theater, the program features comedians handpicked by Murphy, including his close friends Arsenio Hall and Robert Townsend. Marsha Warfield is a veteran of the comedy club circuit whose appearance helps her land a role on the NBC sitcom *Night Court*. Barry Sobel, the token white act, is probably America's first "wigger," as his routine notes the influence of hip hop on white teenagers and uses black slang liberally for humor. The wild card on the show is a very young comic who Murphy saw just a few months before at a New York club. The relatively inexperienced Brooklyn native's best joke ends with the punch line "Bitch, paint my house!" His name is Chris Rock.

Cry Freedom premieres at the Ziegfeld Theater, an example of the kind of frustrating liberal cinema that makes black filmmakers so necessary. Though Richard Attenborough's film is based on a book about the slain South African activist Stephen Biko, the story is told from the point of view of Donald Woods, the white editor who wrote it. The evils of apartheid are documented, but at a certain remove from the pain.

As Biko, Denzel Washington gives one of the steely, morally confident performances that have become his calling card, resulting in his first supporting actor Oscar nomination. A scene in which he testifies resolutely in a hostile South African courtroom is incendiary. Unfortunately, the film doesn't end with Biko's death but anticlimactically, with Woods, played by Kevin Kline, escaping the country. Attenborough is a skilled though ponderous filmmaker who sees the epic nature of the antiapartheid struggle yet is unable to tell it through black eyes. *Cry Freedom* is just one example of the inability of white directors in general to tell black stories from their center. Instead, they use white surrogates as the point of entry.

NOVEMBER 3 The election of thirty-seven-year-old Kurt L. Schmoke as Baltimore's mayor is part of a changing of the guard in local politics that suggests a new direction for black leadership. Schmoke, the first black mayor of this city, is not a product of the civil rights era but one of its beneficiaries. He attended integrated grade schools (he was a local high school football star) and prestigious white universities (Yale, Harvard, Oxford) and held positions of civic authority (serving as a Baltimore state's attorney).

Schmoke is not a big-voiced "Amen"-generating preacher but a calm, just-the-facts speaker, which reflects his studious approach. Grave, youthful, and nerdy, Schmoke is a stark contrast to his counterpart down I-95, Marion Barry, who is reelected to a record third term in D.C. Barry is a verbose, soul-era relic whose fiefdom is built on the cult of personality.

Drugs will play a defining role in the careers of both. In 1988, Schmoke becomes the nation's most prominent elected official to openly endorse the legalization of marijuana, making a thoughtful argument that probably derails his national political career. Details of Barry's own personal involvement with drugs are slowly trickling out.

NOVEMBER 3 Despite the MOVE bombing and its tragic fallout, Mayor Wilson Goode of Philadelphia wins a narrow victory, 51.1 percent to 48.9 percent, over the previous mayor, Frank Rizzo, after a campaign that is much more racially charged than Goode's first campaign.

NOVEMBER 5 President Ronald Reagan announces the appointment of Colin Powell as his national security advisor, making the three-star general the first black to serve in a post with close personal contact with the president in such a sensitive area. Born and raised in the South Bronx by Jamaican immigrant parents, Powell is a career soldier. After serving in Vietnam, he worked as a White House fellow under President Nixon and was then elevated to the role of deputy director of the Office of Management and Budget. After serving several years in the field (and a brief stint as deputy defense secretary in the Carter administration), Powell joined the Reagan administration in '83 as a senior military assistant.

Though a lifelong solider, Powell is viewed as a political moderate and "orchestrator" who moves policy along without bluster or conflict. That he is black yet moves smoothly through corridors of white male power marks him as a gifted crossover strategist.

NOVEMBER 6 To promote the Rick Rubin–supervised *Less Than Zero* soundtrack, Def Jam releases two rap twelve-inchers— Public Enemy's "Bring the Noise" and L.L. Cool J's "Going Back to Cali" backed with "Jack the Ripper." "Noise" is the jam that took the Bomb Squad's production style to the next level—the use of samples creates a wall of sound with a beat like a bomb explosion. As Hank Shocklee describes it, "We use samples like an artist would use paint." If the dense, sample-rich track isn't enough, Chuck D's interplay with Flavor Flav is both forceful and playful, a balance of fury and tomfoolery rarely achieved in any art form. And telling a nation still nervous about Louis Farrakhan that he "is a prophet and I think you oughta listen to him" probably leads hundreds to purchase the Nation of Islam's newspaper, *Final Call*.

"Going Back to Cali" features the loudest scratching sound in hip hop history. How producer Rubin accomplished this feat is one of his trade secrets, but the scratching, contrasted with a saxophone and L.L.'s whispery vocals, both fascinates those who don't think hip hop is music and pisses off many b-boys. L.L. has always been a "you love him or hate him" artist. His arrogance, claims of MC greatness, and tendency to sneer have already made him a polarizing performer.

While "Cali" rubs many the wrong way, "Jack the Ripper" is aimed at one man—Kool Moe Dee. It is the second salvo in one of the great on-vinyl MC battles. Moe Dee dissed L.L. earlier in the summer with the Teddy Riley–produced "How Ya Like Me Now." L.L.'s screaming, rapidly paced, intricately rhymed reply spawns Moe Dee's reply, "Let's Go." The L.L.-Moe Dee rap-off is one of many L.L. participates in. Something about Todd Smith makes people wanna fight him. Despite the verbal blows, no MC proves as durable as L.L. Cool J, who rocks bells into the twenty-first century.

NOVEMBER 24 Jesse Jackson attends a press conference at 777 United Nations Plaza announcing the release of the anti-apartheid twelve-inch "AFRICA" by Stetsasonic.

NOVEMBER 25 Harold Washington's battles with ethnic Chicago end unexpectedly with his death from a heart attack shortly after winning his third term. It is a huge loss for black America, since Washington's strength and adaptability have been an inspiration to many. An acting black mayor, Eugene Sawyer, is named with the aid of Washington's opponents, largely because he isn't a strong figure. In the next election, whites reclaim Chicago's City Hall and the black political dynasty Washington seemed on the verge of building never materializes in the Windy City.

NOVEMBER 27 The original production of August Wilson's *The Piano Lesson* at Yale Repertory Theatre stars Samuel L. Jackson. In a year in which several veteran black actors enjoy commercial film breakthroughs, Jackson is still refining his craft in the theater. He stars in a play, set in 1933, that centers around the value of a piano on which a black family's history is carved. Jackson's Boy Willie wants to sell the piano and buy land the family slaved on down South, while his sister Berniece argues that selling the piano would be ignoring the pain of the family's survival. Complicating the debate is the possible presence of the ghost of Sutter, the white man who once owned the land Boy Willie wants to purchase.

Wilson grapples with the question of whether the black legacy of slavery and struggle should be ignored or honored. Jackson is a tortured, glowering presence full of the fury and humor that later make him a movie star. Unfortunately, by the time the play reaches Broadway in April 1990, Wilson regular Charles Dutton has taken over the role of Boy Willie. Jackson, who has a small but memorable role in Spike Lee's *School Daze,* is still a few years away from prominence.

By the time of *The Piano Lesson* it is generally known that this relatively inexperienced playwright has taken on the ambitious task of writing a play about black life set in every decade of the twentieth century. With only two decades under his belt (another piece, *Jitney,* remains unproduced for years) Wilson has a monumental task ahead to fulfill this dream with the high standards set by his first two plays. It is a daunting, perhaps foolhardy, goal that many doubt can be achieved.

NOVEMBER 28 Tawana Brawley, a Wappingers Falls, New York, teenager, tells a sordid tale of being raped by six white men over the course of four days, after she's found wrapped in a garbage bag and smeared with feces. Coached by a trio of advisors (Reverend Al Sharpton and barristers Alton Maddox and C. Vernon Mason), the fifteen-year-old refuses to cooperate with police, instigating a racial firestorm. Initially there is sympathy for the girl and horror at her fantastic story of Northern racism.

The Brawley advisors had used a similar tactic of withholding access the previous summer in handling the Howard Beach incident, in which a gang of whites chased several black men from a Queens pizza shop, beating them and causing the death of one, Michael Griffin, when he fled into traffic on a nearby highway. They demanded and got a special prosecutor who won the conviction of three men for manslaughter.

But the Brawley case turns out very differently. Her family's silence and the bombast of the advisors (who denounce state Attorney General Robert Abrams as "a pervert" who "masturbated" while looking at Tawana Brawley's picture, and accuse a local prosecutor of being a rapist) erodes the confidence of early supporters (such as Bill Cosby, who offered a $25,000 reward for information). After a seven-month inquiry, a New York grand jury reports that Brawley fabricated the entire story to explain her absence from home.

Lawsuits against the three advisors drag on for years; Maddox and Mason, who had both been effective activist lawyers, are eventually disbarred in New York state (though not just for the Brawley case).

Sharpton, however, survives this debacle. He never admits any wrongdoing or fabrication, sticking by Brawley's outrageous tale. Instead, now established after Howard Beach and Brawley as a leader unafraid of white power, Sharpton evolves into the most prominent nonelected black leader in New York. Much as with Farrakhan, the white media's constant vilification of Sharpton enhances his credibility with blacks.

Sharpton also benefits from the growth of black talk radio on black-owned WLIB-AM. Sharpton uses it to speak directly to black listeners without the filtering of white reporters. On Gary Byrd's influential afternoon broadcast, "Afrocentricity—The Global Black

Experience," Sharpton and many other alternative black voices speak in ways they never could on white radio stations or via mainstream newspapers.

DECEMBER Eddie Murphy's concert film *Raw* is directed by Robert Townsend with a brief comedy short cowritten by Keenan Ivory Wayans. The bulk of the film is recorded at New York's Felt Forum with Murphy, in one of his trademark leather outfits, spending much of his time fixated on women as financial predators. While clearly autobiographical in that Murphy's youth and wealth make him a magnet for mercenary females, the comic's humorously mean-spirited material strikes a chord. The suspicion and cynicism Murphy articulates in *Raw* are echoed in rap records almost immediately after the film opens. The impact of Murphy's performance should not be underestimated. Its $40 million gross is still the record for a concert film, and more than most narrative films earn.

DECEMBER Salt-N-Pepa's single "Push It" is certified gold. This huge pop smash makes the duo the first female mass-appeal stars of a previously male-dominated world. "Push It" is a frankly sexual song driven by a keyboard riff that comes right out of new wave, a blend of old-fashioned pop songwriting and progressive instrumentation that overcomes any resistance. Under the production guidance of Hurby "Luv Bug" Azar, Salt-N-Pepa are no one-hit wonders. In fact, they are among the most consistent hitmakers in hip hop and always walk the line between sexy and raunchy. As once was said of Marilyn Monroe, this duo is the ice cream and cake of sex.

DECEMBER 10 The final episode of Fox's *The Late Show*, a program originally hosted by Joan Rivers, is aired. This attempt to launch a competitor for *The Tonight Show* fails for the new network but not for the broadcast's last host. Arsenio Hall, who took over for the show's last thirteen weeks, is a hit with viewers and critics. The *Los Angeles Times* writes, "Night after night, he presided over the hippest party in town, strutting out in front of an adoring audience and dancing on virtually every racial stereotype around."

Due to a restricting clause in his Fox contract, Hall can't host another talk show for a year. That's fine with the comic, who's about to be in a movie with Eddie Murphy titled *Zamunda Project* (it will be released as *Coming to America*). Says Bob Wachs, who manages both Murphy and Hall, "The end of *The Late Show* is the beginning of Arsenio."

DECEMBER 18   Despite the fact that *The Cosby Show* dominates prime-time television, Bill Cosby stars in the year's biggest cinematic flop, *Leonard Part 6*. While Eddie Murphy and Robin Williams make the leap from TV to film comedy, it proves to be Cosby's Achilles' heel.

Public Enemy in full effect.

1988

1988

This year is marked by two anniversaries and a business transaction that illustrate that the struggle for black advancement in the soul years, while ongoing, has lost its once central place in the consciousness of America. Twenty years earlier the Kerner Commission Report (formally the National Advisory Commission on Civil Disorders) was issued in the wake of the riots that had ripped up Newark, Detroit, Los Angeles, and sundry other major cities. The original report suggested the United States was becoming two very different nations—one rich and white, the other poor and black.

Of course, the Kerner Commission was correct, though it underestimated the number of blacks who'd move into the middle class and the number of whites who'd live in poverty. A follow-up report issued in March of this year concludes that racial segregation still divides the nation and that "the gap between rich and poor has widened."

Two other reports released this year support this thesis. The U.S. Census Bureau notes that six out of ten black families with one or more children are headed by single mothers, while for white families the rate is only two in ten. Continuing the bad news is a report from the U.S. Education Commission and the American Council on Education, which states, "America is moving backward . . . in its efforts to achieve the full participation of minority citizens in the life and prosperity of the nation."

Twenty-five years earlier, Dr. Martin Luther King Jr. led the historic March on Washington where he made the famous "I Have a Dream" speech on the steps of the Lincoln Memorial. In August, 55,000 people march to D.C. to commemorate that long-ago day of black and white harmony. Yet some things haven't changed. The states of Alabama and South Carolina continue to fly the Confederate flag over public buildings despite protests from the NAACP and others. In other states there are persistent signs of white resistance to black achievement. Seven states (Arizona, Hawaii, Idaho, Montana, New Hampshire, South Dakota, and Wyoming) refuse to recognize King's birthday as a holiday.

On a similar note, President Reagan vetoes a civil rights bill designed to strengthen federal antidiscrimination laws, asserting the bill means "unwarranted" federal interference in businesses and religious institutions. Congress later overrides the veto, one of the rare outright victories the Democrats can claim for black America over a Reagan policy edict. Perhaps because he was at the end of his term (and to help Vice President George Bush in the presidential election this November), Reagan signs a bill guaranteeing stronger enforcement of federal open housing legislation. It is a crumb offered from a table covered in cookies.

The most significant business transaction of the year is the sale of a family-owned business to an investment group (Boston Ventures) that, in turn, expects to hand the property over to a large corporation, perhaps breaking up its assets in the process. This type of deal is a staple of the '80s. Except for black Americans, the sale of Motown Records by its founder, Berry Gordy, is incredibly emotionally loaded. In a deal brokered by record distributor MCA in June, Gordy is paid $61 million for the masters, logo, and other distinguishing elements of his record label. (Wisely, Gordy holds onto his publishing company, Jobete, which owns the rights to a rich catalogue of hit songs.)

Motown, the entertainment institution that epitomized the soul-era spirit as a business and cultural symbol, is a victim of the conglomerate control of distribution. The label's success at crossing over its acts (the Supremes, Stevie Wonder, the Temptations, the Jackson 5) to white America leads all the major multinational entertainment companies to emulate its marketing strategies and develop superstar black recording artists.

In 1968, Motown was the dominant label selling black pop music. Twenty years later Motown is just another undercapitalized black business trying to hold on to its market share against well-financed mainstream companies. "It would cost $100,000 just to promote one single," Gordy told *Playboy* later. "That's how expensive it had become. It cost even more when we had to start making videos because MTV had become so strong. So we were losing money. I started thinking about the Motown legacy, I never thought I would sell the business, but I began to realize it was the only way to ensure that Motown would survive."

The sale dismays many. Reverend Jesse Jackson, for one, urges Gordy not to sell. The truth is that Motown has hung on longer than any of its peers, and is the last of the prolific '60s indie labels still functioning as a proprietor-owned business in the '80s. Gordy's Jobete continues as a lucrative business, as the use of Motown songs in movies (*The Big Chill*) and commercials (the California Raisins) generates substantial royalties. Yet there is no question that Motown's sale is another signal that the soul era, like the music that defined it, is dead. Music for black America's new mind-set is everywhere in '88.

JANUARY Tests at two Baltimore clinics that treat sexually transmitted diseases reveal that the AIDS virus is spreading among that city's black population, according to *The New England Journal of Medicine*. Slightly more than 5 percent (about one in twenty cases) of some 4,000 clients walking in the doors of the two local clinics are infected with the HIV virus, and 94 percent of those clients are black. Health officials point out that people entering STD clinics are not representative of the general population—they tend to be more sexually active, poor, and to already have a venereal disease. Still, it is a frightening number if this continues around the country.

Doug Williams leads the Washington Redskins over the Denver Broncos 42 to 10 in the Super Bowl and is named the game's most valuable player. Williams is the first black quarterback to win the National Football League title game. It's not quite as important as Jackie Robinson joining major league baseball in 1947, but Williams's achievement is psychologically important for black sports fans and players.

Williams is the latest in a long line of great players coached by legendary Eddie Robinson at Grambling University. Williams's breakthrough comes after a checkered pro career in which he led the woeful Tampa Bay Buccaneers to the NFL title game in 1979 and then suffered through several injuries. He played in the short-lived United States Football League and returned to the NFL as a backup before becoming the starter under coach Joe Gibbs.

Williams's win is crucial to the evolution of black talent in the NFL. Black college quarterbacks had throughout the league's history either been moved to other positions or viewed as intellectually unable to lead a team. Williams's victory helps crush that stereotype. Within the next ten years, black quarterbacks will be commonplace.

A Compton, California, rap group with a defiantly confrontational name releases its first single. "Dopeman" by Niggas With Attitude, a.k.a. N.W.A., makes no noise nationally but its depiction of a crack dealer is popular in Southern California. During the year this quintet, recording for band member and drug dealer Eazy-E's appropriately titled Ruthless Records, releases other singles that illuminate the darkest corners of the black Los Angeles experience. Eazy, who has a nasal, whiney voice, releases solo efforts that, like N.W.A.'s material, are rife with guns, crack, hos, and cars. Eazy's whiney delivery is hard to take, but Dr. Dre's beats are impossible to resist as they tap into the long tradition of War and other funky L.A. bands. Much of this posse's lyrical direction is provided by Ice Cube, the band's best and brightest MC, though at first few can see past his gleeful use of the word "nigga." Eazy's "Ruthless Organization" taps into the aggression that fires Public Enemy, substituting a mean, ghetto ethos for black nationalism rhetoric. Just as Melvin Van Peebles's arty *Sweet Sweetback's BaadAsssss Song* paved the way for blaxploitation films in the '70s, P.E.'s intensity opens the door for N.W.A.'s nihilism.

FEBRUARY 7   Michael Jordan is named most valuable player of the NBA all-star game before his home crowd in Chicago. Spike Lee's Nike commercials with Jordan are sprinkled throughout the broadcast. CBS's game coverage also includes shots of heavyweight champ Mike Tyson and television actress Robin Givens huddled together at courtside.

FEBRUARY 8   Spike Lee's second feature film, *School Daze,* premieres. This ambitious, critical, and affectionate look at black college life is a major step up for Lee in terms of budget ($6 million) and scale (shot on location at Atlanta's University Center, which houses several black educational institutions). This film, set during the homecoming weekend of a fictional black college, taps into tensions over skin tone and class rarely discussed in public. Spike is particularly critical of the sexism and cruelty embedded in black fraternities, organizations that for decades have nurtured black leaders.

School Daze is an uneven mix of social criticism, teen movie, and M-G-M musical, and serves as a template for Lee's future body of work: big themes, humor, satire, scattershot storytelling, great and bad acting, hit songs, innovative camera work, overbearing scores, and debate-inciting endings.

With the film Spike establishes his eye for discovering talent, behind and before the camera. His production team (director of photography Ernest Dickerson, casting director Robbi Reed, production designer Wynn Thomas, costume designer Ruthe Carter) will stay together for a run of several films before going on to build successful careers on their own. The cast is packed with important young talents, from lead Larry Fishburne to Samuel L. Jackson in a small but memorable role as an angry local resident. *School Daze* is the equivalent of the '80s teen films of John Hughes, introducing the nation to a new generation of black actors, many of them with black theater experience, who'll prosper in the new wave of black films and television. Three cast members (Kadeem Hardison, Jasmine Guy, Darryl Bell) become longtime residents of another fictional black college, Hillman, when NBC revamps *A Different World*.

After a preview screening of *School Daze* for 250 college students at Los Angeles's black-owned Baldwin Hills Theater, director Spike Lee meets a student attending USC film school. The bookish-looking young man tells Spike he wants to direct but right now is concentrating on his screenwriting. The young man's name is John Singleton.

MARCH 5 Richard Pryor's health and career continue to deteriorate. *Moving* is a lifeless vehicle for a star whose body and spirit are clearly flagging.

MARCH 26 In his second run for the presidency, Reverend Jesse Jackson wins a landslide victory in the Michigan Democratic caucus by winning 55 percent of the 200,000 votes cast, double the vote of front-runner Governor Michael Dukakis

of Massachusetts. *The New York Times* reports that a party professional feels it was "remotely, barely, distantly conceivable" that
Jackson could end up with enough votes for the nomination, as
much a reflection of Dukakis's lackluster campaign as Jackson's
mainstream appeal.

MARCH 27 August Wilson's *Joe Turner's Come and Gone*
debuts at the Ethel Barrymore Theater almost a year to the day
that his *Fences,* playing at the 46th Street Theatre, premiered. It is
the first time a black playwright has two plays on Broadway simultaneously. Compared to *Fences, Joe Turner* is a denser, richer,
more complex work that mixes Southern black hoodooism with imagery from the Bible and from African religion. The plot centers
around a haunted man in search of his lost wife in Pittsburgh circa
1911. The production served as the Broadway debut of two remarkable actors—Delroy Lindo as Herald Loomis, the tortured
searcher, and Angela Bassett in the small but crucial role of his
wife, Martha Pentecost.

Fences is the more commercially successful of the two, partly
as a result of the casting of TV and movie star James Earl Jones as
the lead and Broadway vet Mary Alice as his wife. The theme and
structure of this play are also more audience-friendly. Jones is
Troy Maxson, a garbage man in 1950s Pittsburgh, a former Negro
League star who is still bitter he never got Jackie Robinson's shot
at the major leagues. His son Cory, played by Courtney B. Vance,
wants to pursue a college football scholarship but Jones refuses to
give permission.

Troy's own insecurity leads him into an adulterous affair that
undermines his marriage, ruins his relationship with his son, and
ultimately leads him toward a fatal confrontation with his own
demons. As in *Joe Turner,* there is a deep strain of mysticism built
into *Fences.* When Jones faces his moment of judgment, it's up to
the viewer to decide whether he's battling God or his own mind.

The themes of familial strife and infidelity in *Fences* are easier for audiences to grasp than the rituals of *Joe Turner*. Yet both testify to Wilson's ability to create dialogue of Shakespearean richness using slang and colloquial black language. These two plays present Wilson at the top of his game, an artist who translates the legacy of black theater (and song and religion) into a distinctive and very personal voice.

APRIL Living Colour, led by Black Rock Coalition cofounder Vernon Reid, debuts on Epic with *Vivid*. After much touring and groundwork, the anthemic "Cult of Personality" enters MTV's rotation and the band ends up touring, opening for mentor Mick Jagger (and the Rolling Stones) on a U.S. stadium tour.

Following on the heels of Living Colour and, eventually, having a longer, more consistent career is Lisa Bonet's husband, Lenny Kravitz. This Los Angeles–based singer-songwriter's Virgin Records debut, *Let Love Rule,* has hippie-dippy, lovey-dovey lyrics made palatable and propelled by his slavishly retro sound (he even uses studio equipment from the '70s to authenticate his musical direction). A mixed-race person (black and Jewish) like his wife, Kravitz claims roots in the Beatles and Curtis Mayfield that are all apparent in his songwriting.

Because of Bonet's and Kravitz's interracial looks and earthy, gypsy-style dress, they emerge as the first couple of American bohemia, neo-hippie symbols of an aesthetic that reverberates deeply in America.

APRIL Florence "Flo Jo" Griffith-Joyner shakes up the Olympic trials with her own brand of glamour. She competes wearing six-inch-long multicolored nails and her own self-designed, multicolored one-legged unitards. The track and field world is scandalized by this appearance of a style influenced by black beauty parlors and the handmade fashions of ghetto clothing stores. Olympic officials are taken aback, but the NBA's Indiana Pacers pay Flo Jo to design new uniforms.

APRIL 11 To the surprise of everyone at the Academy Awards, presenter Eddie Murphy tells the Oscar audience that blacks are underrepresented in the film industry. Whether or not Murphy felt prodded by the sudden emergence of black directors to make this statement is hotly debated within Hollywood. But Murphy's statement increases the dialogue on the black image that the appearance of *She's Gotta Have It* and *Hollywood Shuffle* has ignited. Murphy will take few other political or controversial stances, but his timing here is impeccable.

APRIL 15 Before "gangsta rap" becomes a catchphrase and black-themed urban films a Hollywood staple, there is Dennis Hopper's *Colors,* a gritty view of South Central street life through the eyes of two cops, played by Robert Duvall and Sean Penn. Though the film suffers from the typical outside-looking-in perspective of liberal white filmmaking, *Colors* does introduce the nation to the warring Blood and Crips, contributing to their notoriety (and inadvertently to their spread). The film's soundtrack gives original gangsta rapper Ice-T his first national exposure with the chilling title song. In a supporting role, young comic Damon Wayans plays a perpetually smoked-out gang banger.

APRIL 18 Tenants at crack-infested Mayfair Mansions housing project in Washington, D.C., invite members of the Nation of Islam from a nearby mosque to begin antidrug patrols. The Nation's security force, the Fruit of Islam, unarmed except for nightsticks and walkie-talkies, guards the project on foot and in vans. The day the FOI arrive, the dealers depart. A follow-up report by *The New York Times* six months later finds Mayfair Mansions is still drug-free.

Viewed as well-mannered yet disciplined men, the Fruit of Islam becomes a highly sought-after security force within the black community. It may have started with anticrack efforts, but the FOI, in their suits and bow ties, are soon doing security at rap concerts and community events and even working as personal bodyguards. In a national black community that is suspicious of local police (even if the city's mayor is black) yet is fearful of homegrown predators, the FOI are viewed by many as proud black champions of order.

APRIL 24   The Los Angeles Police Department conducts gang sweeps, a.k.a. "the Hammer" (so dubbed by Police Chief Daryl F. Gates), that roll through South Central arresting young black and brown people because they "look like" gang members. The LAPD arrest 1,453 during one weekend sweep.

In the *Los Angeles Times,* Gary Williams, an attorney for the American Civil Liberties Union and a South Central resident, wrestles with the implications of "the Hammer." Speaking of crack violence, Willliams writes, "This reign of terror is so complete that while inside my home I can regularly hear gunshots outside, even though the police station is less than a mile from my door. It is a reign so horrifying that I will not even sit out on my front porch at night for fear of being struck by a random bullet."

Like many black professionals, Williams is fully aware of the evil crack has unleashed. But, ultimately, Williams, like many of his peers, is suspicious of enforcement-based cures for societal problems involving blacks. "The more I thought about it, the more I was ashamed that I even had to pause to decide where I stand on this issue. . . . I do not want to see 'the Hammer' fall if the tactics employed include the indiscriminate detention and railroaded arrest of black youngsters because they look like gang members or because they happen to be in the wrong place at the wrong time."

Tracy Chapman does a showcase at the venerable Greenwich Village nightclub the Bitter End in support of her folkie eponymous debut album. With just a guitar, thick, nappy hair, a gorgeous smile, and a clear, powerful ringing bell of a voice, Chapman fills the small room with her songs of love, hate, and intolerance. Born and raised in Cleveland and a recent graduate of Tufts University, Chapman writes songs that are examples of a neo-hippie consciousness that echoes the past but is sharply contemporary. Chapman is ridiculed at a few R&B events for her appearance (the thick, nappy natural, T-shirts, jeans) as much as her music. The truth is Chapman's existence—her music, her style, her social consciousness—challenges narrow-minded views of black essentialism as much as hip hop does. Her "Fast Car" is a surprise pop hit, though the love songs ("Baby Can I Hold You") and political tracks ("Talkin' 'Bout a Revolution") are truer examples of her art. As a pop star and hippie fem icon, Chapman brings forth an alternative black identity that resonates.

JUNE Black radio this summer is dominated by a musical style dubbed "new jack swing" by writer Barry Michael Cooper. This blend of rap rhythms, funk keyboards, and R&B call and response is orchestrated by a Harlem teenager named Teddy Riley, whose handiwork is all over hit records by Bobby Brown, Today, Keith Sweat, Al B. Sure!, Guy, Heavy D, Kool Moe Dee, and others. Riley's deep, seemingly inexhaustible reservoir single-handedly makes R&B relevant again. While some old-school singers try to tap into Riley, it is young hip hop–generation singers who interpret new jack swing best.

Riley is a true Harlem product. As an adolescent he played piano and organ in local churches, while being mentored by ex-cons associated with the drug trade, including Gene Griffin, who serves as his manager. As a teen, Riley hung out at the Rooftop roller rink that was also home to a hip hop label, Rooftop Records. Many local talents performed at the rink (Kool Moe Dee, Biz Markie), while young crack dealers hung out and flaunted their wealth. It is in this ultimate mix of music and danger, celebration and greed, that Riley's artistic outlook is molded.

Versed in gospel chords, the swing beats of hip hop, and the gold-chain glitter of the street, Riley develops an approach that is as immediately identifiable as it is infectious. His impact on black music is so powerful that the two most accomplished producer-writer teams in R&B, Jimmy "Jam" Harris & Terry Lewis and Antonio "L.A." Reid & Kenny "Babyface" Edmonds, adopt some of Riley's techniques to stay competitive. As the new jack swing sound proliferates, the softer R&B sounds of Freddie Jackson, Luther Vandross, Lionel Ritchie, and others suddenly seem as dated as a '60s soul record. New jack swing effectively ends the careers of scores of acts, while making others the new black pop mainstream. Michael Jackson, too shrewd to let any trend pass him by, eventually recruits Riley to replace Quincy Jones as his primary producer.

Perhaps the singer to benefit the most from this new wave of R&B is Bobby Brown, whose *Don't Be Cruel* (released this month) establishes him as the first singing b-boy and confirms the star power he displayed with New Edition. Brown had made one uneventful post–New Edition solo album, *King of Stage,* before. So no one really expected that he would make the most danceable and passionate male R&B album since Jackson's *Off the Wall,* but this street kid from Boston inspires great work from the era's best young producers.

The centerpiece cut and first single is "My Prerogative," a new jack swing classic produced by Teddy Riley that has the testosterone intensity and self-glorifying lyrics of rap. In an era when black male singers rarely shout, Brown spits out an angry denunciation of those judging his behavior over a relentless Riley rhythm track.

The bulk of *Don't Be Cruel* is crafted by L.A. Reid and Babyface Edmonds, who write and produce the title cut as well as "Roni" and "Every Little Step." While not as aggressive as "My Prerogative," these well-composed songs played off the roughest of Brown's vocals, balancing sweetness and soul in a way that recalls the Temptations with David Ruffin singing lead.

B. Brown, as his friends call him, brings an earthy masculinity back to R&B, which was dominated in the '80s by androgynous stars with crooning voices. Brown is a roughneck sex symbol who one day surprises everyone by wooing, and winning, Whitney Houston.

JULY As part of its summer fiction issue, *Esquire* publishes "Men Who Are Good with Their Hands," a sharp, humorous short story by Terry McMillan about the love life of an unnamed female narrator. "Off and on in my life I've mistaken a good lay for love," she writes. "Who hasn't? . . . My instincts always told me that each one would be different—an improvement over the last one. Besides, I've always liked men who were good with their hands." It's a witty preview of her novel in progress.

JUNE 27 Mike Tyson knocks out Michael Spinks in ninety-one seconds in the highest-grossing fight in heavyweight history ($70 million). Mike earns $20 million and barely breaks a sweat.

JUNE 29 Eddie Murphy stars in *Coming to America.* This Hollywood fairytale of an African prince traveling to Queens in search of a bride, while directed by John Landis (*Animal House, Trading Places*), features more black characters on-screen than in all Murphy's previous films combined. Former *Good Times* star John Amos and Murphy buddy Arsenio Hall are very funny.

In a return to his *Saturday Night Live* roots, Murphy does several supporting roles in makeup and is hilarious as the lead singer in Sexual Chocolate, an awful soul band, and along with Hall, as a cantankerous old black barber. In terms of Murphy's leading man charm, his comic cameos, and the range of black talent involved, *Coming to America* is perhaps Murphy's most satisfying film to date.

Satisfying, that is, if you accept it as Hollywood entertainment. Many in the increasingly Afrocentric wing of the black community are not amused by the film's glossy, fanciful depiction of Africa. Murphy takes some lumps in the black media for *Coming to America*.

JULY Public Enemy releases *It Takes a Nation of Millions to Hold Us Back,* a sixteen-song, all-out sonic assault of block-rocking beats and nationalist politics. "Back then artists strove to be different," Chuck recalled about the album in *The Source* ten years later. "We dared to go where no one had gone before and said, 'Fuck it, nothing is going to match it in intensity.' We put it together like rock heads would do a rock album, and were able to perform each song better than it sounded [live]."

Around the time of the album's release, Chuck D begins saying the band's goal is to generate 5,000 black leaders. Another beautiful piece of propaganda is the idea that rap is "black CNN," which tells the stories white media doesn't. On both scores Chuck D is on point. In many buyers this record ignites interest in either political action (the antiapartheid movement), alternative organizations (the Nation of Islam), or black history (the Black Panthers, Malcolm X). *Nation* may not start a new black nationalist movement but, for many, it begins a fruitful internal insurrection that has them question American values.

Nation's lyrics are vivid, pointed, and dramatic, whether describing crack's destructive power ("Night of the Living Baseheads"), attacking the media ("Don't Believe the Hype"), or narrating the vivid tale of a prison break ("Black Steel in the Hour of Chaos"). With Flavor Flav taking the edge off Chuck D's strident delivery, *Nation* is one of the most affecting pieces of political pop ever made, inspiring a wave of other hip hop groups (the X Clan, Paris) and, later, the rap metal group Rage Against the Machine.

Nation is central to a moment in black youth culture when wearing African medallions and Kente fabric from West Africa and using the term "African American" is not simply politically correct, but hip. "Afrocentricity," a phrase popularized by Temple University professor Molefi Kete Asante, looks to African traditions and values as the way to interpret the contemporary black experience. The crisis that crack and AIDS are creating in urban America confirms the need for a fresh critique of racism and this nation's policies. *Nation* puts these ideas on radio and on MTV.

Of course, what makes *Nation* a hip hop masterpiece isn't simply its political agenda. Nothing in hip hop (or pop music history) has sounded quite like it. Chuck D has said, "The key [to the production] is we used a lot of techniques; the basic loop; make a beat then play bits of samples against the beat; sequencing the beat, the samples and a bass line together; and when you're making a record, you'll understand each one of those techniques has a different feel."

Nation was made in an era when the use of sampled material was still the Wild West—you only paid if you got caught. So the layering of samples, from James Brown to John Coltrane, creates a new thing. You can't always tell where the sounds come from, which confounds lawyers who wonder if a client's record is being used. With the exception of another album, *3 Feet High and Rising,* made by Long Islanders De La Soul, no single record extends sampling as an art form quite like *Nation.*

JULY 25 On the cover of Eric B. & Rakim's *Follow the Leader,* the hip hop duo sport Gucci outfits and more gold than Fort Knox. Their jackets are designed by Dapper Dan, an African-born, Harlem-based designer of knock-off outfits who takes top-shelf designer logos (Vuitton, Gucci, MCM) and molds them into hip hop fashion. How he obtains the fabric is not known (or asked about), but every major hip hop celebrity treks to his 125th Street outlet for outfits.

This same month, in front of Dapper Dan's, Mike Tyson has a confrontation with Mitch "Blood" Green, who he'd already defeated in a Madison Square Garden bout. After Green talks trash to the champ, Tyson smashes Green in the face, inflicting a more brutal on-the-street beating than he had in the ring. Tyson's bare hands strike Green so hard he breaks his right hand. And all Mike wanted was to pick up his custom-made "Don't Believe the Hype" jacket.

AUGUST 6 *Yo! MTV Raps!,* hosted by Fab Five Freddy and produced by future feature director Ted Demme, debuts on a Saturday afternoon. It is the first regularly scheduled national rap show and quickly gets the biggest ratings in the music channel's history. Later a daily show, hosted by Long Island MC and DJ Dr. Dre and aspiring rapper Ed Lover, is introduced, bringing hip hop into America's living rooms every afternoon after school and forcing rap records into MTV's rotation. It is no accident that the volume of rap albums sold begins to increase as rap (and black artists in general) finds MTV more receptive.

One of the sad ironies of *Yo! MTV Raps!* is that BET, a network that programs almost nothing but black music videos, doesn't create a competing show until next year and is beaten decisively in a market it could have owned.

AUGUST 12 Graffiti artist turned gallery god and sex symbol Jean-Michel Basquiat dies of a heroin overdose at age twenty-seven at an East Village apartment he is renting from Andy Warhol. Though some of his pieces sold for as much as $50,000 at the time of his death, many in the art world feel Basquiat's work has been in decline since his Warhol collaboration. There is a lot of debate after Basquiat's death about his artistic worth: Was he truly a painter for the ages, or the biggest hype of the overheated '80s art world?

SEPTEMBER Convicted rapist Willie Horton becomes the most famous black criminal of the year and a boon to the Republican party. A GOP attack ad referencing his early release from prison by Democratic candidate and Massachusetts governor Michael Dukakis uses Horton to symbolize America's fear of weak liberal politicians and unbridled black male sexuality. It is a devastatingly effective piece of political propaganda crafted by Lee Atwater, chairman of the Republican National Committee and a huge blues fan. Atwater's handiwork, though only sixty seconds long, is the postmodern equivalent of the racist silent epic *The Birth of a Nation* in the way it indicts Northern whites and sinister blacks. It's not the only reason Bush beats the impotent Dukakis, but it sure didn't help the Democratic cause.

The irony of this situation is that Atwater, because of his taste in music, seems to feel he has a special affinity for African Americans. He is even given a place on the board of trustees of Howard University and is later removed only after persistent student protest.

SEPTEMBER Debbie Allen, who started the decade as an actor and choreographer, has evolved into a respected TV producer and director. She is asked to take over *The Cosby Show* spin-off *A Different World,* which has faltered with Lisa Bonet as the lead. Allen reinvents this look at black college life by promoting three distinctive '80s types: Jasmine Guy's materialistic, misguided yet sweet Whitley, a quintessential BAP; Kadeem Hardison's Dwayne, a humorous, nerdy, kindhearted, proto-buppie man who bounces between caricature and integrity; and Cree Summer's

Freddie, Bonet's heir apparent as America's favorite bohemian black girl.

By bringing these relatively fresh types to national television, Allen gives *A Different World* an identity separate from *The Cosby Show* that makes it feel younger and, for a network show, somewhat hip. In Guy, Hardison (both from *School Daze*), and Summers (a native of Toronto), she showcases actors with good comic timing and distinctive looks. Though never as successful in the Nielsen ratings as *Cosby, A Different World* very much reflects the new energy in black America by balancing tradition (the black college setting) with new opportunities (the wide range of career opportunities and life experiences its characters obsess about).

SEPTEMBER 10 At the Dope Jam rap concert at Long Island's Nassau Coliseum, a young man, Julio Fuentes, is stabbed to death over his gold chain. In the wake of this tragedy and the media's use of the phrase "Rap Violence" to characterize it, a group of performers and industry figures organized by Jive Records vice president of artist development Ann Carli and *Billboard* editor Nelson George works on a pro–hip hop, antiviolence charity record. The loose collective calls itself the Stop the Violence Movement, after a song written by KRS-One. Over the winter the group works to record an all-star rap record, shoot a video, and choose a charity (the National Urban League) to donate the proceeds to. Despite the attacks on hip hop generated by the Long Island death (as well as other incidents), none of the black-owned hip hop labels are interested in releasing a charity record. It is Jive, owned by white South African Clive Calder, that agrees to finance the recording cost and market the single.

SEPTEMBER 20 On the field, the Summer Olympics in Seoul, Korea, are dominated by Florence "Flo Jo" Griffith-Joyner's fingernails (displayed as she triumphs in the 100- and 200-meter dashes) and Jackie Joyner-Kersee's determination (seen in her long jump and heptathlon triumphs).

Those viewing NBC's coverage also witness a confident performance by prime-time anchor Bryant Gumbel, working one of the plum assignments in sportscasting. In a *Washington Post* review of Gumbel, Norman Chad writes, "I had forgotten how surprisingly nasal his voice can be. I had forgotten how irritatingly pompous his style can be. I had forgotten how annoyingly all-knowing he can be. And I had forgotten that, among the few men and women who call the network studio their year-around home, there is no better host in the business. . . . He was born to host. He was born to take us into commercial. He was born to sort out the various venues and scenarios and make it flow, all the while with his legs cross and his pants pressed. His is a reassuring, calming presence like no other."

SEPTEMBER 21   Mike Tyson, Robin Givens, and her mother, Ruth Roper, appear on ABC's *20/20* with Barbara Walters. The champ is uncharacteristically subdued as Givens describes their marriage as "torture." Later it is revealed that Tyson took Thorazine and lithium at the urging of Givens prior to the taping.

It is the latest chapter in one of the most written-about celebrity marriages since Liz Taylor and Eddie Fisher. He accuses her of psychological manipulation; she claims he's beat her. The soap opera ends with each filing divorce papers. While Tyson becomes the sports page poster child for bad behavior, Givens is depicted in all media, but especially rap records, as the ultimate gold digger.

OCTOBER 7   In an effort to assert more control over what they hope will be a burgeoning film career, Run-D.M.C.'s members, along with manager Russell Simmons and producer Rick Rubin, finance the film *Tougher Than Leather*. At one point Simmons passes the script to Spike Lee, but Lee is not interested in the blaxploitation inspired project. Rubin, one of rap's most important producers, proves to be an inadequate director. Despite the presence of Run-D.M.C., the Beastie Boys, Slick Rick, and other MCs, *Tougher Than Leather* makes less than $5 million in a limited release.

Perhaps more important than the film itself is the entity that distributes it. New Line Cinema is a feisty independent film company that becomes famous for the *Nightmare on Elm Street* horror series. *Tougher*, however, opens a new chapter in the company's history, as it begins regularly financing urban films that feature rap stars and are helmed by black directors.

NOVEMBER A couple of white Harvard University students, John Schecter and Dave Mays, begin a hip hop newsletter/tip sheet they call *The Source*. Though based in Boston, the duo and a collection of other young hip hop heads begin building a solid following for their fanzine. At this point most serious coverage of hip hop occurs in alternative weeklies like *The Village Voice* and *The Boston Phoenix*. The mainstream music press coverage is now steady but far from comprehensive or consistent. *The Source* will eventually fill that void and spawn many imitators. But by being the first to cover hip hop seriously, and fanatically, Schecter and Mays build one of the culture's most valuable brands.

NOVEMBER 7 In a single bout, "Sugar Ray" Leonard wins his fourth and fifth boxing titles. After recovering from an early knockdown by Donny Lalonde, Leonard triumphs to capture the Canadian's WBC light heavyweight belt as well as the vacant super middleweight title. For winning his unprecedented five world titles in five weight classes, Leonard is named Fighter of the Decade by several magazines.

DECEMBER 7   D.C. Police Chief Maurice T. Turner Jr. says he doesn't think the city's Operation Clean Sweep, which has produced some 43,000 arrests since it was instituted in August '86, is "having any impact on the demand for drugs. Arrests are not the answer." Looking at crack as a public health—not a crime—issue is a growing trend. This year at D.C. General Hospital, 18 percent of all babies are delivered by crack-addicted mothers. Nationally, the number is 11 percent.

DECEMBER 20   Max Robinson, the first black anchorman on a TV network newscast, dies of AIDS at forty-nine. After his controversial Smith College speech in 1981, Robinson battles alcoholism and other illnesses. It isn't until 1987 that he is diagnosed with AIDS, making him the first mainstream black male figure to acknowledge having the disease. At his funeral, Reverend Jesse Jackson makes a point of emphasizing Robinson's heterosexuality. According to Jackson, Robinson told him, "On this bed and on this Bible, it was not homosexuality, it was promiscuity" that led to his infection.

Robinson, married three times, has a reputation for womanizing, drinking heavily, and drug use. The black establishment rallies around Robinson in his last years, supporting this TV pioneer financially and spiritually. A depressing aspect of this embrace is that as scores of poor, gay, or drug-addicted blacks die of AIDS, there is little public outcry or organizing by African American leaders.

By year's end the rate of new cases is falling among white homosexuals, but increasing among black and Latino gay men, and among intravenous drug users, a large percentage of whom are minority. Blacks and Hispanics make up only 20 percent of the total U.S. population, but 40 percent of AIDS cases. "There continues to be resistance to safer-sex proposals from blacks and Latinos," reports the *Los Angeles Times.* "And many in the minority organizations themselves have not made AIDS a high priority because of their preoccupation with other problems."

The black church, traditionally the crucial instigator of social change in the black community, is in particular slow to make HIV and AIDS a priority. At the time of his death, Robinson, like Magic Johnson later, is the kind of AIDS victim blacks feel comfortable mourning—accomplished and loudly straight.

Citizens of our post-soul nation: Front row (*left to right*) playwright/director George C. Wolfe, art curator Kelli Jones, film director Spike Lee, writer Lisa Jones, actress Alva Rogers, guitarist Vernon Reid. Second row (*left to right*) writer Nelson George, artist Lorna Simpson, rapper Run of Run-D.M.C., filmmaker Warrington Hudlin, record executive Bill Stephney, director/air personality Fab Five Freddy, novelist Trey Ellis. On the stairs (*in descending order*) Def Jam chairman Russell Simmons, director Reginald Hudlin, comic Chris Rock.

1989

1989

Reverend Jesse Jackson will never be president of the United States. In fact, Jackson will never hold elective office in his long and controversial career. Yet in the last twelve months of the '80s he proves he can still throw his weight around. There are two huge black electoral breakthroughs that the Jesse factor—in terms of energizing black voters—definitely affects. The November 7 elections of longtime Democratic pol David Dinkins by a slim margin as New York mayor over federal prosecutor Rudy Giuliani and of Douglas Wilder as the governor of Virginia are both aided by Jackson's endorsement and enthusiastic campaigning.

Dinkins, who was aided by New Yorkers' sensitivity over years of dicey racial incidents in the city, is elected as a calming presence for a combustible town. Jews, in particular, favor him over the combustible federal prosecutor Rudolph Giuliani and help him raise $2.9 million for his campaign. Wilder's victory makes him the nation's first black governor since the 1800s. It is perhaps the greatest black electoral achievement of the post–civil rights era. But Wilder's win isn't all about race. As the unanimous choice of the Virginia state Democratic party, Wider wins running on a strong pro-choice platform in a Southern state balanced between old-fashioned values and the influence on its growing population of more liberal Northern transplants.

Both Dinkins and Wilder have gracious, almost courtly demeanors that match their gray hair and liberal to moderate pronouncements. Call it the *"Driving Miss Daisy* effect" in that both, like Morgan Freeman's dignified driver in the recent hit movie, make whites feel enough at ease that they are able to overcome their innate fear of giving a black person power over their lives. Wilder's honeysuckle charm is crucial in enabling him to woo enough Virginia-bred whites, as well as the state's growing number of expatriate northerners, to win where the nationally better known Tom Bradley of Los Angeles had failed.

Whatever the limitations of Jackson as a leader, which will become more apparent in the '90s, his two runs for president do prove him a rainmaker who raises issues the white candidates ignore and, for a time, makes black voters more optimistic about the potential of mainstream political power.

Jackson's ability to attract voters is also on the minds of the Democratic National Committee when they appoint Ron Brown chairman. A canny and smooth politician, Brown, who has been a close Jackson advisor, goes his own way as chairman, eventually helping to blunt Jackson's power within the party and aiding the rise of William Jefferson Clinton, the two-time governor of Arkansas.

In his now universally acknowledged role as black America's leader, Jackson doesn't just get behind candidates, but supports a profound change in nomenclature. Instead of calling themselves "black," Jackson advocates that people descended from African slaves should call themselves "African American," a phrase that's been circulating for years. (At one point in the '70s "Afro-American" had been in vogue but didn't stick.)

Now, in 1989, a time of great identification with Africa, "African American" gains momentum. Carl T. Rowan, an old-school civil rights political columnist, is peeved by the notion, recalling that "exactly 16 years ago" frustrated leaders convinced the Negro masses to call themselves "black." Rowan sniffs, "There are a lot of things we black Americans must do, some of sacrifice and pain, some difficult, if we are to lift the sons and daughters of African heritage to a point where they can cope and compete in this land. But what's in a name? Nothing."

Roger Wilkins, another venerable civil rights activist and son of Roy Wilkins, one of the NAACP's most famous leaders, embraces the new handle in a *Washington Post* editorial: "The fantasy, writ large across the land in the popular culture of Tarzan movies, the Sambo story and songs nostalgic for the good old South, was that bad as slavery might have been, the Africans sort of brought it on themselves by being so savage and from such a backward place. . . . We had to purge all that garbage from our spirits. . . . One good way to start was to understand that before the European invasion of Africa five centuries ago, the people from whom we got the contours of our lips and the curl in our hair walked their land in their way and arranged their lives according to their own lights."

The majority of blacks in the United States side with Jackson and Wilkins, adopting the "African American" identification either in lieu of or in conjunction with "black." Rowan is right in that this change had no tangible effect on our economic or political status, while causing social confusion for many whites who, for several years, aren't sure which is the politically correct term.

But as an affirmation of Africa, of our pre-slavery past, and as a tool for seeing our existence in a broader, international sense, African American is psychologically helpful. Its widespread adoption is one triumph Reverend Jackson can unequivocally claim.

JANUARY 3 *The Arsenio Hall Show* debuts with the comic making the street slang "Let's get busy!" part of the pop lexicon and bringing new jack flavor to late night television. The thirty-year-old comic's journey to being the first ever black late night television host was long. Raised in Cleveland, Hall began his career on the black club circuit before coming to Los Angeles and working white comedy clubs like the Comedy Store and the Improv. His first regular national exposure comes in the mid-'80s as comic relief on *Solid Gold,* a cheesy show on which current pop hits are interpreted by dancers. Hall didn't come off well on the broadcast but *Solid Gold* gives him a platform at a time when few black comics are being booked on *The Tonight Show Starring Johnny Carson.*

In the mid-'80s he falls in with a set of black comedians who hang around Eddie Murphy. It is that association that leads to his appearance on the HBO Uptown Comedy Express, his mention by Murphy as part of the "black pack," and his supporting role in *Coming to America.* Hall enters the talk show world as a critically acclaimed replacement for Joan Rivers after she exits Fox's sinking *The Late Show.*

When that run ends it is only a matter of time before Hall ends up with his own late night show. Aside from Johnny Carson and, to a lesser degree, his replacement Jay Leno, and David Letterman doing his *Late Night,* no one had really figured out how to make the format's mix of talk, humor, and music work. To his credit, Hall concocts his own distinctive mix of insider jokes, flirtatious women guests, and urban edge. Before *Arsenio* the swelling tidal wave of new black pop didn't have a broadcast television home. Hall's presence means that five nights a week, his sofa is a safe haven for major black crossover stars (Murphy, Oprah, Prince, Whitney Houston, Magic Johnson) and the scores of personalities bubbling under. One of Hall's biggest beneficiaries is MC Hammer, the Oakland rapper-dancer who has made some noise but is by no means a national star. In promoting an upcoming MC Hammer appearance, Hall constantly makes reference to his song "U Can't Touch This" and the hot video that is already burning up MTV and BET.

By the time Hammer and a huge crew of dancers take to Arsenio's large, glossy set, the pop pump has been primed and Hammer delivers a sweat-drenched, dynamic performance that excites non-rap fans. For Hammer, who goes on to sell eight million copies of his second album (*Please Hammer, Don't Hurt 'Em*), being on

Arsenio proves as important as Michael Jackson's appearance on *Motown 25*.

Another star who blows up after an *Arsenio* appearance is Bill Clinton. As a wanna-be presidential candidate in '92, the man from Arkansas pulls out his sax and jams with Arsenio's house band. While it doesn't win Clinton the election, it sure earns him cool points that make many younger nonvoters pay closer attention.

Unfortunately Arsenio's late night cool doesn't last. The talk show is only on for four seasons and ends on a controversial note when Hall decides to have Minister Farrakhan on as a guest, enraging enough white station managers and power brokers to put the already faltering show on life support. It was last broadcast on May 27, 1994. Yet Hall's legacy lingers on as both Leno and Letterman loosen up their booking policies, adding more black music and allowing more black guests to chat while resting their backsides on those very exclusive couches. Several others would try their own version of the *Arsenio* show (Magic Johnson, Keenan Ivory Wayans, *Vibe* magazine with Chris Spencer), but no one has gotten as busy as Hall.

In this same year Hall's buddy Hammer redefines what hip hop success can be even as he alienates the music's hard-core fans. Hammer, a.k.a. Stanley Kirk Burrell, has been a fixture on the vibrant Oakland rap scene for years with his blend of choppy rhymes and dynamic dancing. New York–based A&R people are very familiar with the pushy yet polite MC from music biz conferences, but no one thinks his MC "skills" merit a record deal.

After releasing material independently in the Bay Area, Hammer is finally signed by a major, Los Angeles–based Capitol, which has until then been only a bit player in hip hop. "U Can't Touch This," a simple catchphrase rhyme that rides a sample of Rick James's "Super Freak," explodes on pop radio like no rap record ever has before.

There has never been a rap act who can dance like Hammer. With his kinetic videos and elaborately choreographed concerts (there are often as many as twenty dancers on stage), Hammer merges a Michael Jackson–styled extravaganza with rap rhymes, bringing eager-to-please show biz glitz to a genre that defines itself as antiglitter. This synthesis makes Hammer's *Please Hammer, Don't Hurt 'Em* the number-one album in the country for twenty-one weeks and wins him a slew of endorsement deals (Taco Bell, Pepsi) that, for about two years, make him a commercial pitchman to rival Bill Cosby.

There has also never been an MC whose music is as disliked by others in hip hop. While L.L. Cool J's personality is the chief reason he finds himself being dissed, no one really questions his MC skills. In contrast, Hammer is collectively disdained by the New York hip hop community for his genie pants, cheesy smile, and rudimentary rhymes. The white tap duo Third Base disses Hammer lustily in their video for "Pop Goes the Weasel."

But while the self-appointed gatekeepers of rap have a problem with Hammer, Vanilla Ice makes them absolutely crazy. A tall, handsome dirty blond, Ice tells reporters he's grown up hard in Dade County's ghetto streets. Aided by a team of black producers and rappers, Ice follows the Hammer formula (dancing-heavy video, simple repetitive hook, obvious sample). His "Ice Ice Baby" uses the hook from the great Queen–David Bowie collaboration "Under Pressure" to underscore a video that features a dance routine taken from black fraternity step shows. Vanilla Ice is a real teen idol who taps into the horny market of pubescent girls who usually go for boy bands and don't care if he is a whack MC. Even Madonna, a sexual saleswoman of the highest order, falls (albeit briefly) for the Iceman.

Over time Vanilla Ice's street bio falls apart. Turns out his real name is Robert Van Winkle and he was actually raised in Dallas with a safely middle-class upbringing. Ice's desire for hip hop credibility speaks to a shift in pop aesthetics such that even white boys seek identification with the black underclass. Where the Beastie Boys are smart white kids who love hip hop, Ice (and the many who come after) attempt to somehow submerge their whiteness into a caricatured vision of authentic ghetto blackness. Though Ice is ultimately unmasked as a wanna-be, the idea of marketing one-self as a product of the urban underclass is one of '80s hip hop's silliest legacies.

JANUARY 12 Keenan Ivory Wayans's *I'm Gonna Get Ya Sucka* premieres at New York's Loew's Astor Plaza. Wayans establishes himself as a major comic talent by directing, writing, and starring in this blaxploitation parody. Wayans displays raw humor and a taste for elaborate sight gags as he guides an excellent cast (Damon Wayans, Kadeem Hardison, Anne-Marie Johnson, Jim Brown, Isaac Hayes, Antonio Fargas, Dawnn Lewis). Chris Rock makes a memorable cameo trying to buy one rib at a soul food restaurant.

FEBRUARY DJ Jazzy Jeff & the Fresh Prince win the first ever rap Grammy, for *Parents Just Don't Understand*. As part of a boycott staged by Rush Management, Jazzy Jeff and Will Smith, along with many other MCs, don't attend the awards show. It takes years of lobbying by industry pros and the media for this category to be created and it will be years before the award winners have any relationship to quality in rap music.

FEBRUARY 14 Stop the Violence Movement's press conference and march starts with the carrying of a coffin from the Apollo Theater to the State Office Building across 125th Street and ends with addresses by Chuck D and KRS-One. The record and video for the song "Self-Destruction" is already out on Jive (it was released on Dr. King's birthday) and is one of the first all-star posse cuts:

Public Enemy; KRS-One; Heavy D; Daddy-O, Fruitkwan, and Delite of Stetsasonic; Just-Ice; Doug E. Fresh; MC Lyte (with a rhyme co-written by L.L. Cool J); Kool Moe Dee; D-Nice and Ms. Melody of Boogie Down Productions.

"Self-Destruction," along with a book (*Stop the Violence: Overcoming Self-Destruction*) and a home video, earns over $400,000 that is donated to the National Urban League. It is one of the rare instances of hip hop and an institution of the old soul culture interacting. Throughout the record making and money counting process there is much suspicion on both sides. Yet many of the MCs appear at National Urban League events and the money is funneled toward programs aimed at black youth.

"Self-Destruction" inspires a similar record made by West Coast Rap All-Stars and called "All in the Same Gang," and a lot of conversation about black-on-black crime. However, despite the good intentions of both efforts, the criminal ethos of crack is flowing deeply into the rap game. Not only are gangsta rhymes being kicked, but actual gangstas are financing recording sessions and, in a few cases, even rapping themselves. The Stop the Violence Movement is very much a product of an Afrocentric, politically conscious, Malcolm X revering moment. For much of the early '90s a chaotic "start the violence" movement dominates.

FEBRUARY 27   A book party for Arthur Ashe's *Hard Road to Glory* is held at 75 Rockefeller Center. The former tennis star wrote and compiled the most comprehensive history to date of African American athletes. Though distributed by Warner Books, Ashe volumes are published by black-owned Amistad Press, a reflection of the soft-spoken hero's political consciousness. At this time few know that the frail-looking author is HIV positive. Ashe's final memoir, *Days of Grace,* chronicles his life and acceptance of death.

MARCH Both *The Washington Post* and *The New York Times* print articles on the growth of Afrocentric teaching in public and private schools nationwide. The *Times* reports, "Administrators in several cities in which the student population is largely black or becoming so . . . are considering or are beginning to use the multicultural approach. In these districts, teachers and textbooks emphasize black American and African history and the contributions of blacks in art, science, math, language arts, social studies and music."

Both newspaper stories use the same example of Afrocentric teaching: most Americans know that Thomas Edison invented the lightbulb, but few know that Garrett Morgan, a black man, invented the traffic light.

APRIL 13 Charles Lewis, former D.C. personnel worker, son of a prominent Virgin Islands politician, accused drug dealer, and friend of Mayor Marion Barry, is indicted for cocaine possession. Back in December 1988, Lewis stayed at a local Ramada Inn where Barry visited him on at least six occasions. On December 22, D.C. police visited Lewis's room when a maid complained that Lewis had offered her cocaine. Apparently *The Washington Post* has been tipped about the mayor's visits but the D.C. police have not questioned their boss. Before Lewis is indicted, Barry testifies twice before a D.C. grand jury. In a face-saving gesture, Barry takes a drug test, releasing the negative result to local radio stations. After Lewis's arrest, some in D.C. ask for the mayor's resignation. He tells reporters he's too busy fighting crime. This back-and-forth between the mayor and his critics goes on for the rest of the year, shifting attention from D.C.'s horrific crack problem to whether the mayor is a crackhead.

MAY In American life physical affection between two men is traditionally restricted to a hearty handshake in business or a chaste hug among relatives. Only those fey Europeans kiss. So when Los Angeles Laker Magic Johnson and Detroit Piston Isiah Thomas exchange cheek kisses before several games of the NBA finals, it causes a stir.

This is just not done. The men are close friends, yes. They travel together in the off-season, yes. But only your father kisses you and that is only until you are eight or nine. That two of the most respected athletes in the nation are displaying mouth-to-skin affection in this way is quite a spectacle.

Whatever bond the two share doesn't stop them from competing fiercely through an intense seven-game series. In fact, during game five, Johnson delivers a vicious midair hit on Thomas that further injures an already damaged back. This smackdown comes after Johnson complains that his Laker teammates are too passive in response to the proudly physical Detroit "bad boys." That Johnson's good buddy Thomas has just become a father the day before makes no difference to the Laker star.

Playing in pain, Thomas comes back with a heroic forty-three-point performance in game six of the series. However, ultimately, Johnson's Lakers prevail in game seven, becoming the first NBA team since the 1969 Boston Celtics to win back-to-back titles.

MAY EEOC chairman Clarence Thomas is nominated for a seat on the U.S. Federal Appeals Court that has been vacant since February, when Robert Bork resigned in the wake of his failed Supreme Court nomination. Thomas is the first black nominee for that prestigious court in a decade. The Appeals Court is considered second in importance only to the Supreme Court, because its rulings on regulatory cases and other federal government matters have national impact.

"Clarence has been the first choice of conservatives for elevation in some context in the Bush administration since George Bush won the election," said Patrick McGuigan, of the conservative think tank Free Congress Foundation. "It's probably a safe assumption that judicially he will fall into the conservative wing of that court."

MAY 12 *See No Evil, Hear No Evil* is the third and final collaboration between Gene Wilder and Richard Pryor. It is now widely known that Pryor is suffering from MS, and watching the film it is apparent the disease is inhibiting him. This woeful enterprise is Pryor's last starring role.

MAY 12 The New York City Transit Authority announces the last graffiti-covered subway car is being removed from service today. The NYCTA has developed graffiti-proof subway trains that end the era of car-long graffiti tags and painted windows passengers can't see out of. While rap grows into a career move for urban teens, hip hop's other art forms wane in exposure and popularity. Graffiti doesn't die nor does it completely disappear (in fact, in Europe it gets bigger), but the days of huge graffiti displays on urban transportation end in America.

MAY 22 Public Enemy's Professor Griff uses anti-Semitic dogma to describe the Jewish religion in a *Washington Times* interview, telling black reporter David Mills that Jews "were responsible for the majority of the wickedness that goes on across the globe."

Jews and others urge Chuck to fire Griff and denounce his remarks. Many in the black community, still smarting from Jesse Jackson's "Hymietown" fallout, want Chuck to resist any impulse to remove Griff and to stand up to the pressure. Chuck instead opts to suspend Griff for, essentially, speaking out of turn. Chuck's logic is that Griff violated group discipline with his statements. What Chuck doesn't do is renounce the content of the remarks or his longtime friend.

This compromise doesn't satisfy those on either side but, as controversy does for many pop stars, only makes Public Enemy seem more important, more germane, more essential to the time. While P.E. will never sell as many records as Michael Jackson or even Prince, they are just as culturally important. Public Enemy, off- and on-record, are engaged with all the issues of the moment. Even Griff's gaffe, as thoughtless as it was, once more makes P.E. central to a testy debate—in this case, the state of black-Jewish relations. And the year is far from over.

JUNE De La Soul's *3 Feet High and Rising* on Tommy Boy charts a whimsical new direction for hip hop. This Long Island trio has fanciful names (Posdnous, Trugoy the Dove, Pasemaster Mace); playful, intricate rhymes; and delightfully layered beats and samples, courtesy of producer Prince Paul. The result is a surreal, highly intelligent, clearly nerdy approach to hip hop that attracts scores of adherents. One representative track is "Eye Know," an irresistible love rhyme back when they are still rare, that is anchored by samples from two unlikely sources—soul legend Otis Redding and pop-rockers Steely Dan. These combinations of subject and sound make De La Soul markedly different from everyone else.

For a time De La Soul is the centerpiece of a loosely connected group of MCs, dubbed the Native Tongues Posse, that includes Queen Latifah, the Jungle Brothers, A Tribe Called Quest, Monie Love, and Leaders of the New School. In a general sense, the Native Tongues–affiliated acts bring an Afrocentric consciousness, untraditional topics, and rhyme cadences to rap. Sparked by De La Soul, this vision of hip hop lingers, influencing groups like Black Star, Black Eyed Peas, and J-Live and the Jurassic 5 well into the twenty-first century.

For the listener uninterested in crack-inspired rhymes, De La Soul speaks to the possibilities of a more utopian, nonconfrontational approach to hip hop and life itself. In its way, *3 Feet High and Rising* and the trio's subsequent work are as much a response to the clichés of ghettocentric black pop as Tracy Chapman or Living Colour are.

Queen Latifah's *All Hail the Queen,* released in November and also on Tommy Boy, is less formally radical than De La Soul's debut. Its beats and samples are more conventional, but Queen Latifah is not. This New Jersey–based MC introduced herself with a strong, assertive flow, a Kente crown, and confident, womanist lyrics. Unlike previous female MCs, Latifah doesn't act like a tomboy or a sexy vamp. She is, in a very stylized yet accessible way, a progressive young black woman who doesn't fit into any of the preconceived boxes. A duet with the UK rapper Monie Love, "Ladies First," becomes the first true feminist MC anthem.

Latifah's personality is so forceful that even without huge hits (she doesn't sell over 500,000 copies of an album until into the '90s), her public profile is quite high. She forms a production company and record label called Flavor Unit Entertainment that fosters great talent (Naughty By Nature) as well as her leap into TV (the Fox sitcom *Living Single,* a daytime talk show) and acting, which results in a best supporting actress Academy Award nomination for *Chicago* in 2003.

JUNE 12 A book party is held at B. Smith's for journalist Bebe Moore Campbell's memoir about her father, titled *Sweet Summers.* Moore makes the transition from successful magazine journalist to author by writing an affirmative look at the most important black man in her life. In the '90s this Los Angeles–based scribe will write several best-selling novels featuring middle-class, college-educated women dealing with a rich tapestry of issues, including relations with their white female coworkers, their working-class brothers, and fragile members of their own group. Moore

becomes one of the voices writing the experience of newly em-
powered white-collar black women.

JUNE 23 Batman opens with a score composed by
Prince. The film, directed by the eccentric and visionary Tim Bur-
ton, is both an entertaining popcorn movie and a meditation on
urban paranoia that strikes a chord with the public, earning
$251 million and turning the vintage comic book hero into a movie
franchise. Prince's music for *Batman* is not as easily accessible as
his *Purple Rain* work, but it services the playfully evil undertone of
the film. His standout composition is "Scandalous," an epic of overt
seduction.

The *Batman* album is Prince's last pure pop moment. Over the
next few years, he moves from Warner Bros. corporate star to un-
happy rebel, a change that dovetails with (or causes) a slump in
his media profile and record sales. No other pop star of the decade
has been as consistently musically innovative, conceptually provocative, and plain old fun to watch perform as the man known (for the
time being) as Prince Rogers Nelson.

JUNE 30 Spike Lee's *Do the Right Thing* opens to controversy. Film critic David Denby and political writers Stanley
Crouch and Joe Klein attack this film about twenty-four hours on
a Bedford-Stuyvesant block as muddled and dangerous. "If some
audiences go wild, he is partly responsible," Denby writes in *New
York Magazine*. Because the film references the Tawana Brawley
"rape" and the Howard Beach incident, *Do the Right Thing* arrives
in theaters carrying heavy political baggage.

Thankfully, Vincent Canby cuts through the bull in his *New
York Times* review: "In all of the earnest, solemn, humorless dis-
cussions about the social and political implications of Spike Lee's
Do the Right Thing, an essential fact tends to be overlooked: it is

one terrific movie." Canby notes this "is a big movie. Though the action is limited to one more or less idealized block in Bed-Stuy, the scope is panoramic. It's a contemporary 'Street Scene.' It has the heightened reality of theater, not only in its look but also in the way the lyrics of the songs on the soundtrack become natural extensions of the furiously demotic, often hugely funny dialogue."

Spike has a fondness for Scorsese and M-G-M musicals that he somehow manages to integrate into this film via music-driven montages, characters flinging racial epithets at the audience, clearly artificial storefronts, lovingly photographed sweat, and unexpected eruptions of violence. Occasionally Bill Lee's score competes with the dialogue, but Spike's manipulation of Public Enemy's "Fight the Power" is brilliant. Rap becomes a staple of American films but rarely is it used with the same thematic effectiveness Lee employs in *Do the Right Thing*.

Comparing this film to *School Daze* is like watching a great basketball player in high school and then as a pro. Spike's command of the medium has grown tremendously since his second film, as if every mistake made on that project has been analyzed and corrected. Despite the controversy, the film earns $27 million, makes most ten-best lists, and lingers in the national memory.

AUGUST Terry McMillan publishes her breakthrough novel, *Disappearing Acts*. The book, which features alternating chapters in the voice of Zora (named after Zora Neale Hurston), a schoolteacher who wants to be a singer, and Franklin, a hunky construction worker, creates a template for a wave of commercial black literature that will explode in the '90s.

McMillan taps into the ongoing relationship conflicts between black men and women over commitment, money, and parenthood. Class plays a crucial role as the ambitions and possibilities of Zora and Franklin clash, reflecting the schism between college-educated black women and their potential working-class mates. McMillan writes with an earthy wit, an ear for self-deception, and a common touch that makes *Disappearing Acts* a must-read in black America. By having much of the narrative told by a black male, McMillan blunts much (but not all) criticism that the book is just another example of black male-bashing. "I have about had it with how negatively we supposedly portray black men in our work, because it gets on my nerves that people think of us as sociologists or anthropologists," she tells *Newsday*. "I was trying to portray him [Franklin] as realistically as I could to get the reader to understand what his frustration is, but at the same time not whip out the violins." Though McMillan goes on to enjoy massive crossover success with her next novel, *Waiting to Exhale*, there is a nuanced humanity to the mismatched lovers of *Disappearing Acts* that makes it her most affecting work.

AUGUST 23 Sixteen-year-old Yusef Hawkins is shot dead after being chased and beaten by a mob of white youths in the predominantly Italian Brooklyn neighborhood of Bensonhurst. The locals had been incited when they heard a black guy was coming to a white girl's birthday party in the 'hood. Hawkins actually had traveled to Bensonhurst seeking a deal on a used car.

Coming in the middle of a heated Democratic primary, Hawkins's death becomes topic one. Black candidate David Dinkins visits the family and blames incumbent mayor Ed Koch for the climate of hate in the city. While the attack helps Dinkins's pleas for racial unity, it also becomes the latest platform for Al Sharpton. The notorious reverend organizes a protest march through Bensonhurst that attracts tons of media coverage. Sharpton is routinely attacked by the mainstream media. Yet when black families feel abused by white authority, they increasingly look to the reverend to voice their anger. David Dinkins is just months away from becoming mayor of the world's most important city, while Sharpton builds the constituency that makes him a national figure.

A huge rally is held on 125th Street in front of the State Office Building, marking Hawkins's death. It is a youth-driven event at which many of rap's biggest stars speak and perform. Most are applauded, but L.L. Cool J actually hears some boos, a sign of the audience's intense love-hate relationship with this versatile artist.

AUGUST 26 A *TV Guide* cover story asks the question: "Oprah! The Richest Woman on TV?" The article details the growth of her fortune, from earning $2 million in '86, $12 million in '87, and $25 million in '88. The article estimates that the thirty-five-year-old TV host makes $40 million annually and has a net worth of $250 million. It is a long way from *A.M. Chicago*.

SEPTEMBER The Federal Bureau of Investigation sends a threatening letter to Priority Records about N.W.A.'s "Fuck tha Police." Similar letters are sent out to police departments in the cities where the rap group is about to perform. While it later turns out the letter was the work of one racist federal white agent, the letter's existence speaks to the increasing fears among some elements of the white community over the influence rappers are having on America. "Fuck tha Police" will one day be seen not simply as another example of chief lyricist Ice Cube's flair for nihilistic protest, but as a street prophecy of the fallout from years of repressive policing of black communities in general, and about street life in L.A. quite specifically. At the time the letter is discovered, many left-wing writers run it as an example of Big Brotherism of America. For N.W.A. it is just more proof that, at this moment, they are truly "the world's most dangerous band" and that L.A. gangsta rap is just beginning to create its mythology of bravado and martyrdom.

SEPTEMBER Art Shell, a longtime All-Pro Bowl offensive lineman, now walks the sidelines for the Oakland Raiders as the first black National Football League head coach since Fritz Pollard in the '20s. Shell breaks through by moving up the assistant coaching ranks and being loyal to the Raider organization (and its legendarily demanding owner, Al Davis). The fact that Shell becomes a mediocre coach is probably for the best. It shows that opportunity doesn't necessarily have to be given to a great or innovative African American for it to be significant. Whatever his limitations as a head man, Shell's tenure opens the door for other black head coaches to be hired in the NFL.

OCTOBER Researchers at the National Center for Infectious Diseases suggest that crack cocaine is partly responsible for the spread of the AIDS virus because it leads to both promiscuity and sex-for-drugs trades. The observation is made that crack houses are becoming the heterosexual equivalent of the gay bathhouse of the early '80s, when the HIV virus was widely transmitted. The nearly genocidal numbers of HIV-infected heterosexual black women that we see in the twenty-first century have their roots in the crack houses of the '80s. This vicious drug, which has laid waste to many good people and once livable neighborhoods, continues to bedevil black America like a true force of evil years after its introduction.

OCTOBER "Neon" Deion Sanders, a.k.a. "Prime Time," a fast, flashy, hip hop generation athlete, joins Bo Jackson as a two-sport star. After playing his rookie season as a part-time outfielder with the New York Yankees, Sanders joins the Atlanta Falcons as a starting cornerback. Sanders had been a game-breaking cornerback-punt returner at Florida State while also playing in the College World Series for the school and qualifying for the 1988 Olympic Trials as a sprinter.

The Florida native's athleticism is enough to attract attention, but Sanders decides he wants to be more than just another player. Drawing upon Muhammad Ali's boastfulness and hip hop cockiness, Sanders creates the Neon Deion persona, which involves trash-talking, adopting a self-satisfied demeanor, and wearing as many gold chains as his neck can hold. Sanders is the first athletic superstar in a team sport (Tyson is the first in an individual sport) to match rap's bravado with athletic excellence. He finds a kindred spirit in rapper MC Hammer, who produces Sander's feeble rap single, "Must Be the Money."

Just as Sanders had hoped, big contracts, endorsement deals, and mad celebrity come his way. Though nowhere near as good a baseball player as Bo Jackson, Sanders does become a feared cornerback and a key part of Super Bowl champion teams in San Francisco and Dallas. The Neon Deion persona is the harbinger of a type of athletic star, now typical, then new—the hip hop jock.

OCTOBER After a decade of every-increasing literary excellence by the womanist wing of black literature, a reactionary grassroots literary book emerges as an underground hit. Shahrazad Ali's *The Blackman's Guide to Understanding the Blackwoman* is a best-seller at black-owned bookstores and Afrocentric cultural centers as its Philadelphia-based author articulates a deeply conservative (downright misogynist) view of black women.

Ali writes, "The Blackman and the Blackwoman in America have a problem. They do not get along. Before the Blackman can devise a solution he must know the components of the problem. The first factor is that the Blackwoman is out of control. She does not submit to guidance by her God-given mate the Blackman. Her intention to overpower and subdue the Blackman is motivated by several factors, the most prevalent being her self-inflicted nearly psychotic insecurity."

OCTOBER In the winter issue of *Callaloo* magazine, young novelist Trey Ellis writes an essay titled "The New Black Aesthetic." Originally commissioned by *The New York Times Maga-zine*, the article extends the ideas of Greg Tate's earlier *Village Voice* piece on the generational change in black art. Ellis describes young black artists who "grew up feeling misunderstood by both black worlds and the white. Alienated (junior) intellectuals, we are the more and more blacks getting back into jazz and the blues; the only ones you see at punk concerts; the ones in the bookstore wearing little round glasses and short, neat dreads; some of the only blacks who admit liking both Jim and Toni Morrison."

Ellis further defines his theory by stating, "Though as an aes-thetic the NBA might not be any newer than Ms. Morrison's *Song of Solomon* (1978), yet as a movement we finally have the num-bers to leverage this point of view. For the first time in our history we are producing a critical mass of college graduates who are chil-dren of college graduates themselves. Like most artistic booms, the NBA is a post-bourgeois movement driven by a second generation of middle class." Ellis cites Wynton Marsalis, Eddie Murphy, Spike Lee's *She's Gotta Have It* and *School Daze*, George Wolfe's *The Col-ored Museum*, Terry McMillan's *Mama*, and the rock bands Living Colour and Fishbone as signature examples of the NBA.

Ellis's optimism is not misplaced—as the '80s have evolved there is no question there are profound changes of attitude and artistic temperament afoot. But that's not all that's happened. These changes are too sweeping and intricate just to be defined under the banner of generational change, since they involve shifts in government policy and social transformations in black behav-ior. The most immediately marketable aspects of '80s black cul-ture (hip hop, relationship-based literature) got institutional support first within the African American community and then from corporations that bought into them. But other cultural move-ments born in this period (black rock, truly independent black film) find growth difficult in the coming decade.

OCTOBER 16   *The Nation* publishes *Eyes on the Prizes, Not the People,* by Los Angeles writer-activist Susan Anderson, a piece that succinctly captures the simmering conflict between black leadership and lower-class blacks. Anderson writes, "Even today affirmative action, fair housing, integrated education and voting rights have become the means for only the most privileged or ambitious minorities to gain access to the limited 'opportunities' with the system. The legal and statutory standards that were won by the black freedom movement, as besieged as they are today, are the result of a profound compromise by mainstream black leaders, who withheld any deeper criticism of the economic structure of the nation as long as blacks were 'equally' represented in it. Representation, however, pertained only to 'qualified' blacks. That compromise, with all its class bias, is the hidden reality in black politics today."

Anderson concludes, "If there is to be a renewal of black politics, it will depend upon the ability of leaders to embrace the cause of the poor, and in so doing, challenge the economic order, which creates poverty as casually as it amasses wealth. . . . Such an effort, however, is not likely to come from complacent or corrupt black politicians preoccupied with their own political survival. . . . The civil rights movement, after all, was launched from the seat of a bus, not the seat of political power."

NOVEMBER   The 1990 Sundance Film Festival, the nation's most important platform for indie film, accepts three black feature films (Wendell Harris's *Chameleon Street,* Reggie Hudlin's *House Party,* Charles Burnett's *To Sleep with Anger*), as well as Jennie Livingston's documentary, *Paris Is Burning,* about New York's black gay subculture, and names black critic Armond White to its panel of judges.

The festival, held in January, is a major coming-out party for black directors. Harris's idiosyncratic film, based loosely on the life of two black hustlers, wins the Grand Jury Prize (though it gets only limited theatrical distribution). Hudlin's *House Party,* based on his studio short made at Harvard, wins the filmmakers' trophy (voted by directors) and the award for best cinematography. This delightful film employs two semiskilled but engaging rappers (Kid 'N Play), two great comedians (Robin Harris, Martin Lawrence), and a slew of up-and-coming actors to capture the "party hearty" spirit that inspires hip hop. *House Party* is the most successful film to date tapping into hip hop (it costs $2 million and grosses $28 million for New Line Cinema). After *House Party,* the most important films with hip hop flavor will tap the culture's dark side.

Burnett, whose 1977 film, *Killer of Sheep,* is viewed as one of the most artistically important black indie films ever, wins special jury recognition for the brooding *To Sleep with Anger.* Danny Glover, executive producer of the film, who used his *Lethal Weapon* clout to raise money, plays a Southern trickster whose evil ways almost destroy a stable Los Angeles family. The ghosts of Africa by way of the Deep South inform this parable of how the past can strangle the present. Burnett brings the serious ambition of the original L.A. black indie scene of the '70s into the new age. Though it's not widely released, *To Sleep with Anger* suggests the potential of black film to articulate the range of African American experience as literature and music do. The daunting question *Anger* raises is, will other black filmmakers have the skill and funding to follow Burnett's lead?

Livingston's film brings the spirited world of "the children," a.k.a. black transvestites, to the screen with all its humor, pageantry, and pathos. With the exposure this film gives to "snap queens," their appropriation of mainstream styles (they jokingly call competing groups "the House of Chanel," "the House of St. Laurent") and their posing, a.k.a. "voguing," style of dance leak into mainstream culture in advertising, movies, and music, with Madonna one of those significantly influenced by the *Paris Is Burning* attitude.

The film *Glory* opens. Director Ed Zwick is best known for producing and writing ABC's yuppie hit *Thirty-something* when he ventures into feature film directing with this true tale of an all-black fighting unit during the Civil War. In the canon of liberal Hollywood filmmaking, *Glory* is one of the best because of the casting and the space Zwick gave his actors to create indelible characters. Before becoming a TV star on *Homicide,* Andre Braugher appears here as a bookish Northern Negro, Corporal Thomas Searles. Morgan Freeman, just a film away from his career-defining role in *Driving Miss Daisy,* flashes his Uncle Tom chops as Sergeant-Major John Rawlins, a gentle, all-too-accommodating ex-slave.

But the film truly soars on the angry wings of Denzel Washington. As Private Trip, a potential Nat Turner in training, Washington allows us to imagine what proud black manhood was like during the years before slavery ended. In a classic scene, Washington is tied to a post and whipped for a military infraction. Washington doesn't shout in pain or writhe in agony. Just one single tear rolls down his cheek. It is a great film moment that helps earn him an Academy Award for best supporting actor.

Charles Lane's mostly silent film *Sidewalk Stories* is screened on Fifty-seventh Street in Manhattan. This overlooked feature about a gentle homeless man trying to care for his daughter is a little gem. Lane is part of the community of New York black independent filmmakers whose work has been screened in New York City parks by the BFF. Back in 1976, Lane made *A Place in Time,* a thirty-six-minute silent film about a homeless street artist in New York.

A decade later, Lane is able to capitalize on the post-Spike interest in black indie filmmakers to raise funds for this unusual black-and-white film. Island Pictures, who'd released *She's Gotta Have It* and *Mona Lisa,* picks it up, but lightning doesn't strike for

Lane. Still, *Sidewalk Stories* is a remarkable accomplishment that debuted earlier in the year at the Cannes Film Festival. At the end of that screening, Lane received a twelve-minute standing ovation. Today Lane is remembered, if at all, for directing the truly forgettable 1991 Disney comedy *True Identity,* starring black British comic Lenny Henry as a black man in white skin.

NOVEMBER 5 All year Chuck D has been dogged by the fallout from Professor Griff's *Washington Times* interview. So late one winter evening, Chuck jumps into his Ford Bronco and starts driving, riding from Long Island to Pennsylvania and back. It is during this long solo journey that Chuck writes the majority of the lyrics to "Welcome to the Terrordome."

Over ringing electric guitars and tingling cymbals, Chuck goes solo—no Flavor to lighten the mood—and comes up with a stream-of-consciousness rap reminiscent of the talking blues. It is a very personal, very pained-sounding rhyme that teeters between lament and boast. Of all P.E.'s on-record diatribes, none sounds more anguished than "Terrordome."

And, like almost everything about this remarkable group, "Terrordome" sparks controversy. Several rabbis, who by now are incipient hip hop scholars, cite several lines—"so-called chosen frozen" and "they got me like Jesus"—as having anti-Semitic intent. Following this logic, Chuck went from tolerating anti-Semitism to being anti-Semitic himself.

The irony of these attacks is that much of Public Enemy's support team is largely Jewish. The man who signed them (Rick Rubin), their personal managers (Ron Stoller and Ed Chalpin), Def Jam publicist (Bill Adler), and the president of Rush Management (Lyor Cohen) are all Jewish. And they all support Public Enemy during this year's drama. So Chuck D goes on the *Today* show, along with a Los Angeles rabbi and journalist Nelson George, to explain himself to Bryant Gumbel.

Chuck D and Bryant Gumbel represent two very different paths to prominence—one self-consciously rough and nationalistic, the other as polished as the brass buttons on a soldier's dress uniform. Each man has achieved a kind of social upward mobility impossible the decade before. One sees himself as the voice of the underclass; the other works as a symbol of American normalcy. They speak for two very different (black) American dreams. Gumbel is a by-product of Dr. King's dream of integration and equality; Chuck D is a rebellious political voice of the underclass.

But unlike the '60s leaders, they both work comfortably in a system of commerce in which a color-blind delivery like Gumbel's and a defiantly African American roar like Chuck D's generate income for themselves and the media corporations that give them access to the masses. To that degree the two men aren't very different. While the diversity of popular black expression is probably wider in the '80s than it has ever been, so often it is done in service, whether grudgingly or willingly, of white institutions.

NOVEMBER 6 Charles Lewis, forty-nine, testifies under oath in U.S. District Court that he gave D.C. mayor Marion Barry cocaine at least three times when Barry visited him in a local Ramada Inn in 1988. Barry, while acknowledging making six visits to Lewis's room, denies purchasing, using, or seeing drugs.

NOVEMBER 7 A significant black electoral victory occurs in the great Northwest. Seattle, Washington, is not yet identified with the soon-to-be cultural clichés of grunge music, Microsoft billionaires, and Starbucks. At this moment the city is simply a very white city far from where the majority of black Americans reside, which makes the election of Norman B. Rice as mayor so fascinating. Rice is a black moderate and longtime member of the city council, a policy wonk who wins 58 percent of the vote in a city with a 10 percent black population.

On the same day Seattle makes Rice its mayor, its citizens also approve an anti-busing initiative, Save Our Schools, that Rice opposes. This initiative succeeds by only 1,100 votes. In this wealthy, smart Northwestern city, the majority of residents think a black man is good enough to lead them, but they don't want any of the limited number of black students in town sitting near their kids. The message Seattle sends is a message typical of the age: a black star is more than acceptable, but ordinary black folks are still a problem.

DECEMBER According to the U.S. Census Bureau, black folks are fed up with life in the North and Midwest. A historic reverse immigration is under way that can be traced to shrinking working-class employment opportunities, decaying housing, and crack-spurred social chaos. From 1980 to 1984 only 89,000 non-Hispanic blacks moved to the South from the rest of the country. From 1985 to 1989, the number leaped to 355,000. The black American dream that life in northern and midwestern big cities would bring better jobs, affordable quality housing, and an escape from racism has, for so many, been just an illusion.

A fifty-year exodus up over the Mason-Dixon line is ending. Adults tired of grinding out a living in the cold, grandparents returning to quieter, livable hometowns, and young people looking for a slower pace and a living wage are trekking to black meccas like Atlanta, Virginia Beach, and Charlotte, and then gloating about their new homes to friends still toiling in urban America.

DECEMBER 6 A seventy-nine-year-old black judge sentences a twenty-two-year-old black man to life in prison without parole for possessing 5.5 ounces of crack cocaine, under a 1988 federal narcotics trafficking statute that provides for stiff sentences whenever defendants have two or more prior convictions. In sentencing Richard Winrow of South Central Los Angeles, U.S.

District Judge David W. Williams says, "We have one or two things in common. We are of the same race and we come from the same neighborhood. I grew up on East 109th Street. I know that neighborhood and I know how it's changed. The man is making it one of the neighborhoods you can't live in, can't walk down the streets. My people are the victims."

If Winrow had been prosecuted for these crimes in state court, the maximum term he could have received is four years in prison. His attorney argues that the federal law violates the constitutional protection against cruel and unusual punishment, stripping judges of the discretion to tailor a sentence to a particular defendant. The law under which Winrow is prosecuted is part of the Anti-Drug Abuse Amendments Act of 1988, a bill whose import has been obscured by the controversy over an amendment calling for the death penalty to be leveled against drug kingpins.

One can understand (and even admire) the judge's contempt for drug dealers, while seeing that the Winrow case is just one of many examples of how the crack plague has inflamed the most reactionary aspects of American justice.

In the constant tension between civil rights and sentencing criminals, crack's appearance has tipped the scales of justice decisively toward punishments that are draconian and often racially motivated. Mandatory sentencing policies that make possession of crack cocaine a bigger crime than possession of the same quantity of the powder are clearly aimed at young street dealers who tend to be black and brown. This brand of race-based sentencing is a staple of state and federal legislation well into the '90s, with strong advocates among Republicans and Democrats.

DECEMBER 20 The U.S. military invades Panama to "protect" U.S. citizens and remove General Manuel Noriega from power. On this morning many Americans get their first sighting of General Colin Powell, the recently appointed chairman of the Joint

Chiefs of Staff. As the chief military official of the United States, Powell leads a press conference and explains the army's actions with the crisp aplomb of a talk show host. After years of being a D.C. insider, Powell becomes the last new black media star of the '80s, a smooth-talking, authoritative presence who appeals to whites probably more than to blacks. While Powell's military career has already been blessed, this new prominence gets his name bandied about in a new context (future secretary of state or president?). In explaining how we secured the Panama Canal and beat down the local army, Powell becomes the nation's most beloved general since Dwight Eisenhower and a smooth, accessible voice for American military might. A decade of black stars ends with the most powerful one yet, discussing the invasion of a developing country while most of America is having breakfast.

The Legacy: The History of Our Future

A mercurial quest for leadership. A growing economic and cultural chasm between haves and have-nots. The stealth assassins of drug abuse and sexually transmitted diseases. A redefinition of "blackness" so sweeping the word itself went out of vogue. For those who now called themselves African American, the years between 1980 and 1989 were filled with extreme contrast, a lurching forward and backward that left a legacy that is curious and contradictory.

Hip hop and black women's literature were clear winners; both expressions would continue to grow rapidly in the '90s. The impact of black mayors was inconsistent. Despite the stunning mistake of the MOVE bombing, Wilson Goode was reelected in Philadelphia. Moreover, years later voters in that city would unite under another black mayor. Not so in New York or Chicago, or in the governor's mansion in Virginia, where black power would prove fleeting. Crack, as mania and commodity, has receded, but its human costs are still being calculated in recovering addicts, shattered families, and the perpetuation of jail culture outside of prisons.

Most of the prominent figures of the '80s have stayed on the main stage—some on cruise control, some as afterthoughts, and others in shame. Oprah Winfrey's only misstep in the '90s is producing and acting in an ambitious but incoherent film adaptation of Toni Morrison's classic novel *Beloved*. Otherwise she went from strength to strength with her TV programs, magazine ventures, and book club. Toni Morrison wins the Nobel Prize in literature.

Colin Powell is appointed secretary of state. Three of Terry McMillan's novels are made into movies. Russell Simmons's Def Jam becomes a true hip hop institution and his ventures in cable TV and clothing bear fruit. Henry Louis Gates Jr. remains a ubiquitous, if oft-criticized, force in academia. August Wilson's ambitiously eloquent cycle of plays rolls on. Reverend Al Sharpton bucks the odds and becomes a formidable political power. Spike Lee's career is more complex. No American filmmaker is more prolific, making feature films, documentaries, and commercials, though Lee's once potent culture impact peaks in the early '90s. Public Enemy still tours and records (often for on-line distribution), but no longer is a sales force, though Chuck D (via lectures, television appearances, a Web site) takes on the role of hip hop's conscience. Bryant Gumbel stumbles a few times, but hosts a fine sports program on HBO. Alice Walker is eclipsed by a new generation of women writers, many of whom were inspired by her work. Tracy Chapman's sales are erratic, though her music remains consistently earnest and heartfelt. Today Eddie Murphy seems capable only of $100 million family hits or unfunny adult duds.

Arsenio Hall, David Dinkins, Whitney Houston, Prince (known for part of the '90s as "symbol man"), and Anita Baker are all talents of great '80s import who either disappeared (often of their own choice) or whose personal choices in mate or name held them up to biting ridicule. MC Hammer fell farther than he rose. Mike Tyson transformed from fearsome slugger to circus sideshow, with a briefly sobering stint in jail sandwiched in between.

Michael Jackson and Jesse Jackson, dynamic, exciting, unifying forces in 1984, exist twenty years later with little vitality and deeply tarnished reputations. Sexual transgressions. Lawsuits. Tabloid coverage. Arrogance. False innocence. Time has been cruel to both these Jacksons. Or did they once fly so high their falls had to be equally grandiose?

A friend has a theory that black progress can be charted by the rise of our mediocrities. His argument is that African Americans once had to have the exuberance of Willie Mays, the passion of Shirley Chisholm, or the analytical power of Thurgood Marshall to succeed. No more. An unacknowledged legacy of the '80s is that so many doors were opened that not merely the competent but also the uninspired and, on occasion, the downright bad rose to prominence. If you judge the race's journey by Montel Williams on syndicated television, sundry members of the uninspiring Congressional Black Caucus, and the proliferation of formulaic black romance novels in the '90s, you'd think there was wisdom in this outlook.

Remember black Republicans? Some of those early '80s curiosities hold powerful positions in government in this tumultuous, young century. But Condi Rice and Clarence Thomas prove that the success of one or two individuals, the old role model ideology, sometimes has precious little positive effect on the masses. In the end, it seems, for blacks to participate in this tenuous experiment called American democracy no longer takes exceptional skill or protest marches or the marshaling of moral suasion. It seems all you need now is a desire to fit in and embrace the values of a flawed nation that loves technology, materialism, vast military budgets, false piety, and interventionist foreign policy and hates visionary social programs, independent third-world countries, and paying attention to the views of those who don't accept American values. Mediocrity is a national obsession and, from top to bottom, African Americans joined the chase.

And what of post-soul? I think African Americans have passed through that phase and, in the twenty-first century, are grappling with a new set of identity issues. We are no longer this nation's biggest minority group, though we are part of a huge community of nonwhite people. Many children with mixed-race bloodlines who once, by virtue of custom and racism, saw themselves as "black" now embrace a multiracial identity. Black 'hoods are finding themselves invaded by white homesteaders, seeking their future in places central to the black past. Almost two thirds of black Americans are under forty. In Detroit, the blackest of America's big cities, a thirty-two-year-old hip hop fan, Kwame Kilpatrick, was elected mayor. Things done changed and are changing still. It's time for a new look at our role, as an ethnic community and as part of the United States. We are still instigators, creators, and animators of much of what defines this nation. We are no longer post-soul. We are something else. For now, I leave that new definition to you.

Selected Bibliography

Books

Many books are cited in the text of *Post-Soul Nation,* but those listed here are works that informed the writing either as sources of factual information or by inspiring ideas.

Adler, William A. *Land of Opportunity.* New York: Atlantic Monthly Press, 1995.

Ashe, Arthur R., Jr. *A Hard Road to Glory: A History of the African American Athlete Since 1946.* New York: Warner, 1988.

Asante, Molefi Kete. *The Afrocentric Idea.* Philadelphia: Temple University Press, 1987.

Baldwin, James. *Evidence of Things Not Seen.* New York: Holt, Rinehart, and Winston, 1985.

Bayer, Ronald, and Oppenheimer, Gerald M. *AIDS Doctors: Voices from the Epidemic.* New York: Oxford University Press, 2000.

Bogle, Donald. *Prime Time Blues: African Americans on Network Television.* New York: Farrar, Straus & Giroux, 2001.

Brewster, Bill, and Broughton, Frank. *Last Night a DJ Saved My Life: The History of the Disk Jockey.* New York: Grove Press, 2000.

Christgau, Robert. *Christgau's Record Guide: The '80s.* New York: Pantheon, 1990.

Chuck D, with Yusef Jah. *Fight the Power: Rap, Race & Reality.* New York: Delacorte, 1997.

Dent, Gina, editor. *Black Popular Culture: A Project by Michelle Wallace.* New York: Bay Press, 1992.

George, Nelson. *Blackface: African Americans in the Movies.* New York: Harper Collins, 1994.

———. *Buppies, B-Boys, Baps & Bohos: Notes on Post-Soul Culture.* New York: Da Capo, 2001.

———. *The Death of Rhythm & Blues*. New York: Pantheon, 1988.

———. *The Michael Jackson Story*. New York: Dell, 1984.

Heller, Peter. *Bad Intentions: The Mike Tyson Story*. New York: NAL, 1989.

Magill, Frank. *Masterpieces of African-American Literature*. New York: HarperCollins, 1992.

Marsh, Dave. *Trapped: Michael Jackson and the Crossover Dream*. New York: Bantam, 1985.

Miles, Johnnie H., Davis, Juanita J., Ferguson-Roberts, Sharon E., and Giles, Rita G. *Almanac of African American Heritage*. New York: Prentice Hall, 2001.

Nelson, Havelock, and Gonzales, Michael A. *Bring the Noise: A Guide to Rap Music & Hip Hop Culture*. New York: Harmony, 1991.

Nicholson, Stuart. *Jazz: The 1980s Resurgence*. New York: DaCapo, 1995.

Reid, David, editor. *Sex, Death and God in L.A.* New York: Pantheon, 1992.

Rivlin, Gary. *Fire on the Prairie: Chicago's Harold Washington and the Politics of Race*. New York: Henry Holt, 1992.

Schulman, Bruce J. *The Seventies: The Great Shift in American Culture, Society, and Politics*. New York: Free Press, 2001.

Sontag, Susan. *Illness as Metaphor* and *AIDS and Its Metaphors*. New York: Farrar, Straus & Giroux, 1988, 1989.

Summers, Barbara. *Skin Deep: Inside the World of Black Fashion Models*. New York: Amistad, 1998.

Wynter, Leon E. *American Skin: Pop Culture, Big Business, and the End of White America*. New York: Crown, 2002.

Zinn, Howard. *A People's History of the United States, 1492–Present*. New York: Perennial, 2001.

Periodicals and Newspapers

These publications, some alive, many dead or on aesthetic life support, informed this narrative.

African Commentary	New York Post
American Film	The New York Times
American Visions	Newsday
Amsterdam News	Newsweek
The Atlantic Monthly	One World
Billboard	The Philadelphia Inquirer
Black American Newspaper	Playboy
Black Enterprise	Players
The Boston Globe	Premiere
Chicago Sun-Times	Record World
Chicago Tribune	Rolling Stone
The Christian Science Monitor	San Francisco Chronicle
Cleveland Magazine	Savoy
Daily News	SoHo Weekly News
Ebony	The Source
Emerge	Sport Magazine
Encore	Sports Illustrated
Essence	Time
Houston Chronicle	Times of London
Independent	TV Guide
Jet	U.S. News & World Report
L.A. Weekly	USA Today
Los Angeles Times	Vibe
New Music Express	The Village Voice
The New Republic	The Wall Street Journal
New York Magazine	The Washington Post

Acknowledgments

First and foremost I must thank Ellysha East, a Columbia Journalism School student whose diligence in finding books and articles and navigating LexisNexis saved me years of research. All the best to Ellysha in her exploration of the true meaning of Dog Towns and her return to the Frisbee wars.

Wendy Wolf has edited every nonfiction book I've written since *The Death of Rhythm & Blues* in 1988. As audience, critic, and mentor, Wendy has beaten all my prose into shape. I wouldn't (and probably couldn't) write a nonfiction narrative without her.

Sarah Lazin has been my agent for nearly twenty years, earning my deepest respect and admiration.

A lot of good friends informed *Post-Soul Nation*. In some cases parts of their life stories are chronicled here, so I hope I've done them justice. Thanks to Bill Stepheny, Chris Rock, Regie Hudlin, Russell Simmons, Melissa Maxwell, Ann Carli, Sean Daniel, Stephen Barnes, Akure Wall, Monique Jones, Bethann Hardison, Vernon Reid, Gary Harris, Toure, and Pam Lewis.

I send a special shout out to *USA Today,* Robert Christgau's Consumer Guide column, and the late John Dos Passos for his *U.S.A.* trilogy, all of which influenced this book's format. Much love to Christgau and *The Village Voice* for first giving a home to this crazy post-soul idea in the May 17, 1992, issue, which, over ten years later, formed the backbone of this book.

Index

Page numbers in *italics* refer to photographs.